Praise for Stephanie Coontz's
A Strange Stirring

"Social historian Stephanie Coontz . . . takes a fresh look at *The Feminine Mystique* by examining its effect on the book's original readers. . . . Ms. Coontz usefully debunks some of the myths that have grown up around *The Feminine Mystique* and Friedan." —*Wall Street Journal*

"A timely contribution to the conversation about what constituted progress for women (and for which women) in these days of mommy wars and mama grizzlies. . . . By considering *The Feminine Mystique* as one sturdy strand in the complex arguments we're engaged in to this day, Coontz does Friedan the tremendous favor of pulling her down from heaven and up from hell. . . . It's a relief to have the level-headed Coontz providing perspective and taking Friedan's work and legacy for what it was: stirring, strange, complicated and crucial." —*New York Times Book Review*

"[*A Strange Stirring*] enriches Coontz's impressive body of work on American family life. . . . She continues to deftly make history a personal science, persuading readers to ponder those societal yokes we've taken up to wear around our own necks. . . . *A Strange Stirring* reveals the power of two writers; both are able to see beyond the conventional view and the untold history, and enable the reader to look ahead with new eyes and new questions." —*Seattle Times*

"*A Strange Stirring* gives voice to women whose lives were transformed by Friedan's book, but most compellingly, it sets the historical record straight as far as its impact on families." —*Salon.com*

"[A] useful revisiting of Friedan's book." —Louis Menand, *The New Yorker*

"*A Strange Stirring* is fascinating."

"[An] excellent new social history of the impact of Betty Friedan's landmark book on American women. . . . Coontz is the rare social historian who knows how to weave meticulous research into a compelling narrative of our not-too-distant past. . . . A *Strange Stirring* is, in many ways, better than the original. Today the problem has been named, and A *Strange Stirring* offers poignant personal reactions, accessible history and present-day comparisons to give voice to the modern quest for gender equality."
—Christine Whelan, *HuffingtonPost*

"Coontz recounts the catalytic effect that *The Feminine Mystique* had on a great many women. Her book is full of stories of desperate, suffering people who realized they weren't crazy only when they picked up Friedan's best-seller. . . . But *The Feminine Mystique* is not just an artifact of a benighted era. It still contains important lessons about one of the most important questions of all, which is how to create a meaningful, autonomous life."
—Michelle Goldberg, *The New Republic*

"A thoughtful reappraisal of Betty Friedan's 1960s classic—and a meditation on the ever-evolving role of women in American society."
—*The Daily Beast*, "This Week's Hot Reads"

"A fascinating examination of Friedan's much-misunderstood classic, A *Strange Stirring* should be required reading for any young woman today who believes that she's 'not a feminist.' Not only does Stephanie movingly recount how revelatory *The Feminine Mystique* was to the millions of discontented housewives who read it, but she also details—with examples that had me shaking my head in stupefaction—the unbridled sexism that characterized life circa 1963." —Lorraine Glennon, *Ladies' Home Journal*

"A compelling critique of the impact of *The Feminine Mystique* as an impetus for the profound changes brought by the women's movement in the 1960s and 70s." —*Reuters*

"Coontz shows how Betty Friedan's *The Feminine Mystique* threw a lifeline to U.S. middle- and upper-class white women constrained by conformity."
—*Ms. Magazine*

"[E]xcellent, eminently readable. . . . Coontz's 'demystifying' of both the era and Friedan is an erudite, even-handed look at the explosive feminist undercurrents of the era." —*BUST*

"As the author of several books that challenge the accepted historical narrative of 'traditional' families and institutions . . . Coontz soberly checks facts, corrects misinformation, and fills in holes in the record. Most important, she shows how assumptions and misinformation about the past are used not only to paint a distorted picture of how things used to be, but to justify insidious policies and legislation like the Defense of Marriage Act. In her latest work . . . Coontz focuses on a book we've come to take for granted, arguing that it deserves a closer look. . . . She not only explores the actual content of *The Feminine Mystique* (going well beyond the usual proclamations about its controversiality and importance), but insists that readers (and, presumably, feminists) figure out how to reconcile our idealized version of history with information that complicates it." —*Bitch Magazine*

"[Coontz] shows how profoundly the juggle [between work and family] is shaped by the early-life experiences of each new generation. . . . Coontz also sounds an alarm about prevailing female stereotypes of present times—the 'hottie mystique,' for example, that has young girls believing they should be as sexually attractive as possible, or the 'supermom mystique.'" —*Wall Street Journal*, "The Juggle"

"Nearly fifty years after *The Feminine Mystique* exploded onto the scene, Stephanie Coontz measures Friedan's outsized reputation against a revealing body of research gleaned from archival sources, oral interviews, and surveys she conducted with nearly 200 women. The result is a brisk, even-handed account of the book's literary achievements, political limitations, and enduring legacy. . . . Coontz sheds new light on Friedan's savvy as both a writer and an activist. But Coontz is as intent on demystifying *The Feminine Mystique* and stripping away the exaggerated and false claims surrounding it as she is on recounting its merits." —*Women's Review of Books*

"[Coontz's] slim volume makes an illuminating companion to the book it examines. . . . [The] book is engaging, readable, and brief. . . . [A] worthwhile review of the changes wrought by the past half-century." —*Dissent*

"Engrossing. . . . Here, as in her previous books . . . Coontz does what she does best: differentiates between what we think we know about marriage and family life in previous generations and the historical reality. In this case, that means providing a fresh assessment of the impact that Friedan's book had on women of different classes and racial backgrounds, even beyond its white, middle-class, target audience." —*Psychotherapy Networker*

"*A Strange Stirring* is a much-needed corrective about both Friedan and *The Feminine Mystique*." —*Jewish Exponent*

"Award-winning social historian Stephanie Coontz . . . has written a fascinating new book about the impact of [*The Feminine Mystique*] on American society and how it helped usher in the women's movement."
—*Long Island Woman*

"A book about a book. It's a funny concept, but one that actually works quite powerfully in Stephanie Coontz's new *A Strange Stirring*. . . . There's lots of food for thought here about how to re-imagine our work, our families, and our lives so they can finally, finally transcend mystiques altogether."
—*Feministing*

"Coontz makes abundant use of statistics to dissect the post-war period as experienced by American women more broadly—including African-American and working-class women, who were left out of Friedan's study. She also considers Friedan herself, critiquing her more exaggerated and oversimplified claims, praising her for those observations that remain relevant. . . . As Coontz's enlightening book demonstrates, Friedan's core message about the need to balance meaningful work and family life endures."
—*Barnes and Noble Review*

"Coontz has put together a comprehensive picture of what life was like for women in America during the 1950s and '60s. . . . *A Strange Stirring* is thoughtful and diligent in its research. Educational and incredibly illustrative of this time period in American history, I can't imagine a better study of this pivotal work, and truly appreciate its honesty, clarity, and well-rounded approach." —Kari O'Driscoll, *Elevate Difference*

"Packed with fascinating statistics and research on 20th-century American social history, including the effect of 'liberation' on middle-class, working-class and African-American women, Coontz shines new light on a landmark work."   —*BookPage*

"Coontz's book *A Strange Stirring: The Feminine Mystique and American Women at the Dawn of the 1960s* has an academic title but reads like a sociological thriller."   —*The Spokesman-Review*

"*A Strange Stirring* is a pleasure to read, fascinating and a little bit uncomfortable, like the history recounted in its pages."   —*eHistory*

"For some of us, this is a jolting 'remember when'; for others, a slice of history forgotten all too soon. For all of us, there remains relevance."—*Buffalo News*

"Coontz's dusting off and airing out of the text that became a near-instant feminist legend provides us with an opportunity to reconsider the work and the circumstances it was borne out of, including its flaws as well as undeniable might."   —*Alternet*

"Coontz reconciles Friedan's flawed text with its seemingly outsized influence, and deftly depicts the social context for the dramatic testimonials uncovered in Coontz's research, the revelatory proto-feminist experiences shared by women of her mother's generation. . . . [Coontz's] clear-eyed review of the social data and cultural contradictions of the time . . . comprise a fascinating and important study. *A Strange Stirring* . . . is a book of rigor and undeceiving, one worthy of Friedan's tradition."   —*Bookforum.com*

"This perceptive [and] engrossing . . . book provides welcome context and background to a still controversial bestseller that changed how women viewed themselves."   —*Publishers Weekly*

"Coupling meticulous research with first-person interviews, Coontz challenges a number of Friedan's assumptions and exaggerations while also revisiting the climate in which the work appeared and giving voice to women for whom *The Feminine Mystique* was nothing short of a lifesaver. . . . As women continue to struggle with the effort to balance life and work, Coontz argues that *The Feminine Mystique* remains as relevant today as when it first appeared. In tracing the roots of current discontents, which Coontz dubs the 'Supermom Mystique,' her book is no less required reading than Friedan's trailblazer." —*Booklist*

"Coontz recaptures the impact of Betty Friedan's *The Feminine Mystique* when it was published in 1963. Although Friedan claimed credit for initiating the modern feminist movement, Coontz places the book more dispassionately in its historical context as one of many factors working against entrenched gender roles. Still, Coontz demonstrates persuasively that women readers from many backgrounds found relief—some called it life-saving—in knowing that they were not crazy and not alone in their need to find some work independent of their family roles." —*Library Journal*

"A sharp revisiting of the generation that was floored by Betty Friedan's *The Feminine Mystique* (1963), and how the book is still relevant today. . . . A valuable education for women *and* men." —*Kirkus Reviews*

"[A] compelling read. . . . [T]o begin to understand how we got to where we are today, *A Strange Stirring* is a must-read." —*Spiked Review of Books* (London)

"This book offers a nuanced perspective on the women's movement by ending the invisibility of African-American women." —Donna L. Franklin, author of *Ensuring Inequality: The Structural Transformation of the African-American Family*

"Stephanie Coontz's new book takes you on an engrossing and enlightening tour of the past, with wisdom and meaning for the future." —Nancy F. Cott, Trumbull Professor of American History, Harvard University

"Stephanie Coontz continues to amaze me. In her new book, *A Strange Stirring*, she chronicles the untold story of some of America's greatest pioneers. This is a must read for all who care about our country's growth and maturity. We owe the women described here the same gratitude and respect given to Lewis and Clark and the others who carved out this great nation."

—John Bradshaw, author of
Reclaiming Virtue and the #1 *New York Times*
bestsellers, *Homecoming* and *Creating Love*

"*It Changed My Life* was the title of the book Betty Friedan wrote after her transformative 1963 *The Feminine Mystique*. And change she did the lives of American women. Now in her biography of a classic, Stephanie Coontz imaginatively explores the impact of Friedan's book. Weaving a rich fabric from what women said in letters and interviews, from articles in popular magazines, current scholarship, and her own astute reading of the 1963 work, Coontz compellingly reveals how generations of women—from the flappers of the 1920s to the bloggers and helicopter moms of today—have responded to the challenges modern women face."

—Daniel Horowitz,
author of *Betty Friedan and the
Making of The Feminine Mystique*

"As was written about *The Feminine Mystique*, *A Strange Stirring* is 'a journalistic tour de force, combining scholarship, investigative reporting and a compelling personal voice.' Stephanie Coontz has made a significant contribution to our understanding of the most transformative movement of our lifetimes. Much of what Coontz reports regarding the prevailing ethos of the 1950s as a time of conformity, cultural conservatism and social repressiveness will be fascinating and eye-opening for younger readers. This book is a must read for men as well as for women. And the transformational desire for a work/family balance in life is now reflected not just by gender, but by generation, as both men and women 'need to grow and fulfill their potentialities as human beings,' as Friedan wrote almost a half a century ago."

—Christie Hefner, former chairman and
chief executive officer of Playboy Enterprises
and longest serving female C.E.O.
of a U.S. public company

"Stephanie Coontz is not just one of the most important historians in America, she is also a personal hero of mine and a brilliant writer. This book—like all her books before it—has been a marvel and education for me to behold. I am awed by the scope of this research, of this thinking, and I am struck once more by how much there is learned (and taught) about the slow, stubborn advancement of women in America over the last one hundred years. I will keep *A Strange Stirring* in the forefront of my bookshelf forever."

—Elizabeth Gilbert, author of *Eat, Pray, Love*

"*A Strange Stirring* brings the discussion into the present day, touching on current attitudes toward work, partnerships, parenting, and sexuality. It is a thought-provoking exercise."   —*The News Tribune* (Tacoma)

"[Coontz] takes us back to the 1920s to illustrate the disappointment and yearning that led to *The Feminine Mystique*, then to the release of the book in 1963 and, through nearly 200 interviews with women and men who read Friedan's book when it was first published, Coontz explores why it had such a profound impact on the so-called 'Greatest Generation.'"

—*The Sun Herald* (Sydney)

A Strange Stirring

Other books by Stephanie Coontz:

The Way We Never Were:
American Families and the Nostalgia Trap

Marriage, a History:
How Love Conquered Marriage

The Way We Really Are:
Coming to Terms with America's Changing Families

Social Origins of Private Life:
A History of American Families, 1600–1900

American Families:
A Multicultural Reader

A Strange Stirring

∿∿∿∿∿∿∿∿∿∿∿∿∿∿∿∿∿∿∿∿∿∿∿∿∿∿∿∿∿∿

The Feminine Mystique and
AMERICAN WOMEN at the DAWN
of the 1960s

∿∿∿∿∿∿∿∿∿∿∿∿∿∿∿∿∿∿∿∿∿∿∿∿∿∿∿∿∿∿

Stephanie Coontz

BASIC BOOKS
A Member of the Perseus Books Group
New York

Hardcover first published in 2011 by Basic Books,
A Member of the Perseus Books Group
Paperback first published in 2012 by Basic Books

Designed by Pauline Brown
Text set in Fairfield LT

The Library of Congress has cataloged the hardcover as follows:
Coontz, Stephanie.
    A strange stirring : the Feminine mystique and
    American women at the dawn of the 1960s / Stephanie Coontz.
        p. cm.
    Includes bibliographical references and index.
    ISBN 978-0-465-00200-9 (alk. paper)
        1. Friedan, Betty. Feminine mystique. 2. Feminism—United States—
History—20th century. 3. Women—United States—Social conditions—
20th century. I. Title.

HQ1426.F8443C66 2010
                                                    305.4209'045—dc22
2010022163

ISBN 978-0-465-02842-9 (paperback)
ISBN 978-0-465-02232-8 (e-book)

10 9 8 7 6 5 4 3 2 1

In loving memory of my mother,
Patricia Waddington

Contents

"The thoughts I had were terrible. I wished for another life. I woke up and started to clean and wash clothes and was miserable. No one seemed to understand. My friends didn't feel that way. I just assumed I'd be punished in some way. That's what happens to women who are selfish. My friends said you're so selfish."

CONSTANCE AHRONS dropped out of college to have a child, and as a young wife and mother in the early 1960s was seeing a psychiatrist for depression. Halfway through *The Feminine Mystique* she got up and flushed her tranquilizers down the toilet.

∿∿∿∿∿∿∿∿∿∿∿∿∿∿∿∿∿∿∿∿∿∿∿∿∿∿∿

"There were only two times I understood my mother—when I read the Book of Job and when I read The Feminine Mystique.*"*

KATHY HESKIN'S severely depressed mother wrote her a passionate but "bewildering" six-page letter about *The Feminine Mystique* when Kathy was a teenager. Only years later did she read the book herself.

∿∿∿∿∿∿∿∿∿∿∿∿∿∿∿∿∿∿∿∿∿∿∿∿∿∿∿

"It left me breathless . . . ," recalled Glenda Schilt Edwards, who was twenty-eight when she read the book shortly after it was published. *"I suddenly realized that what I thought might be wrong with me was, in fact, right with me!"*

∿∿∿∿∿∿∿∿∿∿∿∿∿∿∿∿∿∿∿∿∿∿∿∿∿∿∿

"I was trapped in what felt like hell. I had been forced to drop out of school. . . . There were no domestic violence programs and no one ever talked about the issue. . . . I thought I was the only one being beaten and there was something terribly wrong with me. I was ashamed."

ROSE GARRITY married at age fifteen, dropped out of school after just one week in the tenth grade, had her first child at age seventeen, and then had four more in the next five and a half years. She was being regularly beaten by her husband when she read the book, "and it was like the curtain was thrown back on the 'wizard'!"

∿∿∿∿∿∿∿∿∿∿∿∿∿∿∿∿∿∿∿∿∿∿∿∿∿∿∿

"I had everything a woman was supposed to want—marriage to a nice, dependable guy (a good provider), a wonderful little kid, a nice house in the suburbs—and I was miserable."

CAM STIVERS was a twenty-five-year-old wife and mother who thought her life "was over" until she read the book in 1963.

Author's Note

WHEN I FIRST AGREED TO WRITE ABOUT THE IMPACT OF THE 1963 BEST seller *The Feminine Mystique*, I wasn't sure of my ultimate focus. Would the book be about Betty Friedan, the author? Would it be about the feminist movement she helped to organize? Would it be about the ideas of *The Feminine Mystique* itself?

But as I read and reread Friedan's book and other works on the 1950s and 1960s, and especially when I began to interview women who bought the book at the time, the answer emerged. I wanted to tell the story of the generation of women who responded most fervently to what Friedan had to say—a group of women whose experiences and emotions are poorly understood today, even by their own daughters and granddaughters.

Many books have been written and movies made about "the greatest generation." But the subjects of these stories are almost invariably men— the army, navy, and air force men of WWII (only 2 percent of the military in that era were female); the "Mad Men" of Madison Avenue who pioneered America's mass consumer culture in the days of Eisenhower and Kennedy; the ordinary husbands and fathers who created a middle-class life for their families after the privations of the Depression and the war.

What do we know about those men's wives and daughters? As their husbands and fathers moved into a new era, many women felt suspended between the constraints of the old sphere of female existence and the promise of a future whose outline they could barely make out. They were, as one of the women I interviewed told me, "a generation of intelligent women, sidelined from the world." Some were content to provide love and comfort when the men came home. But others felt that something was missing from their lives, though they could seldom put their finger on it.

These women—mostly white, mostly middle class—were at the eye of a hurricane. They knew that powerful new forces were gathering all around them, but they felt strangely, uneasily becalmed. They knew they occupied safer ground than their African-American, Latina, and white working-class counterparts, but knowing that only made them feel all the more guilty about their fears and discontents.

To modern generations, these women's lives seem as outmoded as the white gloves and pert hats they wore when they left the shelter of their homes. Yet even today, their experiences and anxieties shape the choices modern women debate and the way feminism has been defined by both its supporters and its opponents.

Tracing the history of these women and discovering why, despite their privileges, they felt so anxious about their femininity and so guilty about their aspirations was a revelation to me. I came to see how their struggles with their roles and self-images as wives and mothers helped pave the way for succeeding generations of women to have a greater range of choices—choices not free of cost, but requiring far less sacrifice of personal identity and sense of self-worth. And uncovering the pain so many of these women felt was a vivid reminder of what can happen—and still does happen—when their granddaughters and great-granddaughters give up on the dream of combining meaningful work with a fulfilling family life.

My examination of the women and men who read and responded to *The Feminine Mystique* began, as all research on Betty Friedan and her times must, at the Schlesinger Library, in Cambridge, Massachusetts, with its rich store of letters that Friedan received and wrote. I also combed through the oral histories my students and I had taken over the past two decades to find relevant stories from people who had formed families in that era.

In seeking other individuals to interview, I purposely avoided people who had known Friedan personally or had become leaders of the women's movement in the 1960s and 1970s. I use few quotes from such individuals in this book and did not seek interviews with them, although I make extensive use of the tremendously helpful conversations I had with groundbreaking women's historian Ruth Rosen.

To find interview subjects, I posted requests on women's magazines' Web sites; spread the word on professional, religious, and women's studies listservs; and recruited students to ask friends and relatives whether they had heard of or read *The Feminine Mystique*. Staff members at The Evergreen State College were especially generous in relating their own encounters with the book or sending me to their mothers and their mothers' friends they had heard mention the book. Almost everyone I interviewed provided me with still more names.

Unless otherwise noted, the individuals whose full names I use were personally interviewed by me or responded to a detailed e-mail survey and gave me permission to use their names. When a first name and last initial are used, these are pseudonyms for persons who asked not to be named, or for someone described in one of my or my students' oral histories. Quotes from unnamed individuals are from the letters Friedan received, now housed at the Schlesinger Library, although I do identify some of the public figures who wrote to her, such as Helen Gurley Brown, Gerda Lerner, and Anne Parsons.

To make this book more readable, I have substituted a lengthy bibliographic essay for endnotes and pared the number of references to other authors' works in the text. But every page of this book owes a tremendous debt not only to the women and men who shared their stories with me but also to the many historians and sociologists who have made it their life's work to research these matters. I hope readers will look at my bibliography to get a sense of the rich work that has already been done in this field.

Introduction

NEARLY HALF A CENTURY AFTER ITS PUBLICATION, BETTY FRIEDAN'S 1963 best seller, *The Feminine Mystique*, still generates extreme reactions, both pro and con. In 2006, it was ranked thirty-seventh on a list of the twentieth century's best works of journalism, compiled by a panel of experts assembled by New York University's journalism department. But when the editors of the right-wing magazine *Human Events* compiled their own list of "the ten most harmful books of the nineteenth and twentieth centuries" in 2007, they put *The Feminine Mystique* at number seven—not far below Hitler's *Mein Kampf*.

The Feminine Mystique has been credited—or blamed—for destroying, single-handedly and almost overnight, the 1950s consensus that women's place was in the home. Friedan's book "pulled the trigger on history," in the words of *Future Shock* author Alvin Toffler. Her writing "awakened women to their oppression," according to a fellow leader of the National Organization for Women, which Friedan helped establish a few years after *The Feminine Mystique* hit the best-seller list. Following Friedan's death at age eighty-five in February 2006, dozens of news accounts reported that *The Feminine Mystique* ignited the women's movement, launched a social revolution, and "transformed the social fabric" of the United States and countries around the world.

Opponents of the feminist movement are equally convinced that *The Feminine Mystique* revolutionized America, but they believe the book changed things for the worse. Prior to Betty Friedan, wrote one author, middle-class women "were living in peace in what they considered to be a normal, traditional, worthwhile lifestyle." Since *The Feminine Mystique*, "life has never been the same." In her 2006 book, *Women Who Made the World Worse*, *National Review*'s Kate O'Beirne complained that Friedan persuaded women that "selfless devotion was a recipe for misery." Laura Schlessinger, of the *Dr. Laura* radio show, has charged that *The Feminine Mystique*'s disparagement "of so-called 'women's work' . . . turned family life upside down and wrenched women from their homes." And Christina Hoff Sommers of the American Enterprise Institute wrote in September 2008 that although *The Feminine Mystique* was correct in pointing out that postwar America took the ideal of femininity "to absurd extremes," the book was also the source of "modern feminism's Original Sin"—an attack on stay-at-home motherhood. Friedan's book "did indeed pull the trigger on history," Sommers concludes, but in doing so, she "took aim at the lives of millions of American women."

Even people who have never read the book often react strongly to its title. In addition to interviewing people who had read *The Feminine Mystique* when it first came out, I asked others who had never read it to tell me what they knew about it. Their responses were surprisingly specific and vehement. The book was "full of drivel about how women had been mystified and tricked into being homemakers," opined one woman. Another reported that the book explained how women's sexuality had been controlled through the ages and assured me that Friedan had called for an end to marital rape and sexual harassment—ideas that do not appear anywhere in the book's 350-plus pages. The grandmother of a student of mine insisted that this was the book that "told women to burn their bras." Another student's mother told her that *The Feminine Mystique* documented how women in the 1950s were excluded from many legal rights and paid much less than men—although in fact the book spends very little time discussing legal and economic discrimination against women.

Interestingly, many women I talked with were initially sure they had read *The Feminine Mystique*, only to discover in the course of our discussions or correspondence that they actually had not. When they tried to explain the gap between what they "remembered" and what I told them the book actually said, they usually decided that the title had conjured up such a vivid image in their minds that over time they had come to believe they had read it.

As a matter of fact, I was one such person. I first heard of *The Feminine Mystique* when I was an undergraduate at the University of California at Berkeley in 1964. But I didn't hear about it from "Berkeley radicals." Instead, it was my mother, a homemaker in Salt Lake City, Utah, who told me about it. She had attended the University of Washington at the end of the 1930s and married my father in the early 1940s. While Dad was away during World War II, she had done her part for the war effort, working in a shipyard. After the war ended, she quit work to follow my dad around the country as he went to college on the GI Bill, attended graduate school, and established himself in his career.

Mom spent most of the 1950s raising my sister and me. But by the early 1960s, with me away at college and my sister in junior high school, Mom began to get involved in civic activities. Soon she took a paying part-time job as executive secretary of a community group.

Once a week she would call me at college and we would fill each other in on what we were doing and thinking. At one point she asked anxiously whether I thought she could handle going back to school to get her master's degree. At other times she proudly detailed her most recent accomplishments. Once she recounted how bored, lonely, and insecure she had felt as a housewife. The cause, she had recently discovered, was that she had succumbed to an insidious "feminine mystique," which she had recognized only when she read this new book by Betty Friedan.

"Do you know that sociologists misrepresent research to make women feel guilty if they aren't completely happy as full-time housewives?" she asked. Wasn't it scandalous that when a woman expressed aspirations for anything else in her life, psychiatrists tried to make her think she was sexually maladjusted? Was I aware that advertisers manipulated women into thinking that doing household chores was a creative act, and had housewives spending more time on it than they really needed to? "They can make a cake mix that tastes perfectly fine if you just add water. But the box tells us to add an egg so housewives will feel we're actually baking!"

I remember listening to my mother's grievances with a certain amount of impatience, feeling that they were irrelevant to my own life. My friends and I certainly weren't going to be *just* housewives. Looking back, I am ashamed to admit that at the time I believed it was largely a woman's own fault if she wasn't strong enough to defy social expectations and follow her dreams. But it is even sadder to realize, as I did while conducting interviews for this book, that most of these women also believed their problems were their own fault.

I was vaguely aware that women had once organized a long, hard fight to win the right to vote, but that was in the distant past. Far from identifying with other women, I—like many other independent women my age—prided myself on being *unlike* the rest of my sex. In the memorable words of feminist activist and author Jo Freeman, we grew up "believing there were three sexes: men, women, and me." We knew we didn't want to follow in our mothers' footsteps, but it did not yet occur to us that it might require more than an individual decision to chart our own course, that we would need an organized movement to pry open new opportunities and overturn old prejudices. The only movement that really meant something to us in the early 1960s was the burgeoning civil rights movement.

It took a few years for female civil rights activists such as myself to begin to see that we too were subject to many societal prejudices because of our sex. Only gradually, quite a while after the book had inspired my mother and many other housewives, did my friends and I begin to use "the feminine mystique" as a useful label to describe the prejudices and discrimination we encountered.

In fact, it was soon *so* useful that at some point, long ago, the phrase "feminine mystique" became such a part of my consciousness that I was absolutely sure I had read Friedan's book. So when JoAnn Miller, an editor at Basic Books, suggested that I write a biography not of Betty Friedan the author, but of the book she wrote, I jumped at the chance. I was certain that rereading this groundbreaking book would be an educational and inspiring experience. I also decided that I would assign *The Feminine Mystique* to my students to gauge how they would react to a book that had been so influential to an earlier generation.

After only a few pages I realized that in fact I had never read *The Feminine Mystique*, and after a few chapters I began to find much of it boring and dated. As it turned out, so did my students. The book seemed repetitive and overblown. It made claims about women's history that I knew were oversimplified, exaggerating both the feminist victories of the 1920s and the antifeminist backlash of the 1940s and 1950s.

I was interested by Friedan's account of how she had "lived according to the feminine mystique as a suburban housewife" and only gradually come to see that something was wrong with the way she and other American women were being told to organize their lives. But although the story of her journey of discovery was engrossing, her generalizations about women seemed so limited by her white middle-class experience that I thought the book's prescriptions for improving women's lives were irrelevant to working-class and African-American women.

And Friedan's warnings about "the homosexuality that is spreading like a murky smog over the American scene" sounded more like something that would come out of the mouth of a right-wing televangelist than a contemporary feminist. So too did her alarmist talk about permissive parenting, narcissistic self-indulgence, juvenile delinquency, and female promiscuity.

My initial reaction became more negative when I went on to discover that Friedan had misrepresented her own history and the origins of her ideas. Checking her account of the publishing history and reception of *The Feminine Mystique* against the actual historical record, I discovered disturbing discrepancies. I was put off by her egotism, which even her most ardent admirers have acknowledged was "towering," and disliked her tendency to pump up her own accomplishments by claiming that the media, and even her own publisher, were almost uniformly hostile to her views.

I was also indignant that Friedan portrayed all women in that era as passive and preoccupied with their homes. What about the African-American women who had led civil rights demonstrations and organized community actions throughout the 1950s and early '60s, standing up to racist mobs and police brutality—women such as Rosa Parks, Daisy Bates,

Ella Baker, Septima Clark, Dorothy Height, and so many more? What about the female labor organizers of the 1950s or the thousands of mothers who risked arrest in 1959 and 1960, pushing their children in strollers, to protest the mandatory air raid drills that they believed taught Americans to accept the possibility of nuclear war?

But gradually my appreciation of the book grew, as I talked to people who had read the book when it was first published in the early 1960s, went through the letters Friedan received after its publication, and revisited the era in which Friedan wrote. Paradoxically, the less relevant the book seemed now, the more grateful I became to Friedan for reaching out to the many women who, like my mother, had found it a revelation at the time—women who told me over and over that *The Feminine Mystique* transformed their lives, even that it actually "saved" their lives, or at least their sanity. A half century after they read the book, many of the women I talked to could still recall the desperation they had felt in the late 1950s and early 1960s, and their wave of relief when Friedan told them they were not alone and they were not crazy.

Most of the women who wrote to Friedan after her book was published in 1963 and became a paperback best seller in 1964, and most of the nearly two hundred people who took part in my own surveys, were the wives and daughters of families that had lived through World War II. They—or their parents—were born between about 1915 and the late 1930s. Memories of the Great Depression were still vivid in their family culture. They—or their parents, older siblings, or husbands—had experienced the hardships and the solidarities of World War II. The older ones had raised their families in the 1940s or the 1950s and the younger ones had been teenagers in the 1950s.

In the ensuing years, some authors have labeled the older members of this group as "the greatest generation." Others have called it the "silent generation." Both these labels apply to the collective experiences of the men, as soldiers in World War II or as citizens during the Cold War and the Korean War; they have little relevance to the collective experiences of the women of that era.

The women who found solace in Friedan's ideas would not have called themselves, or their mothers, members of the greatest generation. Most felt they were the beneficiaries of their fathers' or husbands' hard work, and many wondered whether they had done anything to deserve the gains their families made in the postwar era. When they did not feel fulfilled in those families, they blamed themselves for being ungrateful or inadequate.

It is not your fault, Friedan told them, that you feel trapped and discontented. The fault lies with the way society has denigrated and wasted your capacities. Not only will you be happier yourselves, but you will be better wives and mothers if you are recognized as individuals with your own social, intellectual, and creative needs. The title of Friedan's 1960 *Good Housekeeping* article that previewed her argument in *The Feminine Mystique* put it simply: "Women Are *People* Too."

Strange though it may seem today, many women in the 1950s and early 1960s had never heard anyone say that out loud. Women were wives and mothers. A few, they knew, were also heroines, brave souls like the female spies who risked their lives for the Allies in World War II. But the idea that an ordinary woman could be a person in her own right, in addition to being a wife and mother, seemed completely new to many women.

Friedan told these women that their inability to imagine a fuller, more complete life was the product of a repressive postwar campaign to wipe out the memory of past feminist activism and to drive women back into the home. As a historian, I knew her argument ignored the challenges to the feminine mystique that already existed in the 1950s. But as I interviewed women for this book and read more about the cultural climate of that era, I came to believe that Friedan was correct in suggesting that there was something especially disorienting—"something paralyzing," as one of the women I interviewed put it—about the situation confronting women at the dawn of the 1960s. Freudian pronouncements about the natural dependence and passivity of females and the "sickness" of women who were attracted to careers may have coexisted with sympathetic assurances that women were in fact capable and did deserve equality. But such assurances only made it harder for women to figure out whether anyone besides themselves was to blame for their feelings of inadequacy.

Friedan captured a paradox that many women struggle with today. The elimination of the most blatant denials of one's rights can be very disorienting if you don't have the ability to exercise one right without giving up another. The lack of support for women's ability to exercise both rights at once forces them to choose half of what they really want, and to blame themselves if that half fails to satisfy their needs. Today many women find this out when they try to balance motherhood and work. In Friedan's time, many women discovered this problem when they fell in love with a man.

The choices women were forced to make in the 1950s were far more starkly posed than ours are today. Contemporary women may resent the pressure to be a superwoman and "do it all," but in that era the prevailing wisdom was that *only* a superwoman could choose to do *anything* with her life in addition to marriage and motherhood, and that such superwomen were few and far between. Yes, pundits admitted, a woman could sometimes achieve a brilliant career or create a great work of art. But before she tried, journalist Dorothy Thompson warned her readers in the *Ladies' Home Journal*, she had better make sure she was a "genius," because if she ended up doing something only ordinary, or "second-rate," she would be wasting the chance to raise a "first-rate" child. One of the most touching letters to Friedan that I read came from a woman who thanked Friedan for delivering her from the tremendous guilt she had felt because she enjoyed working "not in a big business, achieving miracles of economics or science" but at a mundane job that nevertheless made her feel "needed, able, and secure."

So much has changed since Friedan wrote. At that time, many women felt they had too few challenges. Now most of us feel we have too many. At that time, many women believed their minds and talents were being wasted but felt guilty if they wanted to do more. Now we often feel *used up* by the demands on our time and talents but feel guilty when we want to do *less*, either at work or at home.

And yet three themes still resonate today. One is Friedan's forceful analysis of consumerism. "The sexual sell," as she termed it, is even more powerful than in the 1950s, although it is now most destructive for girls and teens rather than for housewives. Second is Friedan's defense of meaningful, socially responsible work—paid or unpaid—as a central part of women's identity as well as men's. And third is her insistence that when men and women share access to real meaning in their public lives, they can build happier relationships at home as well. In this respect, we now know that Friedan's predictions came closer to capturing the reality of twenty-first-century marriage trends and gender relations than more pessimistic prophecies about the supposed "battle of the sexes" that would result if women gained equality.

We still haven't fully figured out how to combine a loving family life with a rewarding work life. But *The Feminine Mystique* reminds us of the price women pay when we retreat from trying to resolve these dilemmas or fail to involve men in our attempts.

The Unliberated 1960s

ON DECEMBER 22, 1962, ONE MONTH BEFORE THE FEMININE MYSTIQUE hit the bookstores, the *Saturday Evening Post* published a cover article purporting to offer a portrait of the typical American woman. The opening page featured a photo of "Mrs. Charles Johnson," surrounded by her husband and children. "I just want to take care of Charlie and the children," the caption explained, summing up what the reader soon learned was the collective attitude of "American women, *in toto*."

The *Post*'s story was based on more than 1,800 interviews and extensive polling by the Gallup organization. According to the author, George Gallup, it was not intended to examine "the extremes" among American women. "Old maids," divorced women, childless women, and working mothers certainly existed in America, he acknowledged, but they were of concern mainly to sociologists, "because they are unusual" and exist "in a society that is not geared for them." The article's aim was to portray how "most" American women lived and thought.

As depicted in the *Post* article, the typical American woman—the one for whom American society was "geared"—was thirty-five years old, had two children (but was hoping for a third), and was a full-time homemaker. She had completed slightly more than three years of high school and had been happily married for fourteen years. And unstated though this was, she was white.

These demographic details meant that the woman they were describing had been born in 1927, just seven years after women won the vote.

As a young child, she would have experienced the Great Depression and almost certainly been aware of the tensions in the household as her parents struggled to get by. She had lived through World War II in her teen years, married a few years after the war's end, and was now taking care of her husband and raising children. But of course the *Post* survey included many slightly older women who had married before or during World War II as well as some who had started their families more recently.

Other publications and commentators, the *Post* editors wrote in the teaser for the article, had variously described American housewives "as lonely, bored, lazy, sexually inept, frigid, superficial, harried, militant, [and] overworked," but the truth was that they were doing fine. While 40 percent of housewives admitted they sometimes wondered whether they would have been better off as a single career woman, only 7 percent said they were "sorry they chose marriage over career." As one put it, "I'm my own boss. . . . My only deadline is when my husband comes home. I'm much more free than when I was single and working. A married woman has it made."

Not surprisingly, given the contrast between their experience as housewives in the newly prosperous 1950s and their still vivid memories of the hardships of the Depression and World War II, three out of four women felt that they got more "fun out of life" than their parents. Almost 90 percent of the married women said that homemaking tasks were easier for them than they'd been for their mothers, and 60 percent believed that their marriages were happier than those of their parents. The typical housewife, the *Post* reported, spent several hours each day cleaning house and taking care of children, but also had time for telephone chats, personal visits, and hobbies such as sewing, reading, or gardening. In fact, observed Gallup, "few people are as happy as a housewife."

American housewives are content, asserted Gallup, because they "know precisely why they're here on earth." Unlike men, women do not need to "search for a meaning in life. . . . Practically every one of the 1813 married women in this survey said that the chief purpose of her life was to be either a good mother or a good wife."

The housewives expressed deep satisfaction about motherhood and often described childbirth as the high point of their lives. But, the pollsters observed, "it takes more than motherhood to make a woman completely happy; it also takes a man." And not just any man. He "must be the leader; he cannot be subservient to the female."

Women "repeatedly" told the interviewers that "the man should be number one." One woman who had worked at a paid job for ten years before quitting to get married commented that "a woman needs a master-slave relationship whether it's husband and wife or boss-secretary." Another explained that "being subordinate to men is a part of being feminine." A third wife declared that what made her "feel equal" was that she always put her husband first and spent her spare time broadening her interests "so I won't bore" him.

One (unmarried) female newspaper reporter did comment that "a woman need not feel inferior while she makes her husband feel superior." But what strikes the modern reader is the degree to which both the women and the pollsters took it for granted that a wife should defer to her husband. Gallup even noted that the task of interviewing so many women had been challenging because some husbands wouldn't allow their wives to participate. One husband "was so angry that his wife had 'talked to strangers' that he refused to speak to her for three days after her interview." Another remarked to the interviewers, "You talk to my wife as if you thought she knew what she was talking about."

Yet neither Gallup nor the women portrayed in the article had any serious complaints about women's status in society. "Apparently," commented Gallup, "the American woman has all the rights she wants. . . . She's content to know that *if* she wants to do [other] things, she can; no one is telling her she can't, and she has made her choice—not business or politics, but marriage."

Gallup found only two small imperfections in the lives of American housewives. One was what he described as the "rather plaintive" desire of wives for more praise from their husbands and children. One woman explained: "A man gets his satisfactions from his paycheck and from being asked advice by others. A woman's prestige comes from her husband's opinions of her."

Still, women assured the pollsters that it wouldn't take much praise to make them happy because, all in all, they were "easily satisfied." "The female doesn't really expect a lot from life," explained one mother. "She's here as someone's keeper—her husband's or her children's."

Gallup's second concern was about what these women, now so focused on marriage and motherhood, would do in "the empty years" after the children were grown. None of the respondents he interviewed mentioned this as a problem, but Gallup was troubled by their lack of forethought. "With early weddings and extended longevity, marriage is now a part-time career for women, and unless they prepare themselves for the freer years, this period will be a loss. American society will hardly accept millions of ladies of leisure—or female drones—in their 40s."

For the time being, however, his report concluded, "the typical American female" is "serene, secure and happy." She loves being a woman and is "well satisfied" with her achievements in life. How odd, then, that just a month later, two of the most influential women's magazines in the country would feature excerpts from a forthcoming book claiming that millions of housewives were in fact desperately unhappy.

A careful reader of the *Post* article might have noted a few signs that not all women the pollsters interviewed were feeling as serene as Gallup suggested. Even though 60 percent of the wives said their marriages were happier than those of their parents, and almost all felt their housework was easier, two-thirds of them did not believe they were doing a better job of child rearing than their mothers had. And 90 percent of them did not want their daughters to follow in their own footsteps, expressing the hope their daughters would get more education and marry later than they had. Furthermore, about half the "single girls," as the *Post* referred to all unmarried women no matter their age, and a third of the married ones "complained about inferior female status."

Nevertheless, the complaints were mild, and these women were certainly not feminist militants. Asked whether they thought it would be a good thing if America someday might have a female president, two-thirds said no.

We often look back on the 1960s as a decade of liberation. By the time *The Feminine Mystique* was published in 1963, the civil rights movement had reached new heights in its long struggle against segregationist laws and practices. McCarthyism still cast a long shadow over American political life, with many people afraid to acknowledge associations or ideas that might expose them to charges of being "subversives," "pinkos," or "fellow-travelers." But the tide of public opinion had begun to swing against the televised hearings where congressmen waved lists of suspected "reds" and demanded under threat of jail time that witnesses name everyone they knew who might ever have attended a left-wing meeting. On the nation's campuses, student groups were beginning to protest the strict rules set up by administrators acting *in loco parentis*. When it came to women, however, the laws, practices, and attitudes of 1963 had more in common with those of the first fifty years of the century than what was to come in the next twenty years.

The homemakers in the *Saturday Evening Post* article may have thought they were *choosing* to defer to their husbands, but they actually had few alternatives. Many states still had "head and master" laws, affirming that the wife was subject to her husband. And the expectation that husbands had the right to control what their wives did or even read was widespread. Many husbands forbade their wives to return to school or to get a job. In 1963, Marjorie Schmiege heard about *The Feminine Mystique* from her local librarian and showed the book to her closest friend, Jan, who lived down the block. The next day, Jan's husband told Marjorie's husband, "Tell Marj never to bring that book into my house again."

In many states, according to the President's Commission on the Status of Women, which issued its report on October 11, 1963, a wife had "no legal rights to any part of her husband's earnings or property during the existence of the marriage, aside from a right to be properly supported." The bar for what constituted proper support was set quite low. In one case that made it to the Kansas Supreme Court, a wife whose comfortably well-off husband refused to install running water in her kitchen was rebuffed when she tried to make the case that this constituted less than adequate support. In community property states, a wife did have a legally recognized interest in the commonly owned property, above and beyond the right to receive basic support from it, but the husband generally had exclusive rights to manage and control that property.

Only four states allowed a wife the full right to a separate legal residence. When a woman married, most courts ruled, she "loses her domicile and acquires that of her husband, no matter where she resides, or what she believes or intends." If a female student in California married a fellow student from out of state, for example, she would lose her in-state tuition. The husband had the right to determine the couple's joint residence, so if he moved and she refused to follow, she could be said to have deserted *him* if he sought a divorce. Even when a wife lived apart from her husband, she could seldom rent or buy a home on her own. In 1972, the *New York Times* carried a story about a woman who could not rent an apartment until her husband, a patient in a mental hospital, signed the lease.

In many states, a woman was obliged to take her husband's surname. In some, she could not return to her maiden name after divorce unless, under the fault-based divorce system, she had proven that he was "at fault." A woman who did not change the name on her driver's license or voter registration upon marriage could have it revoked until she did. In 1971, an Illinois bill to allow married women to use a different surname for legal purposes was defeated, partly on grounds that motel owners could not safeguard "public morals" if married couples could register as Miss Jane Doe and Mr. John Smith.

At least five states required women to receive court approval before opening a business in their own name. In Florida, a married woman who wished to operate a business independently of her husband had to present a petition that attested to "her character, habits, education and mental capacity for business" and explain why her "disability" to conduct a business should be removed. In 1966, an enterprising Texas woman turned this disability into an advantage, claiming that she shouldn't be required to repay a loan she'd taken from the Small Business Administration, because she did not have a court decree removing her disability to enter contracts and therefore shouldn't have been granted the loan in the first place. The U.S. Supreme Court upheld her claim.

Married or single, women had a much more difficult time than men in getting financial credit. Banks and credit card companies discriminated against single women, and if a single woman with her own credit card got married, they insisted that her husband become the legal account holder. In Illinois, Marshall Field's department store would allow a woman to use her first name with her husband's surname if she could prove she had an independent source of income. But in no case could she use her maiden name, explained a credit department spokesman, because "she no longer exists as a person under her maiden name."

In issuing a mortgage or a loan, a wife's income was taken into consideration only if she was at least forty years old or could present proof that she had been sterilized. Until 1967, if a married female veteran applied for a Veterans Administration loan, her own income was not considered in determining the couple's credit risk.

The economic security of housewives who were not employed outside the home depended largely on a husband's goodwill. Some states allowed husbands to mortgage their homes or dispose of jointly owned property without consulting their wives. Others held that rental income belonged solely to the husband. Still others permitted husbands, but not wives, to bequeath their share of the community property to someone other than their spouse. As of 1963, forty-two states and the District of Columbia considered earnings acquired during marriage to be owned separately. This meant that if a couple divorced and the wife had been a homemaker, she was not entitled to share the earnings her husband had accumulated.

The legal definition of marital duties made the man responsible for providing "necessaries" for his wife and children but allowed him to decide whether those included running water or new clothes. A wife's legal duties were to rear the children and provide services around the home. This is why, if a man's wife was injured or killed, he could sue the responsible person or corporation for loss of consortium, but a woman could not do so, because she was not legally entitled to such personal services from her husband.

Such double standards were found throughout the law. Almost all states allowed females to marry at a considerably younger age than men, on the grounds that the responsibilities of a wife did not require the same level of maturity as those of a husband. In Kentucky, a husband could win a divorce if he could prove that his wife committed a single act of adultery, but a wife could not be granted a divorce unless she discovered that her husband was regularly cheating on her. If she had sex with him after finding this out, he could argue that she had forgiven him, and the judge could deny her petition for divorce. Several states allowed a man to divorce a woman if she was pregnant at the time of marriage, "without his knowledge or agency," but no state allowed a woman to divorce her husband if she discovered that he had impregnated another woman prior to their marriage.

The sexual double standard even extended to murder. New Mexico, Utah, and Texas were among states that had statutes codifying the so-called unwritten law that a man was entitled to kill someone he discovered in the act of sexual intercourse with his wife. Such a circumstance could be introduced as "a complete defense" against the charge of homicide. No state allowed a wife to kill a woman she caught having sex with her husband.

It was perfectly legal to ask prospective female employees about their family plans and to make hiring decisions based on the answers. When author Susan Jacoby applied for a reporting job in 1965 as a childless nineteen-year-old, she was asked to write an essay on "How I plan to combine motherhood with a career." There were no laws preventing employers from firing female employees if they married or got pregnant, or from refusing to hire married women or mothers at all.

One man I interviewed noted that his wife had had experience working with early computers before they married, and when she tried to go back to work at the end of the 1950s, she sought a similar job with IBM.

"After taking IBM's specialized exam, she was told that no one had previously scored that high. However, they could not hire her, they said, because they did not place women in the kind of position she qualified for."

One seemingly glamorous job for women in the early 1960s was that of stewardess, but many airline companies required women to quit work upon marriage, and all insisted that they could not work after having a child. Women were expected to resign as soon as they became pregnant. When one airline discovered that a stewardess had kept her child a secret for three years while she continued working, they offered her the choice of resigning or putting her child in an orphanage. Another airline in the 1960s had a unique form of maternity leave: If a woman had a miscarriage or if her child died within a year, she could return to her job with no loss of seniority.

In 1963 and 1964, newspapers still divided their employment ads into two separate sections, "Help Wanted/Female" and "Help Wanted/Male." The advertisements in the Sunday *New York Times* of April 7, 1963, are typical. The "Help Wanted/Female" section was filled with ads such as: "Secretary (attrac) . . . good typ & steno"; "Pretty-looking, cheerful gal for Mad Ave agcy"; "poised, attractive girl for top exec" in a law firm; "Exec Secy . . . Attractive please!" A particularly demanding employer stipulated "you must be really beautiful." One company atypically sought a "career minded college educated" candidate for an executive secretary but specified that she must be single. A few sought Ivy League grads, but the main job requirement for such prospective employees was "good typing skills."

The male section included 281 ads for accountants and 153 for chemists, while the female section had just 9 ads in each of those job categories. Eleven ads sought men for attorney positions, but none sought women. There were 29 columns of "Sales Help Wanted/Male" but only 2 columns of "Sales Help Wanted/Female." The "Help Wanted/Male" section had 94 ads for management trainee positions, while only 2 such ads appeared in the women's job section.

On the other hand, the female section of the want ads contained 162 ads for gal Fridays and girl Fridays, 459 for secretaries, 159 for receptionists, and 122 for typists. Similarly, there were 119 ads for "Household Help Wanted/Female," but just 5 for "Household Help Wanted/Male." One ad, reflecting the racialized as well as gendered nature of job opportunities, touted dependable, live-in maids from the "Miss Dixie Employment Agency," catering to the many white middle-class families that imported African-American servants from the South. Another ad, however, specified that the "Waitress-Parlor maid" they wanted to hire must be "White, well experienced."

Once hired, working women, single or married, were discriminated against in pay, promotion, and daily treatment on the job. In 1963, women who worked full-time earned only 60 percent of what men earned; black women earned only 42 percent. On average, a woman with four years of college still earned less than a male high school graduate.

Women could lose their jobs if their employer no longer considered them "attractive." Airline officials forced flight attendants to retire in their early thirties because, as one company official explained, "the average woman's appearance has markedly deteriorated at this age." Another matter-of-factly explained the business considerations behind the policy: "It's the sex thing, pure and simple. Put a dog on a plane and 20 businessmen are sore for a month."

There was no recourse against what we now call sexual harassment. One high school boy who worked a summer job in a newspaper room in 1964 wrote in his diary that when he entered the compositing room with Doris, the copy girl, "all of the printers and linotype operators started screaming and howling. At first I didn't understand what was going on, but then I figured it out: They were doing it to Doris." When he asked Doris what it meant, she responded, "It's just how they act around women." The boy found the incident startling, but once it was explained to him, he simply accepted it, as Doris had to do, as the way work was conducted in those days.

Women also had little control over their sexual and reproductive destinies in 1963. In 1958, New York City had finally prohibited its hospitals from denying contraceptive counseling to patients, after a newspaper reporter discovered that the city commissioner of hospitals had ordered the chief of obstetrics at Kings County General Hospital not to fit a diaphragm for a diabetic mother of three who had already had two cesarean section deliveries. But in 1963, seventeen states still restricted women's access to contraceptives. Massachusetts flatly prohibited their sale and made it a misdemeanor for anyone, even a married couple, to use birth control. Not until 1965 did the Supreme Court rule that it was an unconstitutional invasion of privacy to deny married women access to contraceptives. It took several more years for unmarried women to obtain equal access to birth control.

In many states, it was illegal for a woman to wear men's clothing, and every state in the union had "sodomy" laws that criminalized sexual relations other than heterosexual intercourse. In California, oral sex, even between a married couple, carried a potential jail term of fourteen years.

Abortion was still illegal everywhere, except to save a woman's life. In 1962, local Phoenix television celebrity Sherri Finkbine, a married mother of four and pregnant with her fifth child, discovered that thalidomide, the sleeping pill she had been prescribed, was known in Europe to have caused crippling and life-threatening fetal disorders. Her doctor recommended a therapeutic abortion, but when Finkbine went public with the news about the risks of thalidomide, the hospital canceled her appointment. Finkbine was forced to go to Sweden for the abortion, where doctors determined that the fetus was too deformed to have survived.

Few women had the resources to get around the laws by flying to Europe. Experts estimated that a million or more illegal abortions a year were performed on American women, with between 5,000 and 10,000 women dying as a result. Such abortions accounted for 40 percent of maternal deaths.

Unmarried women who became pregnant and gave birth faced extreme social stigma, especially in white communities where the new but still tenuous prosperity of the 1950s had created a burning desire, as one woman told me, to "fit in so you could move up." In her words, "having an unwed child in the family just shut you right out of respectable society."

When her own daughter got pregnant, this woman pressured her to go away, have the baby in secret, put it up for adoption, and come back pretending that she had been visiting relatives.

That this was common is confirmed by the testimony Ann Fessler recounts in *The Girls Who Went Away*. More than 25,000 babies a year were surrendered for adoption in the early 1960s, many because young women were persuaded they had no other option. As one later told Fessler: "You couldn't be an unwed mother. . . . If you weren't married, your child was a bastard and those terms were used." "Nobody ever asked me if I wanted to keep the baby, or explained the options," said another. "I went to the maternity home, I was going to have the baby, they were going to take it, and I was going to go home. I was not *allowed* to keep the baby. I would have been disowned."

Before World War II, maternity homes had encouraged unwed mothers to breast-feed after birth and did not pressure them to give away the child, but in the postwar era the philosophy had changed. While young black women who had babies were considered immoral, young white ones were considered neurotic or immature, and by the 1960s many homes put tremendous pressure on them to give up their children. One woman recalled, "I was not allowed to call the father of my child. Even when we would write letters, they would read them. They would either cut out things they didn't like in them, or they would cross through what they didn't like. If the letter really upset them, they would throw it away in front of us or tear it up."

If a woman did keep a child, she and her child faced legal as well as social discrimination. Many companies refused to hire unwed mothers. Children born out of wedlock had the word "illegitimate" stamped on their birth certificates and school records. They had no right to inherit from their fathers, to collect debts owed to their mother if she died, or even to inherit from the mother's parents should the mother predecease them. Until 1968, the child of an unwed mother could not sue for wrongful death if the mother was killed by medical malpractice or employer malfeasance. Until 1972, "illegitimate" children who lived with their father could not collect workers' compensation death benefits if he died on the job.

There was seldom justice for women who were raped. Most state penal codes permitted defense lawyers to impeach a woman's testimony by introducing evidence of previous consensual sex or claiming she had "invited" the rape by wearing "revealing" clothes or "tight" dresses. Many judges required corroboration that was almost impossible to achieve, such as having an eyewitness testify to the rape. In North Carolina, an older man could not be convicted of the statutory rape of a young girl if he could convince a judge or jury she had not been a virgin.

The law did not recognize that a married woman could be raped by her husband. Once a woman said "I do," she was assumed to have said "I will" for the rest of her married life. The courts held that the marriage vows implied consent to intercourse. Not until 1975 did the first state— South Dakota—make spousal rape a crime. North Carolina did not do so until 1993.

Many states also did not take domestic violence seriously, often requiring police officers to see a man assault his wife before they could make an arrest. In some places, the police used the "stitch rule," arresting an abusing husband only if the wife's injuries required more than a certain number of sutures. Until 1981, Pennsylvania still had a law against a husband beating his wife after 10 P.M. or on Sunday, implying that the rest of the time she was fair game.

A 1964 article in the *Archives of General Psychiatry*, published by the American Medical Association, reported on a study of thirty-seven women whose husbands had physically abused them. The authors observed that the wives typically did not call the police until more than a decade after the abuse began, often following an incident where a teenage child intervened in the violence. But rather than lamenting the women's long delay in seeking assistance, the psychiatrists explained that the child's intervention disturbed "a marital equilibrium which had been working more or less satisfactorily." To hear them tell it, most problems in such marriages were the fault of the wives, whom they described as "aggressive, efficient, masculine, and sexually frigid." In many cases, the psychiatrists suggested, the violent incidents served as periodic corrections to the unhealthy family role reversal, allowing the wife "to be punished for her castrating activity" and the husband "to re-establish his masculine identity."

Prejudice and discrimination were pervasive in small things as well as big. Elementary schools did not allow girls to be crossing guards or to raise and lower the American flag each day, nor could girls play in Little League sports. Many universities still required female students to wear dresses to class, even in bitterly cold weather. Women in dormitories faced curfew restrictions that men did not, and college sports were heavily skewed toward men. Often, women couldn't even use school athletic facilities.

Only two of the eight Ivy League schools accepted female undergraduates, while graduate departments often capped the number of women they would admit. Unions routinely kept separate seniority lists for men and women, while professional associations limited the number of female members. In 1963, only 2.6 percent of all attorneys were female, and among the 422 federal judges in the nation, just 3 were women. Not until 1984 did the Supreme Court rule that law firms could not discriminate on the basis of sex in deciding which lawyers in the firm to promote to partner.

Clubs such as the Jaycees could legally refuse to admit women on the grounds that it abridged their male members' "freedom of intimate association." In 1963, the National Press Club in Washington, D.C., was still entirely male. Female reporters who went there to hear a talk by black union leader A. Philip Randolph just before the August 1963 rally where Martin Luther King Jr. gave his "I Have a Dream" speech had to sit in a small balcony away from the rest of the audience, where they were not able to ask questions. And at that historic rally for equality, not one woman was among the ten speakers, although "Mrs. Medger Evers" did introduce a tribute to six "Negro women fighters for freedom," who stood silently on the stage.

In 1957, the federal government finally passed an act ensuring women's right to serve on federal juries, but when *The Feminine Mystique* came off the press six years later, only twenty-nine states allowed women to serve equally with men on city and state juries. In 1963, women, who were 51 percent of the population, composed just 2 percent of U.S. senators and ambassadors and 2.5 percent of U.S. representatives.

Advice books for girls and women hammered home the idea that a woman's greatest goal should be to get married and that she should bury her own interests and impulses in order to please and flatter a man into proposing. Even today some advice books for females are based on this idea, but such books stand out today precisely because they are out of step with mainstream mores. In 1963, Helen Andelin self-published *Fascinating Womanhood*, which became a runaway best seller when it was picked up by a mainstream publishing house in 1965. Andelin counseled women that the way to a happy marriage was to become "the perfect follower." She urged them to cultivate a "girlish trust" in their man and never to "appear to know more than he does." A woman should never let her voice exhibit such qualities as "loudness, firmness, efficiency, boldness." While it was okay to get angry, she told them, you should be sure to display only "childlike anger," which included "stomping your feet" and scolding your man in terms that flattered his sense of masculinity, such as "you big hairy beast."

An article in the January 1960 *McCall's*, "Look Before You Leap," presented a list of questions for prospective brides to answer before they married. The magazine urged the woman to be sure she would be able to press her husband's trousers, iron his shirts, and cook meals he liked. It also asked: "Has he pointed out things about you that he doesn't like, and have you changed because of what he's said?" The correct answer, of course, was yes, but women's magazines and advice books were unanimous in warning women against pointing out anything *they* didn't like in their mates.

Once they were married, women's work was truly never done. Typical of the advice to wives at the dawn of the 1960s was a piece in the December 18, 1960, issue of *Family Weekly* magazine, inspired by the fact that the student council of New York University's college of engineering regularly presented "Good Wife" certificates to "worthy" wives whose "encouragement, collaboration, and understanding" had helped their husbands complete their degrees. "Could You Win this 'Good Wife'

Certificate?" asked the author, a noted marital advice authority of the day. He proceeded to enumerate what it took to make the grade: A good wife makes her husband "feel that he is the boss at home." She "shares her husband's goals, fitting them to her own. She is willing to wait patiently for the ultimate rewards." She understands that "physical love is a symbol of devotion rather than an end in itself, and she is aware that such physical need is usually greater in the male." For this reason, she "never makes him feel inadequate." In conversations, the good wife permits her husband "to take the lead" without interrupting. "She follows an open door policy" for his friends, "even if she finds them dull or sometimes disagreeable." But she also respects her husband's need for privacy, so "she learns when to keep quiet. . . . If he'd rather read or watch a ball game on television, she avoids disturbing him with idle chatter."

Above all, like the women described in the December 1962 *Saturday Evening Post* article, a "good wife" considers "homemaking her profession." "She makes every effort to keep their home . . . a restful haven." And "she does not insist" that her husband share in household chores or child care: "her mate isn't converted into a 'mother substitute.'" Finally, if "she has a part-time career or full-time job, it doesn't take priority in her life, and her own work should not become more important to her than his."

Although advice books often emphasized the tremendous intellectual effort required to manage household chores, the expectations for house-wives' intelligence were pretty low. Many newspapers had columns such as the *Washington Post's* "Anne's Readers' Exchange," where women sent in helpful hints about organizing housework more efficiently. On October 17, 1963, the *Post* printed a letter from one reader who had devised what Anne labeled "a tricky chore combination": "this homemaker claims she can iron and telephone at the same time."

As late as 1969, famed parenting advice author Dr. Benjamin Spock was still reiterating the opinion of most medical and psychiatric authorities that "women were made to be concerned first and foremost with child care, husband care, and home care."

Even well-educated women who themselves worked outside the home joined the chorus. Margaret Mead, a famous anthropologist who had traveled the world and was highly unconventional in her own personal life, wrote several articles expressing concerns about women who sought status or fulfillment in the "competitive world rather than a unique place by a glowing hearth." Frances Perkins, who had been secretary of labor for twelve years under Franklin D. Roosevelt, insisted that "the happiest place for most women is in the home." And although the 1963 report of the President's Commission on the Status of Women decried the extent of inequality in political life, it too affirmed the centrality of women's identity as wives and mothers, noting that women's employment might threaten family life.

It is hard for women today to realize how few role models were available to women who came of age in the 1950s and the first half of the 1960s. Black female civil rights leaders spoke out, faced down mobs, and braved jail, but the only women regularly featured in the news were movie stars and presidents' wives, who were always described by their outfits. Jo Freeman, who would become a leader of the women's movement in the late 1960s and early 1970s, recalled that during the four years in the early 1960s she studied at the University of California at Berkeley, one of the country's largest institutions of higher education, "I not only never had a woman professor, I never even saw one. Worse yet, I didn't notice."

In 1964, the same year Friedan's book came out in paperback, the most blatant discriminatory practices of the era should have come to a halt. In that year the Civil Rights Bill passed, with a last-minute amendment to prohibit discrimination by sex as well as by race, color, religion, and national origin. The Equal Employment Opportunity Commission was set up to enforce the law. But while the EEOC immediately ruled that job ads specifying a particular race violated the act, it balked at concluding the same for ads segregated by sex. The *New York Times* did not abolish gender-segregated ads until 1968.

In September 1965, activists in the stewardesses' union managed to get a hearing before the House Labor subcommittee to protest the airlines' policy of forcing them to retire when they reached their early thirties, but the legislators failed to take their complaints seriously. Representative James Scheuer, a liberal who by his 1991 retirement supported women's rights, facetiously asked the complaining women to "stand up, so we can see the dimensions of the problem." It took the EEOC several years to start enforcing the laws against sex discrimination, and not until 1971 did the Supreme Court invalidate a single state statute on the grounds of sex discrimination.

These attitudes eventually spurred women activists, including Betty Friedan, who had become a celebrity after *The Feminine Mystique* was published, to stop working through established channels and to found an organization devoted to ending all forms of sex discrimination. But when she was writing *The Feminine Mystique* in the late 1950s and early 1960s, Friedan did not choose to tackle issues of legal, economic, and political discrimination. Instead, she asked her readers to take a closer look at the supposedly happy housewife described in articles such as that of the *Saturday Evening Post*.

The Feminine Mystique did not challenge the assertion that most housewives believed their "chief purpose" was to be wives and mothers. Nor did Friedan complain, as some intellectuals had already begun to do in the 1950s, that women were *too* content as housewives. Instead, *The Feminine Mystique* argued that beneath the daily routines and surface contentment of most housewives' lives lay a deep well of insecurity, self-doubt, and unhappiness that they could not articulate even to themselves. And in describing that unhappiness as something more than an individual case of "the blues," Friedan unleashed a wave of recognition and relief in thousands of women. Some of them had already realized that they were "unusual" and not "geared" for what society wanted of them. But many would have agreed with the women who told Gallup and his colleagues that their lives were easier than those of their own parents. Until they read Friedan, that had only made it harder for them to understand why they were not as delighted with those lives as Mrs. Charles Johnson appeared to be.

2

〰〰〰〰

Naming the Problem: Friedan's
Message to American Housewives

The problem lay buried, unspoken, for many years in the minds of American women. It was a strange stirring, a sense of dissatisfaction, a yearning. . . . Each suburban wife struggled with it alone. As she made the beds, shopped for groceries, matched slipcover material, ate peanut butter sandwiches with her children, chauffeured Cub Scouts and Brownies, lay beside her husband at night—she was afraid to ask even of herself the silent question—"Is this All?"

—Page 1, The Feminine Mystique

THE OPENING PARAGRAPH OF FRIEDAN'S BOOK IS ONE OF THE TWO OR THREE passages that women who read the book in the first years after its publication still remember most vividly.

"Everything just clicked," said Sally A., who read it as a thirty-two-year-old housewife in Kansas. She told me she had often wondered whether she should see a psychiatrist because of her tendency to cry "for no reason" in the middle of the afternoon. "But I couldn't afford it, and I was too much the daughter of my working-class folks to imagine doing something as self-indulgent as paying someone good money to talk about myself. Reading that book, though, it was like reading what I would have said to her if we'd been able to sit down for a cup of coffee."

Friedan "called it perfectly," said Lillian Rubin, looking back to her life long before she ever imagined she would become a nationally renowned psychologist and author. "The feeling didn't have a name. It didn't have a reason. So you turned it inward and assumed *you* were the problem. And so did everyone around you."

Ruth Nemzoff's life was changed when a teenage girl who babysat for her made her aware that she was walking through her life in a fog. "'Mrs. B,' she said to me, 'I think you need to read this book.'"

A husband in a small town in eastern Washington gave his wife the book because he had been worried about her moodiness. "I never even realized what I was feeling until I read that first chapter," said Stella J. "I felt like she'd looked into my heart and put into words the feelings I'd been afraid to admit."

Long before a slightly younger generation of women coined the phrase "the personal is political," Betty Friedan used that concept, wrapped in the language of the emerging human-potential and self-help movements, to convince women who were hurting that they could and should do something about it. In fact, sociologist Wendy Simonds considers *The Feminine Mystique* the first modern self-help book for women, noting the similarities in the letters Friedan received and those sent more than twenty years later to Robin Norwood, author of *Women Who Love Too Much*. In both cases, readers experienced a shock of recognition and an overwhelming sense of relief to learn that they were not alone in their feelings. But one crucial difference speaks to the unique impact Friedan had on women who read her book.

In researching her own book, *Women and Self-Help Culture*, Simonds found that many readers of modern self-help books were repeat customers, buying many such books and constantly seeking out new articles on related topics. But they valued the books more for the *feelings* they elicited than for any particular information they imparted. Often the readers could not articulate exactly what they got from a self-help book they had liked, or even remember its central points. "When I don't need it, why do I want to remember it?" asked one woman rhetorically. By contrast, women who read Friedan's book back in 1963 or 1964 could still say, nearly fifty years later, precisely what they learned from it. *The Feminine Mystique* may have been the first self-help book they ever read, but it was also the last many of them ever needed.

"I have a friend who reads those self-help books all the time," Janet M. told me, "and they affect her just like people used to say about a meal in a Chinese restaurant: 'It tastes good, but an hour later you're hungry again.' *The Feminine Mystique* was filling. It stayed with you for the rest of your life."

The Feminine Mystique engaged its fans on both an intellectual and an emotional level. Somehow Friedan managed to write a book that was more than three hundred pages long, with chapters titled "The Sexual Solipsism of Sigmund Freud" and "The Functional Freeze, the Feminine Protest, and Margaret Mead," and still evoke the kind of emotional response we now associate with chick flicks or confessional interviews on daytime talk shows. She took ideas and arguments that until then had been confined mainly to intellectual and political circles and she couched them in the language of the women's magazines she had begun writing for in the 1950s.

There already *was* a name for the overt barriers women faced in American society: sex discrimination. Contrary to some of the myths that have grown up around Friedan's book, plenty of people were already addressing this issue when *The Feminine Mystique* was published. But there was no name for the guilt, depression, and sense of hopelessness many housewives felt.

"Sometimes, a woman would say, 'I feel empty somehow . . . incomplete,'" Friedan wrote. "Or she would say, 'I feel as if I don't exist.' Sometimes she blotted out the feeling with a tranquilizer. Sometimes she thought the problem was with her husband, or her children, or that what she really needed was to redecorate her house, or move to a better neighborhood, or have an affair, or another baby. Sometimes she went to a doctor with symptoms she could hardly describe: 'A tired feeling . . . I get so angry with the children it scares me. . . . I feel like crying with no reason.'"

For more than fifteen years, Friedan told her readers, America's psychiatrists, sociologists, women's magazines, and television shows had portrayed the postwar housewife as the happiest person on the planet. To the extent that women believed this to accurately describe "everyone else," they felt alone and inadequate. So when a housewife failed to attain the blissful contentment that all her counterparts supposedly enjoyed, Friedan said, she blamed herself—or perhaps her husband: "If a woman had a problem in the 1950's and 1960's, she knew that something must be wrong with her marriage, or with herself. . . . She was so ashamed to admit her dissatisfaction that she never knew how many other women shared it. If she tried to tell her husband, he didn't understand what she was talking about. She did not really understand it herself."

When American families settled down to their favorite television shows each evening, contented homemakers such as June Cleaver, Harriet Nelson, and Donna Reed reigned supreme. True, there was the hyperactive title character of *I Love Lucy*, whose unrealistic fantasies about becoming an entertainer like her husband or developing a moneymaking business of her own provided an endless source of screwball comedy. But at the end of each episode Lucy always recognized that her efforts to escape being "just a housewife" had once more backfired and that her exasperated but loving husband had been right again. In 1962, the *Saturday Evening Post* was still assuring readers that few housewives even daydreamed about any life other than that of a full-time homemaker, and that their occasional "blue" moods could easily be assuaged by a few words of praise for their cooking or their new hairdo.

Yet for those who cared to look, Friedan pointed out, signs of trouble had been clear for some time. Some doctors had begun to refer to women's persistent complaints of fatigue and depression as "the housewife's syndrome." Women's magazines were publishing articles with such titles as "Why Young Mothers Feel Trapped" or "The Mother Who Ran Away." Social commentators, revisiting Freud's famous question "What does a woman want?" had fretted about why the American woman was "dissatisfied with a lot that women of other lands can only dream of," as one journalist mused in the March 7, 1960, issue of *Newsweek*.

Most so-called experts, Friedan charged, never questioned the idea that all life's meaning could be found in the role of wife and mother. Rather, they sought to identify what had led women to wrongly devalue these roles. Many blamed higher education for distracting women with lofty academic studies they would never use instead of properly preparing them for marriage and motherhood.

Some commentators noted that modern appliances were not yet efficient enough to compensate for the decline of household help since World War II, so young mothers were overwhelmed with work. Others expressed the opposite view, that mass production had taken over many of women's more challenging household tasks, so that wives needed to try harder to find creativity and novelty in their work as homemakers.

Cultural critics claimed the American gospel of success made too many women desire careers and lose their femininity in the process. Psychiatrists and marriage counselors suggested that women's dissatisfaction originated in sexual maladjustment.

All these explanations, Friedan argued, simply perpetuated the mystique that surrounded the roles of housewife and mother, denying women's need for any other source of personal identity or meaning in their lives. Friedan assured her readers that their pain stemmed from a basic, unquenchable human drive to fully utilize one's own abilities and talents for something larger than darning socks, producing tasty casseroles, and "just being there" for their husbands and children.

The Feminine Mystique introduced its readers to theories such as that of Abraham Maslow, who believed human beings had a hierarchy of needs that must be satisfied in order: first, physiological needs such as hunger and thirst; second, safety and security needs; and then social needs such as love, intimacy, and belonging. But once those needs were met, he said, other needs became equally important—the need for self-esteem and respect, and the impulse to maximize one's creative, intellectual, and moral possibilities. Having moved beyond the hardships of the Depression and World War II, said Maslow and his followers, Americans inevitably yearned for something more than a roof over their heads and a full stomach.

But, explained Friedan, when researchers in this field defined "the mentally healthy man" as "one who has reached the 'highest excellence of which he is capable,'" they meant the male noun literally. They believed that women had no need to search for meaning in their lives beyond their roles as wives and mothers. Indeed, many warned women that if they did desire other avenues of personal growth, it was because they were inadequate sexual partners to their husbands or unnatural mothers to their children. Such ideas were wrong, said Friedan. Women, too, had an inner drive to live up to their intellectual and creative potential.

Friedan reminded her readers that in America's new "affluent society," commentators of many political stripes were expressing concern that the spread of mindless conformity and consumerism was turning men into drones incapable of taking risks, achieving greatness, or contributing to society's progress. Yet the same people were telling women that mindless conformity and consumerism in the service of the family were the deepest fulfillment they would ever find and the greatest contribution they could make to society.

The first chapter of *The Feminine Mystique* lays out the theme Friedan returned to time and time again: Women, like men, have the need and desire to find larger meaning in their lives. The pain that women feel when this need goes unmet should be taken no less seriously just because many of them had satisfied the lower-order needs for safety, security, and physical comfort. "Part of the strange newness of the problem," Friedan wrote, "is that it cannot be understood in terms of the age-old problems of . . . poverty, sickness, hunger, cold. . . . It is not caused by lack of material advantages; it may not even be felt by women preoccupied with desperate problems of hunger, poverty or illness. And women who think it will be solved by more money, a bigger house, a second car . . . often discover it gets worse."

Friedan heaped scorn on the idea that women could solve the problem, as many psychiatrists suggested, by achieving a more satisfying sexual life. One hundred years earlier, when Victorian culture permitted men, but not women, to "gratify their basic sexual needs," many of women's problems may have been sexual in nature. But that was not the issue facing modern women. Indeed, Friedan argued that women had been encouraged to seek too *much* fulfillment in their sexual lives, leading some women to wrongly conclude that an affair or a new husband would assuage their pain.

The source of "the problem with no name," she insisted, was that modern culture did not allow women, as it allowed men, to gratify a need that was just as important as sex—the "need to grow and fulfill their potentialities as human beings." Denied permission to pursue this goal, misled into thinking that service to their family was the highest and only aspiration women should have, many developed "a hunger" that neither food nor sex could fill.

The women most likely to feel this hunger, Friedan said, were those who had chosen not to work outside the home. She noted that "career women may have other problems," but the women who suffered "this nameless aching dissatisfaction" were the very ones "whose greatest ambition has been marriage and children." Having been told that achieving these goals should satisfy their every need and aspiration, these women were afraid to admit their secret doubts and discontents. "There may be no psychological terms for the harm" done when women suppressed their hunger for stimulation and knowledge, Friedan declared. But terrible things happened "when women try to live according to an image that makes them deny their minds."

The response to these ideas was electric. Hundreds of women wrote letters to Friedan after reading a 1960 *Good Housekeeping* article that previewed her book, or the excerpts of *The Feminine Mystique* that appeared in *Ladies' Home Journal* and *McCall's* in early 1963, or the book itself, either in hardback in 1963 or in paperback in 1964.

The *Good Housekeeping* article was far more cautious than *The Feminine Mystique*. Its central argument was summed up in the title: "Women Are People Too," a notion that hardly seems revolutionary today. Yet letters poured in, many of them laboriously written by hand, both to the journal and to Friedan herself. The same excited phrases tumbled off their pages:

"I can't say how grateful I am"; "thank you"; the article "struck at my heart." "Hoorah for giving this 'misfit' courage for self-fulfillment!" "I am one of the people you wrote about." "I felt that the article was written just for me." It is such "a great comfort" to find out I am not "an incurable mental case," to "realize others feel the same," to "know I am not alone in my quest to find who I really am!"

The writers used words such as "desperate" and "overwhelming" to describe their lives. One woman wrote: "My husband cannot understand why I have suddenly turned miserable after 11 years of a good marriage." Until reading the article, she continued, "I had been unhappily living in the belief that my feelings about marriage were all wrong, that no other woman feels as I do. . . . Now that I know I am not alone in feeling as I do the future seems quite a bit brighter."

In a letter dated August 21, 1960, one woman wrote, "For the past year, I have been in a quandary, trying to find an answer to some of the questions you pose in your article. There were times when I felt that the only answer was to consult a psychiatrist and had I the money, prob-ably would have! The times of anger, bitterness and general frustration are simply too numerous to mention, but if I'd had any idea that hundreds of other women were feeling the same way, I don't believe I would have felt so completely alone."

Another woman mentioned that the article had come too late for her: "If I had only had these words and thoughts brought to my attention 10 years ago, perhaps my life would not have taken on the somewhat tragic aspect that it did. Because from just such frustrations as not feeling like a human being, I divorced my husband."

Three years later, the letters responding to *The Feminine Mystique* were filled with similar sentiments. The book, declared one woman, "per-fectly" described the forces that had been "flinging me against a wall of self incrimination." Another explained: "I thought these problems and sit-uations were only mine, and mine alone . . . and the knowledge that my neighbor-housewifes [sic] also have problems" came as such a "relief."

One suburban housewife wrote that she had "everything materially there is to have" but frequently fled into the bathroom "to cry in the towel." She hoped husbands would read the book. "Mine wouldn't. . . . But at least it has helped me understand my feelings and attitudes a little better. Even if I can't change any part of my life now, I will feel better for knowing I'm no[t] an oddball after all."

Another wrote, "Only the other night, while talking to my husband of my discontent at being a housewife and mother only, I cried out in anguish, 'What kind of women [*sic*] am I.' Now it is a comfort to realize that I am a normal women [*sic*], entangled in the world of today. . . . My husband has up to now felt I could not combine being a mother with educating myself for a future role in the world. Since he has been reading your book too, I feel he will realize that these two roles are really one. . . . I'm determined now to make a start, perhaps earning money ironing or baby sitting to pay for each course."

A thirty-one-year-old housewife with four children proclaimed: "You have freed me from such a mass of subconscious and conscious guilt feelings, that I feel, today, as though I had been filled with helium and turned loose!" And a nineteen-year-old college sophomore enthused, "I was so enthralled, my heart beating only for the next word—next fact—next idea—I had to stop and *do something* to express my fervor: I splashed out a big sign, 'YEA BETTY FRIEDAN' to tape on the wall in front of me."

A few housewives sent Friedan poems they had written. "Time goes on," was the first line of one poem. "I stay behind." Another ended with: "She waits/ Listening/ In the dead dark/ To the sea beating itself to death on the beach . . . /She died waiting."

Many women offered themselves as case studies of how the feminine mystique had deformed women's psyches. "I am a classic example of arrested development," wrote one woman, referring to Friedan's description of how women had been infantilized by society's expectations. "I would have been the class of 1953 had I not dropped out of college after two years. . . . But my internal demand for self-expression . . . has been eating away at me for about five years." A Florida mother of four wrote that for years she had been trying in vain to explain to her husband her need "to have a purpose." "All I've ever achieved was to feel guilty about wanting to be more than a housewife and a mother."

Another woman, married eight years with two children, wrote that she had been "fighting a battle with the 'feminine mystique' for four years," with a husband who "is very good as a husband but who believes women are inferior by the will of God, so it hasn't been an easy struggle. Although I stood highest in my high school class and read constantly, none of my ideas were important." She thanked Friedan for giving her "that extra boost I needed to know I am important to myself and my children and not just a diaper changer."

In one letter, a woman described herself as "trapped, with no hope of freedom. . . . After twenty years of home, husband, and children, I finally got a chance to fulfill a dream. I went to college four evenings a week for two and a half semesters and then had to drop out. My husband gave me a choice—school or him. . . . I love my husband and so I gave up school. However, I will try to raise my sons to realize that women are people with the same dreams, hopes, and feelings as men. . . . I will also try to help my daughter realize you can be feminine, a woman, and a full person at the same time. It is too late for me, but not for them."

Some women reported that they were reading the book with their husbands, and a few husbands wrote to say that they now understood their wives' depression better and would try to help them pursue outside interests. One husband, a father to two girls, thanked Friedan for making him feel a little constructive guilt about women's lack of options.

Other women complained that their husbands felt threatened, as one put it, by the idea "that I might have any interest other than him and the children." In a January 1964 letter, a woman who had been "uprooted" by her husband to move "to the boondocks of Alaska" wrote: "All I can say Betty is your husband must be a gem. You should bow down to the East every night and give thanks to the proud, individualistic male who can allow his wife to find her identity without it dissolving their marriage.

To work in your direction would cost me my second husband as it did my first, so I'll be a coward and bake my pies and tend my cottage and dream of all the prose I could write and the conversations I could have with interesting people." As it turned out, Friedan's marriage was not as solid as this woman assumed, and it fell apart soon after *The Feminine Mystique* became a best seller.

Some of Friedan's readers were professionals who already opposed the prevailing cultural prescriptions for women and thanked Friedan for giving them ammunition and validation. Many more had gone to college but dropped out before graduation to marry, or had married immediately after graduation, giving up earlier aspirations of training for a professional career to raise children who had arrived in quick succession.

Still, many readers were women who had never been to college and clearly did not have a middle-class background. Their letters often contained spelling and grammar mistakes, or specifically mentioned their lack of money and resources, sometimes complaining that the book was too expensive. Lisa F. told me that she went through the 1950s without reading any books, and no periodicals except the women's magazines next to the hair dryer on her weekly visits to the beauty parlor. But when she read the article in *Good Housekeeping*, she knew she had to get that book when it came out. When she finally heard that it was in the local bookstore, "I marched right down and bought it out of my weekly food budget. It was the first non-fiction book I ever read all the way through, and I had to look up several words in my husband's dictionary." Journalist and novelist Anna Quindlen remembers that when she was twelve years old, she was struck by the sight of her mother, who was not normally much of a reader, "hunched over this paperback, frowning, twin divots between her dark brows."

In a three-page handwritten letter dated October 20, 1963, one woman wrote in response to reading Friedan's article in *LIFE* magazine, "Education, I have none of. But every single word you wrote was and always did go round and round in my mind till I absolutely had to stop thinking that way, so sure was I that I was some kind of nut."

"My husband cannot understand," she continued. "He needs only me. I need the whole world, in my mind that is." Her children and grandchildren are "a delicious big part" of that world, she wrote, but they "cannot be my whole world."

Laura W. recalled that when she was about fifteen, in either 1963 or 1964, she had seen her mother, who had completed only two years of high school and was married to a brewery worker, hide the book in her closet when she thought no one was looking. Laura remembered sneaking in later to look at it, thinking it might be an "adult book about how to be mysterious and sexy." Instead, it looked disappointingly boring. But she realized she had never before seen her mother read anything except magazines "and I felt somehow that it wouldn't be good for anyone else in the family to find out." Years later, Laura's mother confided that she too had suffered from the problem with no name.

Not all readers felt a shock of recognition. Many disagreed vehemently with Friedan's views. An editor at the *Ladies' Home Journal* wrote to Friedan that she was sorry to report that the "huge" response to the book excerpt in the January 1963 issue contained "more cons than pros," although, she noted, "the pros are extremely articulate." In its next issue, the magazine reported that of the "hundreds" of letters they received, 80 percent were hostile. When *McCall's* published a different excerpt the next month, historian Jessica Weiss reports, 87 percent of the people who wrote to the magazine criticized Friedan's views.

Individuals also wrote directly to Friedan to express their disapproval. A few academics and the occasional businesswoman thought she exaggerated the prevalence of the mystique. But most of the critical letters Friedan received unwittingly confirmed the strength of the ideology she described. "It is reward enough for me to see my husband busy but happy, my children leaders in their own schools, because I am home each day making beds, cooking good meals, and ready to listen . . . to problems, sorrows, and joys," wrote a New Jersey housewife, who thanked God for equipping women with the ability "to be all-loving, self-sacrificing, gentle, feminine." Another letter declared: "Real women are wanted, needed, loved, and desired because we are happy, having learned the finest lesson of all: selflessness."

Most of the angry letters were from people who had not read the entire book, having seen enough in an excerpt or a review to know that they disagreed. A woman responding to an excerpt in the *Chicago Tribune* gave Friedan some acerbic advice: "If you are married, Miss F. I pity your husband and family. If you are not married—*DON'T* EVER MARRY—until you can feel like and be A REAL WOMAN." It was signed "from one who is."

A letter dated February 18, 1963, from a woman who had read the excerpt in the *Ladies' Home Journal*, fairly shouted with indignation: "*Please!* More emphasis on contented homemakers and less on frustrated lost identities. Leave the breadwinner to 'hubby'—result—more inflated male egos." This last result, apparently, was a good thing.

An April 28, 1963, letter from a man who had read a newspaper excerpt inadvertently bolstered Friedan's contention that psychiatry was often used to dismiss women's aspirations. "Any woman who asks herself, 'Is this all?' as in the first paragraph, is in need of psychiatric counseling. . . . Your book-article will only contribute to the further instability of the few neurotic women who take it seriously." Another man had read "the main part" of a speech she gave at Southern Methodist University and was outraged at the idea of encouraging housewives to find jobs: "Do you advocate throwing another 30 million or so males out on the street so women can 'find' themselves?"

Ridgely Hunt, a writer for the *Chicago Tribune*, turned Friedan's argument upside down, suggesting that men had become trapped in their basements because magazines like *Popular Mechanics* had persuaded them to fill their time building plywood commodes and motorized ice sleds. Mocking Friedan's account of women's desire to do something more meaningful with their lives, he described the contemporary man as asking: "Is there no worthier goal toward which I can direct my finely machined intelligence than this tawdry business of earning a living and supporting my family?" But "no one is listening to him," declared Hunt. "His wife is off to a painting lesson so she can express her inner self."

Such ridicule was by no means rare, but Hunt's was intriguing given his personal evolution. A war correspondent who specialized in masculine stories about camping with the Green Berets, riding along in fire engines, and scuba diving to ocean wrecks, Hunt was well known for his hostile attitudes toward women and hippies. Yet by the end of the 1960s he had left his wife and three children and was dressing in women's clothes and growing his hair long. In the mid-1970s, he had sex-reassignment surgery and became Nancy Hunt.

Contrary to many caricatures of the work, *The Feminine Mystique* never urged women to leave their families or even to pursue full-time careers. The final chapter, "A New Life Plan for Women," advocated what social conservatives now suggest women should do as an alternative to working while their children are young. Assuming that most women would opt out of work, or at least cut back to part-time, for several years to raise children, Friedan suggested that during this time they take a few classes or engage in volunteer activities that would be compatible with their family duties, then later pursue or resume a career.

Friedan proposed a "GI Bill for Women" to reintegrate housewives and mothers into public life in the same way the GI Bill had helped the mostly male veterans obtain higher education and job training after their prolonged absence during the war. If women's role in raising families was the valued public service that so many politicians claimed, she argued, why not develop a similar government program to subsidize tuition and books—"even, if necessary, some household help"—for women who had taken time away from work or education to raise children and then wanted to go back to school and prepare themselves for a profession?

"The whole concept of women's education would be regeared from four-year college to a life plan under which a woman could continue her education, without conflict with her marriage, her husband and her children." For women who had not been able to attend college before marriage and childbearing, she suggested that society subsidize a summer immersion program designed to make it possible for them to succeed in future studies.

The Feminine Mystique contained no call for women to band together to improve their legal and political rights. Instead, it urged women, as individuals, to reject the debilitating myth that their sole purpose and happiness in life came from being a wife and mother, and to develop a life plan that would give meaning to the years after their children left home. For all its differences with George Gallup's description of housewives in the *Saturday Evening Post*, *The Feminine Mystique* ended with a similar recommendation, although Friedan encouraged women to develop their additional goals early in life and not put them aside entirely even when the children were young. And she rejected the prevailing view that women who *did* want to work or pursue education throughout their lives would be harming their marriage or their children.

Nowhere does the book advocate that most women pursue full-time careers or even suggest that women ask their husbands to help them with child care and housework if they went to school or took a job. In fact, in the late 1960s and early 1970s, many feminists criticized the book for failing to confront male privilege in the home.

There is no male-bashing anywhere in *The Feminine Mystique*. Friedan actually placed more blame on women than on men for the prevalence of the mystique, which she called their "mistaken choice," and she wrote repeatedly that women would become *better* wives and mothers if they developed interests beyond the home. Indeed, Friedan once suggested that her tombstone should read: "She helped make women feel better about being women and therefore better able to freely and fully love men."

Friedan simply urged women to pursue an education and develop a life plan that would give meaning to the years after the children left home. That her book spurred such outrage in some quarters and such relief in others is testimony to how much many women still needed it, despite the changes already occurring in American society.

Toward its end, *The Feminine Mystique* does contain a few quotes that seem stunningly dismissive of the work of full-time housewives. In Chapter 10, Friedan comments that in decades past, "certain institutions concerned with the mentally retarded discovered that housework was

peculiarly suited to the capacities of feeble-minded girls," adding acer-
bically that in those days "housework was much more difficult" than it is
now. And in Chapter 12 she describes the suburban home as "a comfortable concentration camp," claiming that women who had grown up wanting only to be a housewife were as much in danger of losing their identity
and humanity "as the millions who walked to their own death in the concentration camps."

Still, any serious reader would understand that these quotes are hy-
perbole, because Friedan says repeatedly that women were *not* coerced
into their constricted lives, but rather chose them. And after these in-
flammatory statements, she quickly concedes that the suburban home
"is not a concentration camp, nor are American housewives on their way
to the gas chamber." All she is really saying, she assures her readers, is
that many housewives "are in a trap, and to escape they must . . . live
their own lives again according to a self-chosen purpose. They must
begin to grow."

That message—that they could and should begin to grow—was what
most of the women who read the book cover to cover took away. Nine of
the women interviewed for this book still had their original copies of *The
Feminine Mystique* and allowed me to go through their yellow, dog-eared
pages. Not one had underlined any of the acerbic quotes in the book,
and few even remembered her saying these things.

Friedan was not looking for an audience of militants. She wanted to
reach beyond the academics, career women, feminists, and leftists who
had already questioned the feminine mystique in the 1940s and 1950s,
although without calling it by that name, to women who were not yet aware
of the sources of their unhappiness. And she managed to strike a chord
in the kind of woman who knew at some level that her aspirations for life
went beyond the recipes and homemaking hints in women's magazines
but who hesitated, out of guilt or self-doubt, to acknowledge those other
needs and desires. The question is, why were so many women in that position in an era when so many social changes were already under way?

3

~~~~~~~~

After the First Feminist Wave: Women from the 1920s to the 1940s

MANY DIFFERENT WOMEN RECOGNIZED THEMSELVES IN FRIEDAN'S PORTRAIT of Americans brainwashed by the feminine mystique. Some were "ordinary housewives" or their daughters, who had never known a family that was not organized on the male breadwinner–female homemaker model and had never been exposed to the kind of social criticism they encountered in Friedan's work. They often wrote to Friedan that until they read her book, they had never imagined any alternative to the lives women were living. Others were self-described "spinsters," "divorcees," or "neurotic malcontents" who said they had always thought of themselves as "freaks" because they didn't fit the norm.

But many women I interviewed reported having gone through a puzzling evolution—or devolution—in their lives. They had attended college, worked at jobs they enjoyed, or been raised in families that supported women's aspirations for education and equal rights. Over and over, women described having been honors students, community activists, political organizers, or competent "working girls" before they married and had children. But somewhere during the late 1940s or the 1950s, they had abandoned any dream of resuming their former pursuits and lost the sense that they had anything to contribute to the world aside from being wives and mothers.

Friedan argued that this collective loss of confidence and aspiration was part of a major transformation that occurred after World War II, when a social sea change wiped out the memory of what feminism had accomplished in the early twentieth century. One of her first tasks in the book was to remind women of what they had done in the past.

From the 1850s through the 1920s, Friedan explained, women had struggled to gain access to education, win the right to vote, and break down other barriers preventing them from entering the public world of work and politics. "The ones who fought that battle won more than empty paper rights," she wrote. "They cast off the shadow of contempt and self-contempt that had degraded women for centuries," finding a new confidence in their own capabilities.

Friedan described the "sense of possibility" that women felt in the 1920s, 1930s, and 1940s. The public was captivated by daring pilots Amelia Earhart and Elinor Smith Sullivan and by female athletes such as nineteen-year-old Gertrude Ederle, who not only was the first woman to swim the English Channel but also did it faster than any of the five men who had previously made it across. The "spirited career girls" of those decades—from such widely admired real-life women to the feisty heroines portrayed in films by Katharine Hepburn and Rosalind Russell—were celebrated in popular culture, including by women's magazines.

But after World War II, Friedan continued, "the image of the American woman as a changing, growing individual in a changing world was shattered. Her solo flight to find her own identity was forgotten in the rush for the security of togetherness. Her limitless world shrunk to the cozy walls of home."

How, asked Friedan, had the exhilarating embrace of individual identity and feminist ideals in the 1920s given way to a vision of feminine fulfillment that prevented a woman from using her capabilities, from "even dream[ing] about herself, except as her children's mother, her husband's wife"? What produced the "strange paradox" of the 1950s and early 1960s, when just as professions finally were opening to women, the term "'career woman' became a dirty word"? How was it that in the space of little more than a decade, the feminine mystique had become "so powerful that women grow up no longer knowing that they have the desires and capacities the mystique forbids"?

Friedan's answer, described in painstaking detail in eight chapters packed with facts, figures, and quotations, was that the feminine mystique developed as part of a postwar backlash against the feminist movement of the late nineteenth and early twentieth centuries. The attempt to drive women back into the home, she argued, was spearheaded by Freudian psychiatrists, conservative social scientists, and educators who increasingly claimed that when women prepared themselves for anything other than marriage and motherhood they were turning their back on their true feminine nature.

Friedan acknowledged that women had not been forced into accepting the feminine mystique. The call for women to return to the home had tapped into pent-up desires for stability among people whose families had been disrupted by the hardships of the Great Depression and World War II. Focusing on the family also seemed to alleviate the anxieties unleashed by Cold War tensions. Responding to these inducements, and misled by so-called experts who explained that it was abnormal to want anything else, women made the "mistaken choice" to retreat into domesticity. "What happened to women is part of what happened to all of us in the years after the war. We found excuses for not facing the problems we once had the courage to face."

In Friedan's view, women withdrew from the responsibilities and challenges of independence in the 1950s "just as men shrugged off the bomb, forgot the concentration camps, condoned corruption, and fell into helpless conformity." It was easier and safer "to think about love and sex than about communism, McCarthy, and the uncontrolled bomb. . . . There was a kind of personal retreat, even on the part of the most far-sighted, the most spirited; we lowered our eyes from the horizon, and steadily contemplated our own navels."

Business interests enthusiastically promoted this retreat into personal life because they saw in it a tremendous opportunity to expand the consumer goods sector of the postwar boom economy. In an exhaustive review of 1950s advertising manuals and surveys, including studies provided by Ernest Dichter, the decade's leading advertising guru, Friedan showed that manufacturers explicitly defined the ideal consumer as a homemaker who could be convinced to see housework as a way of expressing her individual creativity and affirming her femininity.

Friedan used the stunningly frank statements of the motivational researchers to reveal how they consciously tried to persuade women that buying household goods and foodstuffs would provide self-realization, sexual fulfillment, and a sense of eternal youthfulness. Advertisers became "the most powerful of [the mystique's] perpetuators . . . flattering the American housewife, diverting her guilt and disguising her growing sense of emptiness."

The chapter titled "The Sexual Sell" still elicits a shock of recognition and resentment today, and it had a tremendous impact on readers at the time. In each of the original copies of the book that I reviewed, this was the most heavily underlined section. Following on the heels of Friedan's trenchant critiques of psychiatrists, social scientists, educators, politicians, and popular magazines, this chapter provided the clinching piece of evidence for many readers that they had indeed been targets of a massive and cynical campaign to erase the feminist aspirations of the 1920s and turn women into mindless consumers.

In the years since *The Feminine Mystique* was published, historians have faulted Friedan's account of the decline of feminism and the rise of the feminine mystique. They point out that she exaggerated the popular approval of feminism in the 1920s, 1930s, and 1940s, as well as the novelty of the antifeminist propaganda of the 1950s. The feminine mystique was not a postwar invention, but rather a repackaging of old prejudices in more modern trappings in the aftermath of the suffrage movement. Indeed, the effort to convince the "New Woman" to turn her back on the rights she had gained during the first two decades of the twentieth century began before the ink was even dry on the Nineteenth Amendment, giving women the vote. It is true that Freudian warnings about the sexual abnormality of the career woman gave antifeminists new weapons in the 1940s and that the blandishments of the sexual sell in the 1950s added the carrot of consumerism to the stick of antifeminism. But there was no golden age of feminism in the 1920s and 1930s.

Yet Friedan's account rang true to many women who had raised families in the1940s and 1950s. Again and again, women told me there was "something different" about the postwar era, "something deadening." By the 1950s, women were marrying at a younger age than at any time in the previous hundred years, and this may have made them more susceptible to the sexual sell. And three decades of relentless attacks on feminism as antimale and antifamily had taken their toll. Even women who had experienced other models of family life and female behavior said that during the 1950s they came to believe that normal families were those where the wife and mother stayed home, and that normal women were perfectly happy with that arrangement.

FRIEDAN WAS CERTAINLY CORRECT THAT IN THE FIRST DECADES OF THE twentieth century, the final push for female suffrage, along with the overturning of many restrictive conventions from Victorian days, stirred an excitement about female achievements and capabilities that had largely receded by the 1950s. Suffrage activists collected millions of signatures on petitions and held mass meetings that garnered enormous public attention. From street corner rallies organized by fiery labor orators to dignified delegations of middle-class "ladies" who gently lobbied small-town mayors and state legislatures, the suffrage movement was highly visible across the country.

Not everyone agreed with the women's rights activists, but their opponents' hostility often worked in the suffragists' favor. In 1913, suffragists holding a mass march in Washington, D.C., two months after President Woodrow Wilson's inauguration were attacked by an angry crowd. The women were jeered at, pelted with burning cigars, and knocked to the ground. Some had their clothes torn off. The police and national guard refused to defend the women, and journalists reported that the suffrage marchers had to fight their way "foot by foot" up Pennsylvania Avenue, taking more than an hour to traverse the first ten blocks. But the incident became a national scandal that embarrassed opponents of women's rights and galvanized more women into action.

By 1916 the National American Woman Suffrage Association had 2 million members, and the more militant National Woman's Party had 50,000 members. During World War I, Women's Party leader Alice Paul built a "watchfire" in an urn outside the White House gates. Every time Wilson made a speech that referred to the need for freedom abroad, Paul and her supporters burned a copy of the speech to dramatize the hypocrisy of condemning other countries for lack of freedom while more than half of America's own citizens still were not allowed to vote.

When demonstrators were arrested, they went on hunger strikes, which prison authorities tried to break by forced feeding. Protests against the jailings and the prison treatment were held throughout the country. Eventually public outrage became so great that the suffragists were released and their sentences nullified. Feeling the heat, President Wilson pressed his allies in Congress to stop blocking the suffrage bill.

The campaign for the vote challenged the nineteenth-century image of women as passive and timid. Friedan quoted the memoir of an English feminist who recalled that women's organizational capacities, courage, and solidarity "were a revelation to all concerned, but especially themselves. . . . We were often tired, hurt and frightened. But we . . . shared a joy of life that we had never known." The dramatist Jesse Lynch Williams, a supporter of women's rights, described the stunned reaction of hostile members of a Fifth Avenue men's club to one of the massive suffrage demonstrations that periodically clogged New York City's major thoroughfares:

It was a Saturday afternoon and the members had crowded behind the windows to witness the show. They were laughing and exchanging the kind of jokes you would expect. When the head of the procession came opposite them, they burst into laughing and as the procession swept past, laughed long and loud. But the women continued to pour by. The laughter began to weaken, became spasmodic. The parade went on and on. Finally there was only the occasional sound of the clink of ice in the glasses. Hours passed. Then someone broke the silence. "Well boys," he said, "I guess they mean it!"

The constitutional amendment to approve women's suffrage passed the Congress in 1919 and was ratified by the states in 1920. Jubilant women vowed that America would never be the same.

Changes in cultural mores about gender and sexuality during the first two decades of the twentieth century contributed to the heady sense that a revolution was under way, even among women who were not political activists. The World War I era saw the overthrow of nineteenth-century norms that had prevented respectable young women from going out in public alone or with a member of the opposite sex. The middle-class custom of "calling," where a young man socialized with a young woman in her parents' parlor or on the front porch, gave way to dating, where the man picked up the woman and then took her, without a chaperone, to a film, cabaret, dance hall, or amusement park.

His date often left the house wearing clothes that would have marked her as a prostitute just twenty years earlier. One authority has estimated that in the late nineteenth century a respectable middle-class woman wore more than thirty pounds of clothing when she went out in public. Now women were free to wear sleeveless dresses that ended at their knees, smoke cigarettes, drink liquor, bob their hair, and even talk openly about sex.

For most women, such personal freedoms merely opened up a new route to marriage and provided more opportunity to find sexual satisfaction within marriage. But for others they were part of an unprecedented insistence on the right to an independent identity. Many career women saw themselves as participating in a feminine revolution. They presented themselves as examples of what their gender could achieve rather than as exceptions or anomalies, as so many career women of the 1940s and '50s were wont to do. Movie star Mary Pickford declared that she was "proud to be one of . . . the girls who make their own living" and delighted to see other members of her sex make good. Amelia Earhart was an outspoken supporter of the Equal Rights Amendment.

The successes of the early-twentieth-century feminist movement permanently changed the discussion of women's roles in society. Even defenders of traditional gender roles could no longer argue that women were innately incapable of physical heroism and political, professional, or athletic achievement. Few dared to maintain that society had any right to legally prevent women from exercising the same rights as men. Suddenly it was hard to find anyone who had been against the Nineteenth Amendment, even though the vote had been so close that one congressman refused to have his broken arm set for fear of missing the vote, while another left the deathbed of his wife, an ardent suffragist, to cast his vote for her cause.

The Roaring Twenties were indeed heady times. But Friedan exaggerated the extent of women's gains. Equal rights may have been increasingly accepted in the abstract, but in practice acceptance of female independence did not gain much traction in the 1920s. Opponents of gender equality shifted tactics and changed their rhetoric, arguing that while the women's movement had led to necessary reforms, it had gone too far. People who had initially condemned feminism because it encroached on men's traditional prerogatives now presented themselves as the true defenders of the female sex, faulting the movement for taking away women's traditional privileges.

In August 1920, the month the Nineteenth Amendment was ratified, the *Ladies' Home Journal* printed a "Credo for the New Woman." The editors offered a backhanded endorsement of women's rights that stressed the limits to equality they felt American women should accept. "I believe in woman's rights; but I believe in woman's sacrifices too." "I believe in woman's suffrage; but I believe many other things are vastly more important." "I believe in woman's brains; but I believe still more in her emotions." And "I believe in woman's assertion of self," as long as "through her new freedom [she] elects to serve others."

In November 1923, the *Ladies' Home Journal* printed an article by Corra Harris in which she remarked that modern women had been "acquiring a new set of adjectives, such as 'able,' 'efficient,' 'influential,' 'distinguished.'" Harris conceded that many of the activities of these "up-and-coming women of the present moment" were useful, and she even admitted to an "anxious hope" that they would stay in public service long enough to give "the national household a cleaning." But Harris believed that women must and soon would once more embrace the old adjectives, such as "'meek,' 'matronly,' 'maternal,' 'kind,' 'domestic.'" They would recognize, Harris predicted, that nothing was to be gained from reforming the world at the price of their "mental and spiritual" happiness, and they would return to "the ancient duties and pleasures" of home.

"We can amend the Constitution," Harris concluded, "but it is my belief that we cannot change the nature of women by doing so. They belong to love, goodness, faith in all things. . . . They will never endure the revolting revelations of political life nor the fierce competitions of public life. They are only trying on a new-fashioned garment to see if it becomes them. It will not. Therefore they will not wear it or pay for it."

Not everyone shared Harris's confidence that American women would get over their infatuation with the new freedoms. As the 1920s progressed, warnings about the excesses of feminism became more strident. One especially popular ploy in agitating against further progress was to publish testimonies of purported former feminists, or daughters of feminists, about the costs of "too much" liberation.

Typical was "I Rebel at Rebellion" by Marian Castle in the July 1930 *Woman's Journal*. Castle acknowledged that an older generation of women had become understandably "tired of being classed with children and imbeciles at the polls" and "ashamed of having to search their husbands' pockets in the wee small hours for even smaller change." But her generation, she claimed, had "carried the banner of freedom to unforeseen heights," and these had become as oppressive as the old restrictions.

The freedom "to smoke, to drink, to sit up all night, to discuss the hitherto undiscussible, and to work like men with men," Castle claimed, had become "desperately confining." So, she announced, she had "become a rebel once more" and was fighting to "be free of this new freedom." Castle described herself as now singing "paeans of joy over the fact that I may depend upon my husband for money instead of earning it myself."

The onset of the Depression tilted the discussion of women's place in society even further toward the antifeminist side. The persistence of high unemployment increased hostility toward working wives, who were thought to be double-dipping into an already shrinking pool of jobs. In a 1936 Gallup poll, 82 percent of people said wives should not work if their husbands had jobs. By 1939, the percentage had risen to almost 90 percent.

Women's support for equality as an abstract principle did not disappear. In a 1938 poll conducted by the *Ladies' Home Journal*, 60 percent of the female respondents disliked having the word "obey" in marriage vows, 75 percent favored joint decision-making between husband and wife, and a whopping 80 percent felt that an unemployed husband should keep house for his wife if she were working. In practice, however, 60 percent said they would not respect a husband who earned less than his wife, and 90 percent believed a wife should give up her job if her husband asked her to do so.

The Depression also undermined the allure of work outside the home for women. In the 1920s, joining the workforce had been an adventure for many young women, but in this gigantic economic catastrophe, more women were pushed into segregated, low-wage jobs. During the 1930s women lost ground in the professions and in the better-paid manufacturing work they had begun to enter in the previous decade.

Employed wives found themselves working a longer "double shift," as they tried to save money at home by sewing more of their own clothes, canning their own preserves, and baking goods from scratch. Jenny L. reported that her mother often baked more than the family really needed because bulk flour came in cloth bags that could be used to make clothes. Her mom calculated that it was cheaper to purchase more flour and crowd some extra bread into the oven than to buy separate cloth for the girls' dresses. Sometimes she traded the extra bread for fresh vegetables or sent Jenny to give it to other unemployed families.

Many women who had expected to be full-time homemakers were forced to join the workforce when their husbands were laid off. A study of white working-class and middle-class men and women who grew up during the Great Depression found that children of both sexes associated such changes in parental roles with high levels of family tension. They saw their mothers' work outside the home as a failure of their fathers rather than a success of their mothers. Compared to the previous two generations, youths raised in the Great Depression were more eager to marry early, start a family, and have a stay-at-home wife.

Articles by "reformed" feminists remained popular through the 1930s. Rose Wilder Lane, daughter of Laura Ingalls Wilder of *Little House on the Prairie* fame, and a woman who had worked outside the home since she was eighteen, wrote the article "Woman's Place Is in the Home" in the October 1936 *Ladies' Home Journal*. She claimed that thirty years earlier, she had been one of the young women fighting for the freedoms the younger generation now enjoyed. "You can hardly imagine the world as it was then," she wrote. "You do not know how much you owe us." But if you did realize how much you owe us, she continued, "you would slit our throats."

By encouraging women to become "personally independent," Lane declared, she and others like her had thrown away the "deep-rooted, nourishing, and fruitful man-and-woman relationship." Lane was an economic libertarian who believed that the New Deal had undermined the manly self-reliance that made America great. But she believed that feminism had undermined the womanly dependence that was equally important to society, creating a "self-centered self-reliance" that, for females, was as "imprisoning as armor." Give up such self-defeating independence, she urged women, and abandon the attempt to use any of your talents as anything more than "adornments . . . for your femininity." Your true "career is to make a good marriage."

Dorothy Thompson was another well-known and successful journalist who warned women against the hidden costs of "emancipation." In her column "If I Had a Daughter" in the September 1939 *Ladies' Home Journal*, she claimed (with considerable overstatement) that "there is scarcely an occupation, whatever the intellectual requirements, that is not open to women." Thousands of women had therefore come to believe that they could "enter engrossing and demanding occupations . . . and at the same time have happy and productive marriages." But, she declared, that is "an illusion. One woman in a thousand can do it. And she is a genius."

If I had a daughter who wanted to be a novelist, Thompson wrote, I would tell her "that little talent of yours" is unlikely to produce anything truly worthwhile and urge her to abandon any dream of a career. She would do better to raise "a fine man" than to write "a second-rate novel."

Most women who had been feminists in the early twentieth century did not renounce their views, but in the absence of a central unifying issue, such as the vote, the movement lost its momentum. And women who remained activists were deeply divided over where to put their energies. The National Woman's Party devoted its efforts to lobbying for an Equal Rights Amendment that would prohibit politicians and employers from passing laws and work rules that applied to only one gender. Such rules, known as "protective" legislation, excluded women from jobs that required heavy lifting, included night shifts, or were thought to pose particular threats to health and safety.

Proponents of the ERA argued that many of these regulations kept women from well-paid work. Protective legislation allowed women to work as waitresses, where they rushed back and forth from kitchen to dining room balancing heavy trays of hot food, but prevented them from standing behind the bar and mixing drinks.

However, most activists, including most labor-union women, supported protective legislation, fearing that women's health and economic prospects would suffer if they were put into direct competition with men in a social environment where health-and-safety regulations were minimal. So old allies went in separate directions, often in mutual animosity.

Women on both sides of the ERA issue increasingly worked behind the scenes to influence legislation rather than attempting to reach a mass audience. During the New Deal, an unprecedented number of female activists who supported protective legislation were appointed to policy-making positions, especially in the Women's Bureau of the Labor Department.

The networks they constructed later served as the organizational base for the revived feminist movement in the 1960s. But in the meantime, feminism lost its public face. And in the economic and political climate of the 1930s, activist women and men who might otherwise have supported campaigns to extend female equality turned their attention to building a social safety net for families and countering the growing threat of fascism.

WORLD WAR II INTRODUCED NEW ELEMENTS INTO THE DISCUSSION OF women's place in the public sphere. The United States entered the war in December 1941, and before the war's end in August 1945, the female labor force would increase by almost 60 percent, with married women making up three-fourths of those newly entering the workforce. As part of the war effort, women worked in jobs that had previously been unthinkable for their sex: They became pipe fitters, mechanics, welders, carpenters, and shipfitters, their efforts glamorized in the image of "Rosie the Riveter."

Their war work renewed a national sense of pride in women's capabilities. In 1943 a Senior Scholastic poll of 33,000 female high school students found that 88 percent aspired to have a career other than homemaking for at least a portion of their lives. And by May 1945, according to a Women's Bureau survey in Detroit, 60 percent of female workers who had been housewives before the war said they wanted to remain employed once the war ended.

Nevertheless, national polls found that fewer than 20 percent of American women as a whole thought the ideal life should combine marriage and a career. Despite the patriotic approval of women who worked in the war industry, strong hostility was directed at wives who worked for any other reason.

Many people were suspicious even of temporary war work when it came to mothers. J. Edgar Hoover, director of the FBI, argued that paid jobs were not appropriate for mothers in any circumstance. A mother "already has her war job. . . . Her patriotic duty is not on the factory front. It is on the home front!"

The government's creation of child care centers to accommodate working mothers stirred tremendous controversy, and a growing school of thought claimed that mothers' war work was spawning an epidemic of juvenile delinquency. In 1943, Margaret Riddle wrote a widely cited book blaming modern mothers for not giving their children enough "Tender Loving Care." An article in one women's magazine suggested that such neglectful mothers be drafted by the government and assigned "to duty in their own homes."

One survey of popular periodicals from the 1920s through the 1950s found that women portrayed in articles in the mid-1940s were more likely to hold jobs than in those from the 1920s, 1930s, or 1950s. But favorable attitudes toward such working women were confined to wives without children and mothers who worked from home or in their husband's business. Women who worked in independent professions or sought careers for their own sake were actually vilified more often in 1945 than in 1925, 1935, or 1955.

Somewhat paradoxically, a new strand of hostility directed at stay-at-home wives and mothers also escalated in the early years of the war. Historian Rebecca Jo Plant notes that many "modern" thinkers in the 1920s and 1930s had criticized the nineteenth-century cult of domestic motherhood not because it limited women's rights but because it gave women too much moral authority within the home. In 1942, building on this anti-maternalist sentiment, Philip Wylie published his vituperative *Generation of Vipers*, which blamed women for dominating the home front to the point that they emasculated their husbands and smothered their sons. Wylie drew on the writings of Freudian psychiatrists to support his attack on "momism," and the Freudians in turn embraced his label as their own.

In the view of most psychiatrists and the writers who popularized their works, "momism"—whether it took the form of overly strict or overly indulgent behavior—was the cause of almost every social ill. It produced sissies, murderers, and homosexuals. It even produced Nazism. Had Adolf Hitler's mother not coddled her son as a child, claimed medical author

Amram Scheinfeld in a November 1945 *Ladies' Home Journal* article, "history might have taken another course." The title of the article posed a question that many Americans answered with a resounding yes: "Are American Moms a Menace?"

Edward Strecker, a psychiatrist who studied soldiers found unfit for military duty, certainly thought so. He argued that unprecedented numbers of men were too "psychoneurotic" to cope with the rigors of military life, and he traced the problem back to the overprotective, smothering "mom and her wiles." Society was "veering toward a matriarchy," he claimed, in which mothers kept their sons "paddling about in a kind of psychological amniotic fluid rather than letting them swim away . . . from the emotional maternal womb."

These attacks on women's influence inside the home coexisted and sometimes merged with the attacks on their power outside the home, so that women got it coming and going: They were blamed for devoting too much attention to their children as well as for devoting too little.

The end of the war spurred more efforts to get women out of the workforce and back into the home. During the war, the government's *Magazine War Guide* had urged the editors of women's magazines to encourage women to get involved in civilian defense efforts outside the home. However, historian Nancy Walker reports, once the war ended the *War Guide* publishers suggested that editors "replace discussions of child care with articles on juvenile delinquency." This, they reminded the editors, was "one of the social ills blamed on working women."

As the veterans came home and began readjusting to civilian life, women were advised to set aside any independent aspirations they had developed. Sociologist Willard Waller declared that women had "gotten out of hand" during the wartime emergency. It was time to reaffirm two rules: "women must bear and rear children; husbands must support them."

Other experts argued that wives had a duty to rebuild their husbands' self-esteem, which had been damaged when they came home to find that women had been successfully running their households. A wife should make a special point of deferring to her husband's needs and wishes, they advised. "He's head man again," the magazine *House Beautiful* reminded its female readers. "Your part . . . is to fit his home to him, understanding why he wants it this way, forgetting your own preferences."

Women had little choice but to comply. When the war ended, thousands of female war workers showed up at their jobs only to find their final paycheck waiting. By 1947, more than 3 million women had been laid off from their wartime work.

Many were outraged at being dismissed so cavalierly. They took to the picket lines, carrying signs reading "Ford Hires New Help. We Walk the Street," "How Come No Work for Women?" and "Stop Discrimination Because of Sex." Several unions, including the United Auto Workers, held discussions about how to balance the rights of veterans with those of women.

But the public was in no mood to back any serious initiatives on women's behalf. In 1946, a *Fortune* magazine poll found that only 22 percent of the men they interviewed and barely 29 percent of the women thought women should have an equal chance at employment.

For many women, especially younger ones who had a family or planned to start one, regrets about losing good paychecks and the camaraderie of the workplace were outweighed by the relief of having their men home from the war. My own mother recalled forty years later how hurt and angry she had been at being let go with so little ceremony or thanks. "But we knew the veterans deserved their old jobs back," she told me when I recorded her oral history back in the 1980s. "And I was looking forward to finding a better place to live and settling into family life for a while."

At the beginning of the war there had been a surge in hasty marriages, and during the war sexual experimentation had been widespread, both at home and on the front. Not surprisingly, the end of the war saw a huge spike in divorces, which only led to new concerns about the need to strengthen marriage. It also had the benefit of immediately weeding out many marriages whose endings might otherwise have been spread out over the 1950s, producing a deceptive appearance of marital stability in that decade.

Unmarried men and women were eager to settle down after the disruptions of depression and war, and the average age of marriage dropped sharply. In 1940, only 24 percent of eighteen- to twenty-four-year-old women were married. By 1950, 60 percent of women in that age group had tied the knot. Men also began marrying younger and in greater numbers; by 1950, more than 40 percent of American males between twenty and twenty-four were married, compared to just 22 percent back in 1900. And the birthrate, which had been falling for most of the previous hundred years, soared after the war.

These changes were accompanied by a new romanticization of the nuclear family as the main source of security and happiness. The first half of the 1940s, historian William Graebner argues, was a time of social activism around such public issues as opposing fascism and supporting the war effort. But the second half of the decade was characterized by a "private, familial" culture, "committed to consumption and the consequent reversion to traditional gender roles." It was now almost a patriotic duty, Americans were told, to become "blissfully domestic," furnishing their homes, yards, and garages with the most modern goods and appliances the postwar economy could provide.

Most wars and other historical events that destabilize family formation or result in couples being separated for long periods of time are followed by a brief bump in weddings and births, as people make up for delayed marriages and childbearing. Typically, however, the spike is followed by a quick reversion to preexisting trends, and this is what demographers of the 1950s initially expected to see. Instead, the postwar "adjustment" lasted long enough that it seemed to have established a new norm for family behavior in America. The age of marriage continued to fall for the next fifteen years: By 1960, half of all women were marrying while still in their teens. The postwar rise in fertility continued until 1957, when it peaked at 123 births per 1,000 women, up from 79.5 per 1,000 in 1940. The birthrate for third children doubled between 1940 and 1960, while the birthrate for fourth children tripled.

Looking back at the late 1940s and the 1950s from the late twentieth century, many observers mistakenly believed that the family norms of that era were natural or traditional. For them the question was why the postwar family model disintegrated and diversified so rapidly after 1965. But it may be more instructive to ask why the postwar increase in marriages and birthrates was not the short-lived "correction" most demographers expected, and why the retrenchment into domesticity lasted so long.

Immediately after the war, many observers believed that the example of Rosie the Riveter had permanently shattered the idea that women's place was in the home. The editors of the *Saturday Evening Post* predicted that millions of American women would now "sniff at postwar bromides about woman's place." And in fact, the postwar campaign to get women back into the home did not go unchallenged. Resistance to the reestablishment of older gender stereotypes was especially strong in 1946 and 1947, although it faded thereafter.

In 1946, Elizabeth Hawes published a vigorous defense of working women titled *Why Women Cry: or Wenches with Wrenches*. In the same year, Mary Beard issued a searing attack on Freudian theories about women. And the February 1947 *Ladies' Home Journal* featured the most unapologetic argument for gender-neutral marital roles that I found in any mainstream magazine published between 1945 and 1963. In "I Wear the Apron Now," David Duncan reported that he and his wife had switched roles after their second child was weaned. His wife left every day at 8:30 A.M., returning between 5:30 and 6:30 P.M. He spent the day caring for their two daughters, cleaning, marketing, and cooking, while trying to find time to write. The result, he concluded, completely contradicted the "popular belief that children need the care of a mother, which cannot be replaced by a father."

"After the first few days," Duncan wrote, "I was accepted as the logical person to whom to turn in case of a skinned knee, a bumped head, or desire for a graham cracker. My wife has become the charming lady who returns home in the evening, listens to a recital of the day's events, reads them a story, and assists in putting them to bed. The children hold her in considerable awe and proudly tell their playmates that *their* mother goes to work each day. When asked about their father, the reply is generally, 'Oh, he just stays home and takes care of the house and sometimes writes on the typewriter.'"

A similarly modern note was struck in the June 16, 1947, issue of *LIFE* magazine, which featured a series of stories about "The American Woman's Dilemma." The typical young woman, the editors explained, was "just as interested in getting married and having children as she would have been a few decades ago. But housework and child care alone no longer seem interesting enough for a lifetime job." Articles in this issue profiled several mothers who held down invigorating full-time careers, as well as a stay-at-home mother of three who worked one hundred hours a week. The magazine also described one mother in a dual-earner family who could not afford a nanny and had to board her child during the workweek. Remarkably, they did not imply that she was neglectful or unloving, merely noting that such separations are painful for parents and "sometimes breed insecurity in children."

The dilemma, as *LIFE* posed it, was whether a woman should combine a full-time job with marriage and motherhood, which was "likely to be very hard when her children are young" but "will leave her well-rounded in interests and experience when she has reached the free years after 40," or devote herself to full-time homemaking, which would ease the strain of raising a family but leave her "unprepared for what to do with her life once the children are no longer young."

The magazine sympathetically explored the lives of women who made each of these choices, as well as a third choice that the editors seemed to favor: "to combine part-time work with housekeeping while she is young and to use this experience more fully when her children have left home." This is exactly what Friedan suggested as a good option for most women in *The Feminine Mystique*.

But 1947 was also the year that journalist Ferdinand Lundberg and psychiatrist Marynia Farnham published *Modern Woman: The Lost Sex*, in which they described feminism as a "deep illness" and accused career women of seeking to symbolically castrate men. They calculated that two-thirds of Americans were neurotic and that most of them had been made so by their mothers. They saw no contradiction in saying that overinvolved stay-at-home mothers were as great a problem as neglectful career women, explaining that this was because such women's natural contentment with their domestic roles had been disturbed by "pernicious" feminist agitation.

In *The Feminine Mystique* Friedan quoted liberally from *Modern Woman* to illustrate the viciousness of postwar attacks on women. In fact, *Modern Woman* had more critics at the time of its publication than Friedan acknowledged. Still, it was an instant best seller and was featured in weekly news reports shown in movie theaters. And by the early 1950s, Farnham and Lundberg were quoted more often in popular magazines than their critics.

The antifeminist counteroffensive was reinforced by the political climate of the age. By the late 1940s America was in the midst of a massive anti-communist crusade that came to be known as McCarthyism, after Senator Joseph McCarthy of Wisconsin, one of its most strident and shameless practitioners. Politicians built entire careers around identifying and attacking communists, communist sympathizers, "queers," and "pinkos"—not to mention "liberals," who were, one intelligence officer testified before a congressional subcommittee, "only a hop, skip, and a jump" away from being communists. When President Harry Truman established a Loyalty Review Board for government employees, its director explained that the government was entitled to fire any worker on any "suspicion of disloyalty . . . however remote," without holding "any hearing whatsoever."

Private companies, unions, newspapers, and the entertainment industry soon claimed the same right, and many industries compiled blacklists of people who were suspected of subversive beliefs or supported such supposedly un-American causes as racial integration or nuclear disarmament. When women in New York organized to pressure officials to retain the day-care programs instituted during the war, the *New York Times* declared that their actions had "all the trappings of a Red drive, including leaflets, letters, telegrams, petitions, protest demonstrations, mass meetings, and hat passings." Readers were left to wonder why an organization supposedly funded by Moscow had to resort to passing the hat.

By the early 1950s, American culture was steeped in fear and suspicion. A 1953 poll found that 80 percent of Americans believed it was their duty to "report to the FBI relatives and acquaintances suspected of being communist." My mother recalled that "it was a good time to keep your head down. There was plenty to do getting resettled as a family instead of trying to take on McCarthyism, and at first it was a full-time job because there were still so many scarcities. Gradually, we got things that had been almost impossible to get for so many years—from little ones like sweets and stockings to big ones like a home and car. Then I had another child. Before I knew it, it was the middle of the 1950s and everything I'd done and thought in the late 1930s and during the war seemed like another world. I wasn't really happy with my life by then, but I could no longer imagine any other alternative."

The seductions of consumerism and the silencing of dissidents by political suppression were certainly factors in encouraging people to hunker down into the nuclear family, but something more subtle was also at work. Friedan exaggerated when she argued that a postwar counterrevolution wiped out feminism, leaving the marketers and women's magazines of the 1950s unchallenged in their campaign to instill the feminine mystique in women's psyches. Yet she was right to remark that, more than in other eras, American housewives in the 1950s seemed especially likely to either forget they had ever had any other options or to believe they were no longer capable of exercising them.

Louise Beecher, born in 1922, spent the Depression in Flint, Michigan, where her father ran a small grocery and her mother helped out in the shop. Many of their friends and customers were factory workers in the auto industry, and Louise remembers sitting enthralled, at age fifteen, as members of the Ladies Auxiliary of the United Auto Workers recounted how they had braved tear gas and billy clubs to protect their husbands, brothers, and fathers, who had occupied several auto plants in a sit-down strike. One woman showed her how to fold a newspaper into a makeshift weapon for use in a clash with police or strikebreakers. Louise also babysat for a woman who worked in a printing company and was proud of her skills. "I had lots of role models for independent women who weren't the least bit neurotic," she recalled. "But twenty years later, I could hardly remember that."

Louise was nineteen when the war started. Her boyfriend immediately enlisted, and Louise spent the war working in her father's store. She married her boyfriend in 1946, and they had their first child in 1948. For a couple of years, Louise worked part-time while her husband went back to school on the GI Bill. She quit when he graduated and landed a good job. Soon they moved into a new home, "with plenty of room for a family," away from the working-class neighborhood where she'd grown up. By 1957 she had three children, ages nine, seven, and four, and was "not bored, exactly—the kids were too much work for that—but restive, dissatisfied."

"Suddenly, out of nowhere, I got this urge to go to school and train to be a pharmacist. But I didn't know what I'd do for child care. What kind of a bad mom would I be if I left my kids with a babysitter? Now it seems silly, because I had babysat all through my teens for a perfectly normal, well-adjusted family where the woman worked and the kids were doing fine and nobody thought there was anything wrong with her. But still, I was afraid the neighbors would look down on me. I thought there was something wrong with me for not being content with my nice home and my three kids and my weekly appointments at the hair salon."

"And it wasn't just like I felt I shouldn't work. I was afraid I couldn't handle the pressures. I worried it to death for the next six years, first deciding one thing, then another, wondering if I ought to see a psychiatrist. Then someone at the hairdresser's—maybe it was the hairdresser herself—told me about this book I ought to read. *The Feminine Mystique*."

For all of Friedan's exaggerations and sometimes selective use of evidence, she was right that for many women there was something peculiarly disorienting about the postwar ideology of domesticity. The sources of that disorientation were more complex than Friedan's account of feminist victories before the war and an antifeminist counterrevolution afterward suggests. And the cultural currents of the 1950s were not as monolithic as she claimed in supporting women's confinement to the home. But in many cases, rather than providing women with maneuvering room, the mixed messages and contradictory trends in that era actually contributed to their sense of paralysis.

During the late 1940s and the 1950s, many women—especially those in the middle class—came to internalize society's ambivalence about women's nature and role in postwar America as a personal shortcoming rather than a societal contradiction. And precisely because they recognized how much better off they were than their parents and many contemporaries, those who did feel discontented also felt deeply guilty about it. Until they read *The Feminine Mystique*, these women had no language to understand their conflicted feelings and no way to justify their inchoate desire to get "something else, something more, out of life."

4

~~~~~~~~

The Contradictions of
Womanhood in the 1950s

FRIEDAN PAINTED THE 1950S AS A TIME OF POLITICAL CONFORMITY, cultural conservatism, social repressiveness, and female passivity. Although this was true for many Americans, revolutionary changes were occurring below the surface in women's behaviors and options. One puzzling question is why these changes, which were well under way by the mid-1950s, did not undercut the media definition of women as homemakers long before the 1963 publication of *The Feminine Mystique*, and why so many of Friedan's readers found her defense of women's right and need to work a revelation.

Although women's employment had fallen dramatically in the immediate aftermath of World War II, by 1947 it was growing again. And by 1955 a higher percentage of women worked for wages than ever had during the war. In fact, their employment rate grew four times faster than men's during the 1950s. The employment of wives tripled and the employment of mothers increased fourfold.

The social acceptability of women working also increased during the 1950s. In the era's romantic comedies and popular love stories, it was often the girl who worked at a fun job, not the "girl next door," who got her man. Once she got him, she usually quit work. But polls showed enthusiastic approval of an engaged woman taking a job so the couple could marry sooner.

There was even growing acceptance of wives earning extra money for the family, as long as the husband did not object and the wife did not go back to work before her children were in school. Many opinion-shapers even encouraged women to take jobs once their children were grown, arguing that with the age of marriage and childbirth continuing to fall, most women were still healthy and active in their empty-nest years and should do something useful rather than fritter away their time in bridge parties and other idle pursuits.

In the 1930s, laws and policies had prohibited employers from hiring married women if their husbands were employed by the same company or government agency. By 1941, almost 90 percent of the nation's local school districts refused to hire married women, and 70 percent required female teachers to quit work when they married. Married women were welcomed into the workforce during the war, but as soon as the war ended they were urged to go home and tend to their husbands' needs. The government even reformed the tax law to give a special bonus to male-breadwinner families. Framers of the new provisions explicitly argued that this would encourage women to turn "to the pursuit of homemaking."

But as the demand for service and retail workers soared in the postwar boom, politicians and business leaders began to see women as an untapped resource for filling labor shortages and making America more competitive with the rival Soviet Union. In the 1950s, the National Manpower Council exhorted employers to hire women and urged women to seek paying jobs, although it tended to favor policies that encouraged wives to withdraw from work after childbearing and reenter when the children were older.

In 1956, President Dwight Eisenhower asked Congress to pass a bill requiring equal pay for equal work, something women's lobbyists had long urged. The bill, which made no provision for equal access to jobs, didn't pass. But Eisenhower's approach represented a change from the attitude of President Truman, who in 1948 had labeled any talk of women's rights in the public arena as "a lot of hooey."

Women also made substantial gains in education during the 1950s. More girls completed high school in that decade than in any previous era, and a higher percentage of them went on to college. One study of young white women found that they were twice as likely to go to college as their mothers had been.

And yet even as ever more women joined the labor force, there was a concerted effort to define the limits of what was acceptable. Marynia Farnham and Ferdinand Lundberg, authors of the virulently antifeminist 1947 work *Modern Woman: The Lost Sex*, had conceded that there was some work women could do without violating their natures. But they insisted that pursuing a "career," which they defined as work plus prestige, was antifeminine to its core and an assault on men's self-respect. This theme, stripped of its antifeminist vitriol and sugarcoated as concern for women's true happiness, became increasingly prominent in the 1950s.

Movies, Broadway plays, and popular literature depicted women who had prestigious or high-paying careers as ready to quit them the instant they landed a man. In *All About Eve* (1950), Bette Davis plays a successful, award-winning Broadway actress. But once she marries the man who has long loved her, she gives up an acting part she always coveted because "I've finally got a life to live" and something "to do with my nights." In *The Tender Trap* (1955), Debbie Reynolds's character gets picked for her first part on Broadway. But when Frank Sinatra asks her if she is excited, she responds halfheartedly that it's "all right." "A career is just fine," she explains, "but it's no substitute for marriage."

It was acceptable for a woman to keep her job after marriage if her husband didn't object *and* she didn't like her work too much. It was not acceptable for a woman to want a job that would be satisfying enough to compete with her identity as wife or impinge on her husband's sense that he was the primary breadwinner.

This point was made over and over in advice columns. In the March 1954 issue of *Coronet*, one expert held up the example of "Jacqueline M." as a model for working women. Jacqueline had been earning more money than her husband when she married him, but she promptly "gave up her job, and took one that paid less, because she knew how important it was for her husband to feel he was unquestionably supporting her." In Lena Levine's 1957 advice book, *The Modern Book of Marriage*, Levine told women that they could work for pay and still have a happy marriage only "if they remember one important thing": A woman must "let her husband know that her job is secondary, that her first interest is always the home."

Popular culture encouraged wives and mothers who worked for pay in the 1950s to lead what film critic Brandon French has called a "double life" rather than a "full" one. They were urged to completely "dissociate their identities from their jobs . . . defining themselves entirely through their roles as wives, mothers, and homemakers, regardless of what else they did." To the extent women were willing to do this, society was happy to have them fill the lower rungs of the occupational ladder, freeing up men for more important and remunerative jobs. The October 16, 1956, issue of *Look* magazine assured its readers that working women "gracefully conceded" the upper levels of the work world to men. A March 17, 1962, editorial in the *Saturday Evening Post* opined that society could welcome women into the workforce now that "they have finally outgrown their childlike need to compete with men."

Even as more opportunities opened for men to move into middle-class or upper-middle-class professions and unionized blue-collar workers saw dramatic increases in their earnings power, women's employment gains were mostly in the lower-echelon, nonunionized segments of the workforce. Between 1947 and 1966, the inflation-adjusted hourly wages of men increased by 50 percent, with men in their twenties making the greatest gains of all. Reflecting these income gains, home ownership rates of men in their thirties more than doubled between 1940 and 1960.

But the wages of young women remained relatively low and flat. Accordingly, historians Jordan Stanger-Ross, Christina Collins, and Mark Stern note, women's "best opportunity to share in the wealth of their young male counterparts was to marry."

From 1951 to 1955, female full-time workers earned 63.9 percent of what male full-time workers earned. By 1963, women's pay had fallen to less than 59 percent of men's. Meanwhile, the proportion of women in high-prestige jobs declined: Fewer than 6 percent of working women held executive jobs in the 1950s.

The experience of Sandra Day O'Connor illustrates the obstacles faced by women who aspired to a challenging career. In 1981, a decade after the women's movement had begun to open up unprecedented opportunities to talented women, O'Connor became the first woman to sit on the U.S. Supreme Court. But when she entered the job market in 1952, having graduated second in her class at Stanford Law School and served on the prestigious *Stanford Law Review*, she got only one job offer from all the major California firms to which she submitted a résumé. This firm explained that it did not employ women as attorneys but would be happy to hire her as a legal secretary.

For the typical single woman, such discriminatory attitudes and narrow opportunities made marriage look especially attractive. Polls conducted by the Survey Research Center at the University of Michigan found that in 1957, single women were much *more* likely than their married counterparts to hold positive views about marriage and to regard it as their best option for self-fulfillment and happiness. Twenty years later, when single women had many more educational and occupational opportunities, their view of the benefits of marriage had dropped sharply.

The idea that marriage was the best possible investment in a woman's future was heartily endorsed by parents. While many mothers and fathers did not think it worthwhile to invest heavily in their daughter's education, by the end of the 1950s, the typical expenditure on a daughter's wedding represented 66 percent, or two-thirds, of an average family's yearly income—a higher proportion than in 2000, when the average wedding cost only 53 percent of median family income and the bride and groom often shared the cost with their parents.

Still, with almost a third of married women working for pay by the late 1950s, why didn't their existence challenge society's definition of women exclusively as wives and mothers? One reason was the demographic characteristics of the married women who entered the workforce. Most of the wives and mothers who got jobs did so when they were in their late thirties or older and their children were well along in school. One recent estimate suggests that no more than 250,000 women with small children were in the paid labor force, although this probably undercounts the numbers of African-American, Chicana, and Latina mothers working for pay. And the majority of working wives worked only part-time or seasonally.

Cultural perceptions were also skewed by the tendency of the press, then as now, to devote more attention to what was happening in new segments of the population than to the average experience. The explosive growth of suburbia preoccupied the media then, and people tended to move to the suburbs to start their families. The suburbs had not existed long enough to have many empty-nest families or opportunities for part-time employment. As a result, less than 10 percent of suburban wives worked for pay.

Finally, there is much truth in the common perception that the 1950s were the height of the male-breadwinner family. The total female labor force participation was growing, but the number of families where the wife did unpaid work on a farm or in a small business was falling and the number of families who relied on the labor of children and teens was sharply down. Add to that the falling age of marriage, the rising birthrate, and the expansion of male earning power, and it's fair to say that never before had there been so many families where young children were being raised by full-time homemakers supported by their husband's earnings rather than by a wider family labor force.

For all these reasons, most Americans believed that the "normal" life for a modern mother was to become a homemaker in a male-breadwinner family and live according to the cultural stereotypes about womanhood that Friedan described as the feminine mystique. If a woman with younger children *did* have to work, it was often at a job that was unsatisfying and poorly paid, with a husband unwilling to help her with the housework when she got home. So it is not surprising that many such women aspired to become full-time homemakers. And even though married women were more likely to express negative views of marriage than single women— or than their own husbands—most believed that they *ought* to be happy homemakers and that almost every other woman in the nation was.

Those assumptions and aspirations were reinforced by the mass media and advertising industries. Today the media makes a point of niche marketing, targeting diverse segments of the audience and trying to cater to their perceived needs and fantasies. But the opposite was true in the 1950s and early 1960s, when older local sources of knowledge, values, and even entertainment were displaced by a homogenized national culture that literally whited out America's diversity.

The astounding growth of television was one potent disseminator of this national, homogeneous culture. In 1948, 500,000 homes had televisions. By 1952, the number was 19 million. By 1960, 87 percent of all households had a television, including 80 percent of rural households. Unlike radio, which featured some ethnic, regional, and class diversity in its programming, television portrayed an idealized white middle-class male-breadwinner family as the norm.

Another important influence in shaping women's understanding of "normality" were women's magazines, which reached a much higher percentage of female readers than they do today and accounted for a much larger segment of what women read. In 1964, *McCall's*, which had invented the "togetherness" slogan of 1950s domesticity ten years earlier, had 21 million readers, mostly between the ages of eighteen and forty-nine, in a population of about 37 million women that age. The *Ladies' Home Journal* and *Good Housekeeping* each had almost 15 million readers.

In *The Feminine Mystique*, Betty Friedan claimed that during the 1950s these influential women's magazines "printed virtually no articles except those that serviced women as housewives, or described women as housewives, or permitted a purely feminine identification like the Duchess of Windsor or Princess Margaret." She reported that in 1958 and 1959 she "went through issue after issue of the three major women's magazines . . . without finding a single heroine who had a career, a commitment to any work, art, profession, or mission in the world, other than 'Occupation: housewife.'"

Friedan exaggerated the ubiquity of the happy housewife. In a survey of monthly magazines from 1946 to 1958, historian Joanne Meyerowitz found that the mass-circulation magazines of the postwar era frequently profiled women who combined marriage with careers or public service outside the home. Although the sharp critiques of Freudian antifeminism found in magazines of the late 1940s had faded by the early 1950s, leftist journalist Eve Merriam wrote witty dissections of the cult of the happy housewife in the pages of *The Nation*. In 1953, sociologist Mirra Komarovsky, whose work Friedan relied on more than she acknowledged, wrote a well-reviewed book decrying society's failure to understand the importance of work and education in women's lives. And sociologists Alva Myrdal and Viola Klein, anticipating many of Friedan's points, argued in their 1956 book, *Women's Two Roles: Home and Work*, that the "glorification" of homemaking and motherhood substituted flattery for respect. They noted that this exaltation of homemaking constituted "the cheapest method at society's disposal of keeping women quiet without seriously considering their grievances or improving their position."

But most of this discussion was confined to the pages of "highbrow" journals, such as *Harper's* and *Atlantic Monthly*, and the academic press, both of which were suspect in the atmosphere of McCarthyism and the Cold War. Liberals and leftists had largely been driven out of the mass media by anticommunist blacklists, such as the 1950 publication *Red Channels: The Report of Communist Influence in Radio and Television*, which listed 151 composers, writers, announcers, singers, and actors whose support for liberal or left-wing causes, or even for the work of the United Nations, made them "potential subversives." Allies of Senator Joseph McCarthy sat on the Federal Communications Commission, keeping their eyes peeled for shows that did not abide by such ever-widening blacklists.

In the political realm, the Civil Service Commission fired almost 3,000 people as "security risks" and reported that more than 4,000 others had resigned under the pressure of investigations into their political associations and beliefs. Feminists, and educated women in general, were particularly suspect. The House Un-American Activities Committee warned that "girls' schools and women's colleges contain some of the most loyal disciples of Russia. Teachers there are often frustrated females."

In this atmosphere, most women who continued to focus on women's rights during this period tended to do so behind the scenes. They were, in historian Linda Eisenmann's words, "quieter, less demanding, and more accommodating than women's advocates before 1920 and after 1965."

Friedan may have overstated her case, but considerable evidence supports her contention that women's magazines became more traditionalist on marriage and gender roles during the 1950s. Sociologist Francesca Cancian surveyed articles on marriage from high-circulation magazines such as the *Ladies' Home Journal, McCall's,* and *The Readers' Digest* for each decade from 1900–1909 through 1970–1979 and found that during the 1950s there were fewer articles endorsing flexible gender roles than in the 1920s, 1930s, or 1940s. She also found that advocacy of egalitarian marital values, such as communicating openly with one's husband or expressing one's own individuality, became less frequent, while there was more emphasis on women's sacrifice of aspirations beyond the home. Another detailed examination of magazine articles, TV scripts, and child-rearing manuals of the 1950s found a marked reassertion of traditional gender roles and male dominance in marriage during the latter part of the decade.

A similar trend occurred in popular entertainment, according to historian James Gilbert's analysis of scripts for *The Adventures of Ozzie and Harriet*, which began on the radio in the 1940s and then moved to television. In the years immediately after World War II, episodes often mocked Ozzie's illusion that women were incapable of doing "men's" tasks and found humor in setting up occasions for gender role switching. During the 1950s, however, the show abandoned these themes. In addition, the visual portrayal of Harriet in the TV series, where she was constantly holding a tray of cookies or running a vacuum cleaner, overshadowed the verbal give-and-take that had characterized the radio broadcasts.

In movies as well, the images of acceptable female behavior narrowed, especially when it came to portraying women and work. Friedan's claim that during the late 1940s and the 1950s the career woman replaced the seductress as the femme fatale who must be punished for her sins is supported by film critic Peter Biskind, who argues that the "Scarlet Letter A," symbol of the ultimate female transgression, increasingly stood for "ambition" rather than "adultery."

Friedan was also correct in contending that the media paid less attention to women's rights during the 1950s than in earlier decades. A study of how newspapers and popular magazines covered such issues between 1905 and 1970 found that coverage was highest during the suffrage struggle, between 1905 and 1920. It reached its lowest point between 1950 and the early 1960s and did not rise again until the late 1960s. Coverage by the *New York Times* was fairly high at the beginning of the 1950s but then declined steadily to a low point in 1960 before beginning a gradual recovery.

What the media *did* cover incessantly during the 1950s—along with the refrain that smothering homemakers created homosexuality, narcissism, and neurosis—was the drumbeat of claims from politicians, psychiatrists, social workers, and judges that working mothers were the cause of all other childhood ills, including delinquency, insanity, and all forms of criminality. Lynn Parker recalls that her mother "had been a career woman before she married my father" but then became a stay-at-home wife. Parker's mother went back to work when Parker was in high school, and she noticed that this improved her mother's depression. "I could see that it was very good for her to be working and I admired her for going to work," she recalls. But Parker had also absorbed the tremendous social disapproval of working mothers, so she chose to "lie on school forms that asked for mother's occupation. I continued to check the housewife box, because I feared my teacher would judge her poorly."

Friedan blamed these conservative cultural trends on the growing influence of Freudianism. In the 1920s, she noted, Freud's emphasis on freedom from sexual repression made his theories appear to support women's emancipation. But from the 1940s on, Freudian ideas "became the ideological bulwark of the sexual counter-revolution in America." Psychiatrists increasingly focused on Freud's notion of "penis envy," which, they declared, led many women to reject the passivity that women needed to reach true sexual fulfillment, thus dooming themselves and their families to maladjustment and misery. "Narcissism," dependence, and even "masochism," traits seen as pathological in men, were considered normal or healthy in women.

The most vicious psychoanalytical attacks on women began in the 1940s rather than the 1950s, with books such as Philip Wylie's *Generation of Vipers*, Marynia Farnham and Ferdinand Lundberg's *Modern Woman: The Lost Sex*, and Edward Strecker's *Their Mothers' Sons*. But during the 1950s Wylie and others continued to heap invective both on "castrating" career women and on overly controlling stay-at-home mothers. By 1955, *Generation of Vipers* had gone through twenty printings. In the early 1960s, Wylie was still finding a wide audience for his attacks on "The Womanization of America," brought about, in his view, by an unholy alliance of career women and housewives who had established a "she-tyranny" over American men.

Perhaps even more damaging to women's sense of self were the gentler, and hence more insidious, versions of these ideas that were endlessly recycled in the media during the 1950s. Studies of postwar culture show that Freudian notions of sexual difference permeated popular culture, becoming a major explanatory device for human behavior in movies, magazines, and news stories. As Friedan put it, Freudian antifeminism settled over the American landscape "like fine volcanic ash."

In 1953, *Collier's* ran an article whose banner headline asked: "Does Your Family Have a Neurosis?" If the family was "mother-fixated," the answer was definitely yes, but even happy and devoted families could be neurotic, the article said. By the mid-1950s, it was scarcely possible to find a magazine that did not talk knowingly about one or another form of neurosis, usually caused by women's failure to conform to their feminine "instincts."

The assignment of women to a passive, secondary role in social life, which had once been ascribed to duty, social custom, God's will, or innate differences in ability, was now declared to be a woman's only route to personal fulfillment. Psychiatrist Helene Deutsch declared that the modern woman renounced "originality" and personal aspiration not out of coercion but "out of her own needs," which were best met by identifying with her husband's achievements. A normal woman found complete satisfaction in her role as homemaker, mother, and sexual companion to her husband. Any woman who did not find such complete fulfillment, psychiatrists explained in circular reasoning disguised as the latest scientific thinking, was clearly not normal.

Sociologists argued that unless society encouraged a clear differentiation of the sexes, everything from the nuclear family to the economy itself could disintegrate. The renowned Harvard sociologist Talcott Parsons and his collaborator Robert Bales claimed that the most functional form of family for modern industrial society was one where the husband played the "instrumental" role, earning the family living, and the wife played the "expressive" role, providing emotional support to the wage earner and nurturing the children. From this it followed that boys must be reared to accept the masculine identity that would prepare them to be family decision-makers and breadwinners, and girls should be channeled into activities that would prepare them for homemaking and motherhood.

Farnham put it succinctly in a 1952 article in *Parents* magazine: Boys could not develop into successful men nor girls into fulfilled women if society made the mistake of regarding its citizens "not primarily as male and female, but as people." Clearly the title of Friedan's 1960 article, "Women Are People Too," was not as self-evident as it now sounds.

In 1947, *LIFE* magazine's June issue on the dilemmas facing women in the postwar world had taken a relatively neutral view about the choices women made concerning work and family. Revisiting the topic in December 1956, the magazine took a stronger stand against combining work with motherhood. The introduction to the issue, by "Mrs. Peter Marshall," praised feminism for making women healthier and "more attractive than ever before" and for increasing the infant survival rate. But, she warned, feminism often led women to lose sight of their real source of fulfillment, and that was when "their troubles begin." A normal woman's most satisfying moments in life, Mrs. Marshall declared, occurred not when she got her first job or proved her intellectual abilities, but when she wore her first formal gown, was taken into the arms of the man she loved, or held her baby in her arms.

The same issue did feature one article by a husband who took the controversial stand that his wife's full-time job was "good for her, good for him, good for their children—and good for the budget." But his opinion could hardly compete with Robert Coughlin's interviews with five psychiatrists, all of whom agreed that the primary cause of marital unhappiness, divorce, and disturbed children was "wives who are not feminine enough and husbands [who are] not truly male."

In 1947, *LIFE*'s editors had balanced the antifeminist views of Farnham and Lundberg with acerbic criticisms of Freudian pronouncements by several well-known female authors, but in 1956, not one rebuttal of Coughlin's experts was to be heard. Several of the psychiatrists conceded that some women had no choice but to work, but they were unanimous in telling Coughlin that those who *wanted* to work—especially at a full-time job—were "rejecting the role of wife and mother." A woman who made this choice, as Coughlin summed up the consensus, "may find many satisfactions in her job, but the chances are that she, her husband and her children will suffer psychological damage, and that she will be basically an unhappy woman."

Freudian ideas about gender difference even seeped into women's colleges, the one arena where women had traditionally been encouraged to aspire to a life of the mind. Some educators used Freudian precepts to argue that traditional subjects such as physics, philosophy, and calculus were not relevant to women's role in society and were causing "discontent and restlessness." Friedan quoted Lynn White, president of Mills College from 1943 to 1958, who suggested in 1950 that colleges should educate women to be housewives rather than train them in skills they would never use. "Why not study the theory and preparation of a Basque paella, of a well-marinated shish-kebob, lamb kidneys sauteed in sherry, an authoritative curry?" asked White.

Not all educators took the ideas of "sex-directed education" as far as White, but in March 1962, psychiatrist Edna Rostow, writing in the *Yale Review*, chastised those who failed to put into practice what modern researchers now knew about the needs of "femininity." It is a psychological fact, she contended, "that many young women—if not the majority—seem to be incapable of dealing with future long-range intellectual interests until they have proceeded through the more basic phases of their own healthy growth as women"—marriage, childbearing, and child rearing.

Or as Grayson Kirk, president of Columbia University from 1953 to 1968, put it, "It would be preposterously naive to suggest that a B.A. can be made as attractive to girls as a marriage license."

"Ideally," Rostow wrote, a woman's life in the prime years of family-building "should contain no elements of competition with men in the world of work." Instead, "it should reflect her full emotional acceptance of the role she is living: receptive, bearing, nurturing." Encouraging a young woman to embrace any other goal "can adversely affect the development of her full identity." Only after she has fulfilled her natural destiny as wife and mother should she consider what other occupations and identities she might wish to assume. Rostow recommended that women not even begin training for any profession until they were between the ages of thirty and forty (about ten to twenty years after most women in that era had their first child). That was "the natural starting point for serious professional study in the rhythmic pattern of modern woman's life."

All this did not mean, as Friedan claimed at one point in her book, that for more than fifteen years, "there was no word . . . in the millions of words written about women to challenge the myth of the happy housewife." In fact, as Friedan acknowledged elsewhere in the book, the one women's issue that regularly did make it into the mass media, right alongside the celebration of domesticity, was the puzzling question of why so many women seemed unhappy or dissatisfied with their lives. Young mothers felt exhausted and "trapped," magazines lamented; older housewives were bored. As early as 1949, *LIFE* reported that "suddenly and for no plain reason" American women had been "seized with an eerie restlessness." Under a "mask of placidity" and an outwardly feminine appearance, one physician wrote in 1953, some housewives were "seething" with resentment and anxiety. Long before Friedan labeled their discontent "the problem with no name," doctors were puzzling over the mysterious "housewife syndrome."

But until Friedan attributed women's unhappiness to the contradictions between women's needs and the precepts of the feminine mystique, there was no widely publicized alternative to the psychiatric explanation of female discontent as an individual problem of sexual or gender maladjustment. When women described being trapped in their homes, dominated by their husbands, or resentful of their economic dependence, this was taken as a symptom rather than a potential cause of their disturbance, something to be treated by analysis, medication, and even electroshock therapy. As sociologist Carol Warren notes in *Madwives*, a study of women hospitalized for schizophrenia in the 1950s, there was at that time, unlike today, "no legitimizing cultural vocabulary" for housewives who felt isolated in their homes, unhappy in their marriages, or damaged in their sense of self.

So the prescribed treatment for "the housewife syndrome" was not to figure out how a discontented woman could change her life to gain a stronger sense of self, but how she could change her feelings to reconcile herself to her role in the family. In 1963, psychiatrist Herbert Modlin described his success in dispensing such treatment to five "paranoid" women. Their "distorted perceptions" about male persecution disappeared, he reported, once he and his colleagues helped them learn to value their "feminine social role."

The patients Warren studied were pronounced cured only when they admitted that their discontent had been unjustified. One woman reported in her discharge interview that she had been advised to enter the hospital in the first place because "I felt that I was dominated." Since then, "I've had a chance to think things out." Another wife described how her treatment had helped her: "I feel like baking cookies . . . and that's because I've made up my mind to be a homemaker instead of always worrying about a career."

Less extreme than commitment to a mental hospital but much more widespread was medication. When tranquilizers became readily available in the second half of the 1950s, they were initially prescribed for high-charging businessmen such as those portrayed in the TV series *Mad Men*. Yet by the second half of the 1960s, women were twice as likely as men to use tranquilizers, and most consumers of "mother's little helper" were white and better educated than average.

NOT EVERYONE IN AMERICA CONSIDERED IT CRAZY FOR WIVES AND MOTHERS to have interests outside the home before they reached middle age. Many educators persisted in believing that women should be taught to use their minds and imaginations for something besides cooking. And the same popular magazines that disparaged "the career woman" as an ideal or goal often commended individual women who had successful careers. In many of the magazines she surveyed, historian Meyerowitz writes, "domestic ideals coexisted in an ongoing tension with an ethos of individual achievement." She found many articles that celebrated both domestic devotion and public success—"sometimes in the same sentence."

A 1953 *Coronet* article about the female mayor of Portland, Oregon, was titled "The Lady Who Licked Crime in Portland." The mayor was described as "an ethereally pale housewife" who tipped "the scales at 110 pounds." But she was also labeled a feminist, intensely concerned "with the status of women." And no one suggested that she needed to be institutionalized or medicated.

So there were more mixed messages, exceptions, and contradictions in the media's depictions of the ideal feminine life than Friedan admitted in her book. In the long run, these mixed messages, combined with the trends toward increased workplace participation and education for women, helped pave the way for a new women's movement that would have happened with or without Betty Friedan. Indeed, by the time Friedan's book appeared in 1963, many young women were already rejecting "the feminine mystique" without ever having heard it called that.

But many women never heard the exceptions and caveats to the feminine mystique that historians now recognize in retrospect. And the few who did hear them seem to have found them all the more confusing. "It would have been easier if everyone had been as negative as Philip Wylie," Joan C. told me. "Then you could have gotten indignant. But it was like being enveloped in a big cloud of cotton candy, sweet and sticky. You couldn't punch your way out."

Anne Parsons, the daughter of sociologist Talcott Parsons, wrote to Friedan describing her sense of isolation and marginalization as an intelligent woman trying to build a research career in the 1950s. "I began to wish that someone would call me names or throw stones or threaten to send me to a concentration camp so that at least I would know for certain that the world was against me."

A strong-minded woman determined to pursue a career could have cobbled together enough supportive quotes and celebrated role models to justify her resolve, and many did. But the individuals praised in women's magazines for successfully reconciling family life with a career were painted in such heroic, larger-than-life terms that they could not possibly serve as role models for most women. The descriptions of how these women pulled off their successes underscored Dorothy Thompson's 1939 warning that only one in a thousand could manage such a thing. Articles on successful women would invariably marvel at their "ceaseless activity," "amazing" energy, and ability to "get along without sleep." Many readers admired these women, and perhaps even envied them, but few could imagine emulating them.

Today women often resent the psychological pressures created by the pressure to "have it all." But in the 1950s, women were firmly told that they could "have it *or*," meaning they could be anything they wanted to be in the public world, *or* they could be happy.

You are free to choose, the prevailing ideology said. You can do anything you want and society will no longer try to stop you. But modern science has proven that if you do not first devote yourself to being a homemaker, you will probably end up desperately unhappy, and your choice may be a sign that you already suffer from a deep illness.

Prior to the 1940s and 1950s, a woman was condemned if she did not do what was expected of her. In the 1950s, she was pitied if she did not *want* what was expected of her.

For most of American history, a woman's role as wife and mother had been seen as a sometimes painful duty. People talked about a woman's lot, not a woman's choice. And a woman's lot involved self-sacrifice, not self-realization. But in the world of 1950s advertising, all that changed. One of the marketing research books Friedan accessed informed its clients that "the modern bride is deeply convinced of the unique value of married love, of the possibilities of finding real happiness in marriage and of fulfilling her personal destiny in it and through it." She "seeks as a conscious goal that which in many cases her grandmother saw as a blind fate and her mother as slavery"—to "belong to a man . . . to choose among all possible careers the career of wife-mother-homemaker."

Postwar ideology was particularly disorienting for many women because it often came in the guise of a forward-thinking rejection of "traditional" ideas about gender and sexuality. The new ideology of marriage promised women satisfaction in their home life that their mothers and grandmothers would never have dreamed possible. The modern woman would find joy and creativity in the housework that had been pure drudgery for her grandmother. She would experience sexual pleasures unimaginable to her repressed Victorian foremothers. And she would reach new heights of egalitarian intimacy with her husband, who would come home each evening eager to participate in the joys of togetherness.

In the long run, such heightened expectations about marriage helped make many women more assertive in their relationships and gave some women the courage to end empty and unsatisfying marriages. But in the short run, these expectations often added to a woman's guilt and confusion, because they were not yet attached to any new expectations about men's behavior. Women were encouraged to expect more than ever from marriage, but they were told that when a marriage fell short, it was almost invariably because they were not good enough wives. If a husband's bad behavior threatened the marriage, it was up to the wife to figure out what she had done to trigger this behavior and how *she* must change to bring out her husband's better side.

Studying the advice of marital experts in this era, historian Rebecca Davis found a widespread consensus that the path to marital happiness lay in the wife adjusting her own wishes to her husband's needs, whims, and even neuroses. After four counseling sessions at Ohio State University's marriage clinic, for example, a twenty-year-old pregnant wife dutifully concluded that her husband's infidelities were probably due to her failure to take enough care with her own appearance and that of her home. She therefore resolved to be "better groomed, cleaner." If such rededication to domesticity did not create the bliss that a true woman ought to find in marriage, "resignation," one social worker remarked, could offer "protection from excessive frustration."

Other mixed messages abounded. A woman was told that she should put nothing above her devotion to her children, her love for her husband, and her delight in her home, but she was sternly warned against devoting so much attention to her family that she smothered her children and emasculated her husband. In the nineteenth century it would have been unthinkable to call a woman *too* devoted a wife or mother. But by the 1950s, the woman who focused too intensely on being a housewife and mother was deemed as big a menace to society—and to men—as the woman who rejected domesticity in favor of a paid career. The pursuit of domestic bliss—the one outlet for a woman's dreams and aspirations—turned out to damage the men on whom women were supposed to rely.

And in the hierarchy of cultural concerns during that era, the dilemmas facing American women paled in comparison to the "crisis" facing American men. Pundits bemoaned the eclipse of the risk-taking entrepreneur by "the organization man." They worried that men were losing their hard edge because they increasingly worked in impersonal bureaucracies where "feminine" characteristics such as teamwork, compromise, and concern for others' opinions were more important than individual initiative and aggressiveness. Men, said sociologist David Riesman, were becoming "other-directed" instead of "inner-directed."

The material comforts that were promised as the reward of a successful family were simultaneously feared as a threat to the nation's moral fiber. Some commentators fretted that modern affluence had created a culture of leisure that was undermining the work ethic of yore. Others worried that "status-seeking" men were working too hard to amass material goods. But however contradictory the problems described, almost everyone agreed that they were the fault of women.

If a woman left home to get a job, she was threatening the last bastions of masculinity. But if she devoted all her attention to making her home a place of comfort and fulfillment, she was either overdomesticating her husband or putting too much pressure on him to keep up with the Joneses. If she left a child with a babysitter to take a part-time job, she was neglecting the next generation. But if she lavished too much attention on her children, she might produce a whole generation of homosexuals.

Even the mutually satisfying sex life that was supposed to be one of the rewards of conforming to the 1950s model of masculinity and femininity contributed to the sense of masculine crisis. Sociologist Riesman warned that as women became avid consumers of sexual and romantic advice, "the anxiety of men lest they fail to satisfy the woman also grows."

One of the quickest routes to a best-selling book in the 1950s was to explain how women's behavior—whether as wives, mothers, or career women—was to blame for the "crisis of masculinity" that supposedly characterized the era. An issue of *Look* magazine titled "The Decline of the American Male," reprinted as a book in 1958, squarely laid the blame for men's problems on that same domesticity that was elsewhere being celebrated as women's best hope for happiness and society's best hope for stability.

The book described a litany of problems facing American men, all of them stemming from the power their wives supposedly exerted. "Women's new rank in the family has encouraged her to make extraordinary and often frustrating economic demands on her husband." Women were making new sexual demands as well, so that the poor man could no longer "concentrate on his own pleasure; he must concern himself primarily with satisfying his wife." The upshot? "Men overwork themselves to supply their wives with material possessions" and then exhaust themselves trying to satisfy them sexually. Adding insult to injury, the "fad of togetherness" had led wives to ask husbands to do "things around the house that their fathers didn't even know had to be done."

Even critics of suburban domesticity in the 1950s, liberal as well as conservative, directed their anger not toward the system that kept women trapped in the mystique of housewifery and consumerism, but toward the wives themselves. In 1956, *The Crack in the Picture Window* gathered widespread attention for its searing indictment of suburbia. The author,

John Keats, combined sociology and satirical fiction to chronicle the lives of two hapless suburban dwellers, Mr. and Mrs. John Drone. Keats quoted Dr. Harold Mendelsohn of American University's Bureau of Social Research about the "terrifying monotony" of suburbia and the loneliness of wives whose husbands could at least escape during the day. But in the next breath he argued that suburbia was producing a "matriarchal society" that turned the average woman into a "nagging slob" and her husband into "a woman-bossed, inadequate, money-terrified neuter."

Keats's prescription for Mr. Drone was to throw off his domination by women and reject his wife's attempts to domesticate him. But he advised Mrs. Drone to isolate herself even further in the lonely job of homemaking, becoming someone who "baked her own bread, painted her own pictures, and had as little to do with her neighbors as was humanly possible."

ON A BREAK FROM COLLEGE IN THE EARLY 1960S, I WORKED FOR A WHILE at an institution for autistic and schizophrenic children. At that time, a leading psychiatric explanation of schizophrenia was that it was caused by mothers who subjected their kids to "double binds," or conflicting messages. "Don't be a sissy; be careful not to hurt yourself." "Come kiss Mama; don't muss my makeup."

One day I watched a female television reporter drop off her child at the center on the way to work. She was trying to get him to let go of a glove he had taken from her during the car ride. Fearing she would be late to work, but not wanting to traumatize her child by grabbing the glove from him, and acutely aware that psychiatrists and aides were watching her every move, she followed him around the room with an anxious smile, saying, "Give Mommy the glove, honey. That's a good boy. Give Mommy the glove. Mommy has to go now."

When she left, a watching psychiatrist explained to me and another attendant that this was "a classic double bind." The mother's smile gave the boy permission to play the keep-away game with her even as she scolded him, while her use of the words "good boy" suggested that she wasn't really serious about wanting the glove. "Magnify that by a thousand more incidents of the same nature, and voila—you have a schizophrenic," said my fellow aide knowingly, and I blush to admit that I nodded in agreement, believing that I had gained a new insight into the dynamics of family life.

Today we know that the "double bind" theory does not explain schizophrenia. Mothers were not driving their children crazy by giving them mixed messages. But the double binds facing women in the 1950s made many believe *they* were going crazy. In fact, one of the phrases I heard most often from the women I interviewed for this book was "I thought I must be crazy."

5

∧∧∧∧∧∧∧

"I Thought I Was Crazy"

THE FEMININE MYSTIQUE "LEFT ME BREATHLESS," RECALLED GLENDA SCHILT Edwards, who was twenty-eight when she read the book, shortly after it was published. "I felt as though Betty Friedan had looked into my heart, mind, and psyche and . . . put the unexplainable distress I was suffering into words. I was astonished that before [reading the book] I could not express why I felt so depressed, even though my distress drove me to see two therapists at different times. Both therapists seemed to feel that I was having trouble 'accepting my role as a wife.'"

Janice K. was thirty-six and the mother of ten-year-old twins when a friend sent her *The Feminine Mystique* in 1963. The year before, she had seen a psychiatrist for eight months without ever getting to the bottom of her "troubles." She became so indignant when she read the book that she sent a copy to her therapist "with a note saying he should read it before he ever again told a woman that all she needed was to come to terms with her 'feminine nature.'"

Laura M., now a veteran journalist, read it in high school. "My most vivid memory is that I finally realized I wasn't crazy. I was still part of a generation expected to embrace family life as the 'end all and be all,' to subsume my ambitions to my husband's goals. But I didn't want to! What was wrong with me?" Reading Friedan's book made Laura realize that having aspirations beyond being a housewife might actually be healthy, not sick.

"I had forgotten all about *The Feminine Mystique*," wrote Mary Lee Fulkerson, whose husband was a career military officer in the 1960s.

"Reading it now, more than 45 years after it was written and maybe 40 years after I first read it, it seems so superficial and mealy-mouthed. It took me a few days to remember how it was for me back then. And then the agony and despair of those times came flooding back to my heart and mind."

For some women, the book was literally a lifesaver. When Rose Garrity read the book she was a young mother whose husband regularly beat her. She had married at age fifteen, dropped out of school after just one week in the tenth grade, had her first child at age seventeen, and then had four more in the next five and a half years. "I was trapped in what felt like hell," Rose recalls. "I had been forced to drop out of school. . . . There were no domestic violence programs and no one ever talked about the issue. . . . I thought I was the only one being beaten and there was something terribly wrong with me. I was ashamed."

Rose worked on getting her high school diploma in secret, hiding her study materials from her husband. "When I read this book it was like the curtain was thrown back on the 'wizard'! I suddenly understood what was going on, how sexism works, and was energized to begin to survive as an individual person." Today Rose runs a domestic violence program in rural New York and serves on the board of directors of the National Coalition Against Domestic Violence.

Most women had less burning reasons for their discontent, which made them even more likely to feel there was something "terribly wrong" with themselves. "I didn't think I had any 'excuse' for what I was feeling," says Sharon G. "My dad used to hit my mom, and I swore I would never put up with that. But no one was hitting me. I loved my husband and he loved me. Yet I was miserable."

Judy J. remembers crying helplessly as she tried to explain her depression to her unsympathetic mother. "What more could you want?" her mother kept asking. "Do you remember what my life was like when I was raising you and your brother, with no washing machine and a wood stove I had to feed four times a day? What's wrong with you?" Friedan's book told Judy it was okay for her to want more, and helped her figure out what that "more" might be.

Cam Stivers recalls that around the time she read *The Feminine Mystique*, "I had the feeling (at 25!) that my life was over, and that nothing interesting would ever happen to me again. . . . I told myself that the fix I was in was my own fault, that there was something wrong with me. I had everything a woman was supposed to want—marriage to a nice, dependable guy (a good provider), a wonderful little kid, a nice house in the suburbs—and I was miserable."

"I didn't know why I was so unhappy," recalls Danielle B., "until I read *The Feminine Mystique*. Then something clicked." The letters Friedan received at the time were full of similar phrases: "Like light bulbs going off again and again"; "What a sense of relief"; "Now I know I'm not alone"; "It's not just me"; "Suddenly I understand." Nearly fifty years later, women recollected the same tremendous sense of relief. "I suddenly realized maybe I wasn't an outcast"; "I wasn't a nut-case"; "I wasn't going mad"; "I recognized what was missing from my life"; "I understood what I was feeling and felt validated!!"

Cam Stivers remembers thinking, *Your unhappiness isn't just you. There's something wrong with the whole arrangement.* "I can't express how freeing it was for me to realize that my predicament was not all my own fault."

After finishing the book, Glenda Schilt Edwards, who still felt terrible after being treated by two different psychiatrists, "realized that what I thought might be wrong with me, was in fact, right with me!" "It was a real 'click' moment for me," commented Linda Smolak, who went on to become a professor of psychology and women's studies. "It literally changed (and perhaps saved) my life."

Jeri G., then a thirty-six-year-old mother of three, read *The Feminine Mystique* in 1963. She had taken an overdose of sleeping pills the year before. "Maybe it was just a 'bid for attention,' as the cliché goes, and not a serious attempt at the time," Jeri said, "but if so, no one gave me the kind of attention I needed. My doctor sent me to a psychiatrist, but he only made me more ashamed of my feelings. I truly believe that if I hadn't found that book when I did, I might really have killed myself the next time."

A look at the life of Anne Parsons reveals how tormented some women were by the pressures of the feminine mystique. Anne was the daughter of Talcott Parsons, the renowned Harvard sociologist who insisted on society's need for "normal" families consisting of male breadwinners and female homemakers. Even though Anne's parents encouraged her to develop her own intellect, she felt pressured to live the kind of life her father prescribed for most women. In an eight-page letter she wrote to Betty Friedan in 1963 after reading the book, Anne recalled that she had chosen not to take fourth-year math in high school "for fear of being called a brain," and while in college had agreed to a marriage based more on the desire for security than anything else.

When she came to grips with her motivation, Anne explained, she broke off the engagement and pursued advanced work in psychiatric theory and anthropology, but at age twenty-five she was haunted by the price she felt she had been forced to pay for her choice. The unmarried career woman, she complained, was not seen "as a person at all." Instead, she was stereotyped as "aggressive, competitive, rejecting of femininity and all the rest." It "is like being a Negro or Jew," she commented, "with the difference that the prejudices are manifest in such subtle ways that it is very hard to pin them down, and that the feminine mystique is so strong and attractive an ideology that it is very hard to find a countervailing point of view from which to fight for oneself."

Feeling increasingly marginalized in her relations with colleagues, Anne committed herself to a mental institution in September 1963, where she kept a diary recording her fears about the Cold War and the arms race and her frustration with her psychiatrist's insistence that she was "resisting insight into my feminine instincts." Page-long sentences veer back and forth between Anne's anxieties about the state of the world and the refrain, written in caps, "you CANNOT COME TO TERMS WITH YOUR BASIC FEMININE INSTINCTS." Nine months later, after writing to her father that she thought the psychiatric treatments had made her worse and trying in vain to get released from the hospital, Anne committed suicide.

Anne Parsons might have developed her mental problems even in a world where single female intellectuals were not regarded as defective women and psychiatrists did not tell patients they were resisting their feminine instincts if they held strong political opinions or harbored intellectual ambitions. But many other women insisted it was the tenets of Freudian psychiatry that had made them feel crazy, and it was Friedan's book, not talk therapy or medication, that allowed them to reclaim their sanity.

Some, like Edwards, echoed Anne Parsons's claim that seeing a psychiatrist had made things worse. Edwards recalls: "My presenting complaint was that I did not know why I had such sad and distressed feelings, as I had everything I thought I should have to feel happy; a successful husband, three wonderful children, a house in the suburbs, a station wagon and a family dog, what else could possibly be lacking? They told me I was having trouble 'accepting my role as a wife.'"

A self-described "ex–newspaper woman" with two young children wrote to Friedan in November 1963 that when she talked to a psychiatrist about the sense of emptiness she felt in being a full-time homemaker, he kept asking "if I was *sure* there wasn't 'Another Man' involved and whether I really loved my children."

Other women reported a better experience, finding psychiatrists who sympathized with their frustration or depression and made useful suggestions about how to alleviate it. But most of the women I interviewed told me that the turning point in their lives came when they started seeing their anxiety as a legitimate social grievance rather than an individual problem. This insight gave them the courage to pursue their dreams, or sometimes just the permission to *have* a dream. For that, most credit *The Feminine Mystique*.

CONSTANCE AHRONS IS THE LAST PERSON IN THE WORLD I WOULD HAVE expected to have subscribed to any form of the feminine mystique. When I met her back in the early 1990s, she was already the author of a groundbreaking book challenging the conventional wisdom about divorce and directed the Marriage and Family Therapy Doctoral Training Program at the University of Southern California. Having heard Ahrons explain complex topics in interviews and give no quarter when confronted with sloppy thinking, I found her thoroughly intimidating. Well groomed and self-assured, she seemed the kind of woman who would simultaneously notice the holes in my arguments and the ones in my stockings.

But when I interviewed Ahrons for my research, I learned that she was not born to the professional, capable role she seems to inhabit so effortlessly. She might have gone down a very different path had it not been for reading Betty Friedan's book.

Ahrons was the daughter of immigrant parents from Russia and Poland. Her father had three years of college and was a small merchant. Her mother was a high school graduate who alternated between being a full-time homemaker and helping her husband in the store. When Ahrons was growing up, she never thought about preparing for a profession. She entered college in 1954, the first woman in her family to do so. But she and her family saw college "more like a finishing school" than a training ground for work. She almost flunked out the first year, in part because she had never thought of herself as smart. In the family folklore, "my brother was the bright one, and I was the pretty one."

Ahrons got married in her sophomore year, at age nineteen, and had her first child at twenty. At that point she dropped out of college to become a full-time housewife and mother. Getting married, she recalls, was such an overriding dream that once she achieved it, she had no idea what to fantasize about next.

This was a common theme among the women I interviewed: Having been raised to believe that finding a husband and having children would be the crowning achievements of their lives, many said that they looked into the future a few years after having children and found that they had no compelling goal left to pursue. As Cam Stivers said, it felt as if her life was already over.

When *The Feminine Mystique* came out in 1963, Ahrons had two children and had been deeply unhappy for several years. "The thoughts I had were terrible. I wished for another life. I woke up and started to clean and wash clothes and was miserable. No one seemed to understand. My friends didn't feel that way." Her husband could afford to hire household help, which was the norm in the upper-middle-class family into which Ahrons had married. But her friends used their babysitters to get their hair done, go shopping, or play bridge. Ahrons longed for something different. "I tried to sell *LIFE* magazine over the phone," she recalls, "which resulted in a terrible sense of rejection. I took a Christmas job three evenings a week, without telling my husband, and he made me quit after a week." None of her friends worked, and none understood her dissatisfaction with a life that they enjoyed. In 1961 she began seeing a psychiatrist, who put her on tranquilizers.

Ahrons began to think about going back to school, and her psychiatrist was supportive, "but he saw it mostly as a way for me to keep myself busy." Almost everyone else was furious at the idea. Her mother told her she would be neglecting her children. Her friends said she was crazy. Her husband couldn't understand what the point was. After all, he earned more than enough to support, even indulge, her. Connie's father was the only person who approved of her returning to school.

Then she read *The Feminine Mystique* and "it slammed me in the face." Four decades later, Connie can "distinctly remember reading the book and crying the entire time." The second chapter "said you aren't the problem, society is the problem. It never occurred to me before that I wasn't the one who needed treatment." She felt a weight lift from her shoulders because "now I could name the problem, and know it didn't originate in my own psyche." She got up from her reading and flushed her tranquilizers down the drain.

When Ahrons applied to return to college, she did so mostly to relieve her boredom and depression rather than to train for a career. "The most daring goal I could imagine was to be a substitute teacher." But she did well in her studies and got interested in new subjects, and as she did, her horizons broadened. She went on to earn a PhD and become a distinguished researcher. "It was Friedan's book that opened those doors."

Ahrons knows now that Friedan's arguments had been anticipated by earlier writers such as Simone de Beauvoir and Mirra Komarovsky. "But for women like me who had never read anything else, this was life changing. . . . For us it wasn't derivative, it was a bombshell of new ideas and information."

Many women who read the book at the time told me they were astounded by the women's history Friedan recounted. In reading about what the suffragists did, they came to believe that their feelings of incompetence and helplessness were not natural, but were a learned response to the way society had infantilized women.

It is difficult for modern American women, steeped in the power of positive thinking, to realize how pervasive negative thinking was for women in the 1950s and early 1960s. Friedan gave many of her readers their first exposure to what is now a self-help cliché: that individuals can achieve their full potential when they reject the stereotypes that have been laid on them and realize they have the power to change.

In the early 1960s, stereotypes about women were so prevalent that even those who consciously rejected the status quo and protested inequities elsewhere in society seldom applied their political insights to their own experiences as women. A case in point is Lillian Rubin, now an internationally known social scientist who has published twelve books over the past thirty years.

Rubin was raised in the Bronx by an immigrant working-class single mother who had a very clear view of how her daughter could better herself. "I work in a dirty factory," her mother told her when she was young. "You'll work in a clean office. And then you'll get married."

Rubin wanted to go to college, and she was a better student than her brother, who didn't even want to attend college. But her mother believed "college was reserved for a boy; I was a girl who'd have a husband to take care of her." Like Ahrons's family, Lillian's mother discounted her daughter's intelligence. "My mother's line was: 'He's the smart one, you just study harder.'"

Although Rubin was disappointed to miss out on college, she accepted that her brother would go to school and she would go to work and help pay his way. But she became increasingly anxious to escape from her mother, and the only way she could even contemplate not living at home was to get married. So in 1943, at age nineteen, she married "the first man who asked me."

Rubin's husband became a certified public accountant after the war, which moved them into the middle class, fulfilling her mother's ambitions for her. Lillian stayed home with her daughter until the child turned three, after which she worked outside the home for several years. She was also active in politics in Los Angeles, where the family lived. "But despite the work and the political activity, I still felt trapped. My life never felt like my own. Friedan called it perfectly. The feeling didn't have a name. It didn't have a reason. So you turned it inward and assumed *you* were the problem. And so did everyone around you.

"I thought I was a troubled person who couldn't be satisfied with the fine life I now led—at least fine in comparison to where I came from. I had moved into this pretty house on a pretty street with a wonderful kid I adored and an okay-enough husband. So what did I have to complain about? I had climbed up to where I was supposed to—higher than my mother had hoped—and I wasn't happy. And I didn't know why."

As time passed, Rubin began to feel that her husband wasn't really "okay enough," and she initiated a separation. "When my mother heard we'd separated, she called my husband and told him, 'If Lillian wants to come back, treat her like a dog in the street. She doesn't deserve what you've given her.'" Fearing that she would not be able to support her child, Lillian agreed to reconcile three months later. She also consented to move from central Los Angeles, where she was a community activist, to the suburbs where her husband worked.

For several years, she tried to be the supportive wife. When her husband brought clients home, she entertained them. "I was constantly putting on a show. I didn't like the clients, and I didn't want to be doing this, but I felt I had to. I'd look at the young mothers walking in the park and they looked very happy. How much easier their lives seemed to me. But I couldn't do it, so I would run off to do politics. At the time, I was helping to organize the black community in Watts (what they now call South Central), where we ultimately succeeded in electing the first black congressman in California. I loved the political work. That's what kept me in the marriage and made the suburbs bearable."

Rubin got home for dinner every night and did "everything expected of a wife. But I didn't like it. And I always thought there was something wrong with me." So did her husband, who not only couldn't understand her discontent but feared her political activism would hurt his own reputation.

Rubin ended up leaving her husband and holding down several responsible jobs during the 1950s, first as a politician's campaign manager and then as personnel manager in an electronics firm, where she was fired when the FBI came around asking about her political activities. She next got a job at a nonprofit company, where her boss decided to keep her on even after the FBI visited again.

Yet Rubin still did not recognize the parallels between the racial and class inequalities against which she was organizing and her own situation as a woman. She met her present husband in 1961 and married him in March 1962. "Then the rest of my life started. I sat around trying to figure out what that meant. I'd changed a man I didn't care for, for one I adored, but that didn't do anything for my internal life, for the things that had made me restless."

In January 1963, Rubin went back to school at the University of California. Shortly afterward, she read *The Feminine Mystique* and "it was a revelation. It was like having a pain and finally your doctor tells you, your pain actually has a source. You aren't imagining it." For the first time she felt "total reassurance" about what she wanted to do with her life.

Rubin had already embarked on a new path, but Friedan's book helped her to understand what had led her there and to avoid the second thoughts about her choices that had plagued Anne Parsons. "I had lived the life Betty described. I woke up every day wondering if this was all there is, berating myself for not appreciating my good fortune, my nice suburban house, and my neighbors, all of whom seemed so much happier than I. I had no way to relate to them. Until I read *The Feminine Mystique*, I thought my feelings were unique and that I was somehow flawed, not a proper woman." But Friedan's book told Lillian that the course she had embarked on was exactly what "a proper woman" would do.

EVEN BEFORE THEY READ FRIEDAN'S BOOK, MANY OTHER WOMEN HAD already begun to take steps to build a different life than that prescribed by the feminine mystique. But surrounded by disapproval of their lives and denigration of their capacities, they thirsted for validation. Pat Cody, co-owner of Cody's Bookstore in Berkeley, California, was the fourth of eight children of Catholic working-class parents and the first to go to college. "I did not feel guilty about working," she recalls. "It had been a necessity in my life since I did babysitting when I was fourteen." But once she went into business with her husband, she was puzzled and angered by the way men treated her. Often, when she asked a sales rep a question, he would reply to her husband. When her husband brought home *The Feminine Mystique*, her reaction was "At last, a name for a situation!"

When Barbara Bergmann graduated from Cornell University in 1948, her mother asked, "How come you've come back without a husband? What do you think I sent you there for?" When *The Feminine Mystique* was published, Bergmann was in her mid-thirties and an untenured associate professor at Brandeis University. "I was unmarried, and fairly sure I had missed out on having a family. So when the book came out, I was in a state of envying housewives. Reading the book didn't make me any happier with my single state, but it showed that the most common alternative wasn't so hot either." Her mother died in 1965, "and later that year I married the first man that walked in. We are still married, both just turned eighty." But she made sure to marry someone who did not ask her to give up the career she had once thought could preclude marriage.

IT HAS OFTEN BEEN CLAIMED THAT *THE FEMININE MYSTIQUE* MADE women dissatisfied with their marriages. Certainly many women who felt trapped in unhappy marriages credit Friedan with giving them, as Janet C. said, "the courage to decide that the world wouldn't end if I left my husband."

Sandra G. wrote that in 1953, at age eighteen, she had married the first boy she had sex with, "and he threw that up to me every time we had a fight. I had 'given in' to him, he said. How did he know I hadn't 'done it' with other boys? And I felt bad, but I also kept thinking, 'He was the one who slept with other people before me; why am I the one who has to feel so bad?'" Reading Friedan made Sandra feel "like I had a right to get respect from a man, and if I didn't get it I could actually fend for myself."

Joanne Kinney was married with two children when she read the book "in pieces and parts when time permitted" in 1963 and 1964. Joanne and her sister would discuss Friedan's views and their husbands' reaction to the book's publicity. Both husbands hated the ideas they were hearing.

Joanne had always resented that she had to ask her husband for permission to buy clothing. She was also frustrated because "working outside the home was not allowed." He claimed it "would be too embarrassing for people to think I had to work." *The Feminine Mystique* showed Joanne that there were other unhappy housewives in America. It also made her think that a woman didn't necessarily have to stay with someone just because she wasn't sure where she would live and who would support her if she left. In Joanne's words, "I guess Friedan gave me the right to divorce . . . or so I thought."

But few of these women took an antimarriage attitude away from *The Feminine Mystique*, which made a point of not criticizing husbands for their wives' unhappiness. Instead, they took Friedan at her word when she said marriages would be happier when women no longer tried to meet all their needs through their assigned roles as wives and mothers. Many of the women who left their husbands in the wake of discovering feminist ideas practically glow with happiness when describing their second marriage. Joanne told of her joy at being able to marry the close friend who "is and was the love of my life since I met him in my second year of high school."

Jocelyn M. makes a similar point. "Once I gained the confidence to expect more out of life, I learned just how happy a marriage could be.

But it took a second marriage, after a lot of miserable years as a passive wife, before I knew that happiness."

Other women reported that their marriages were improved or even saved because they read the book. Several said that before they read Friedan they had tried to deal with their feelings of emptiness by flirting with other men or drinking too much. "For a while I and a couple of my neighbors lived a *Desperate Housewives*–lite sort of life," recalls Jolene W. "I never actually committed adultery, but I came close a couple of times. But once I took Betty's advice and got the part-time job I had been interested in, I didn't seem to need that kind of gratification anymore."

Heather Kleiner first heard of *The Feminine Mystique* in the early 1960s, but she didn't immediately relate to it because she and her husband, then in graduate school, "were part of a group of other student-parents, beset with similar problems of juggling work, studies, and parenting. So I did not feel the loneliness and isolation of my suburban counterparts."

But after the birth of her second child in 1966, recalls Heather, "I became a housewife, and my 'days of rage' began. . . . I remember being very, very angry. . . . And I blamed my poor husband for contributing to my stultifying unhappiness." Reading *The Feminine Mystique* helped her realize "that my problems were societal and that my husband and other family members were as much 'victimized' as I by gendered role expectations."

A few women said they might have saved their marriages if they had read *The Feminine Mystique* sooner. One woman, after reading an article by Friedan in *Good Housekeeping,* wrote her a letter in August 1960, saying, "If I had only had these words and thoughts brought to my attention 10 years ago, perhaps my life would not have taken on the somewhat tragic aspect that it did. Because from just such frustrations as not feeling like a human being, I divorced my husband."

Journalist Laura M. credits Friedan's book with reinforcing a cautious approach to marriage that ultimately stood her in good stead. "I was surrounded by girls who were very into becoming a Mrs., getting a teaching certificate along the way, 'just in case.' When I read the book, it confirmed that there was good reason for my distaste for this 'domestic goddess' lifestyle. When I fell in love and became a mother years later, I feared I would be like a bird flying into a cage and having the door shut after her." In fact, "domestic life turned out to be wonderful. . . . But that was only because I took care to choose a man who wanted me to have a career and would participate fully as a parent. The book was life-changing for me."

Ruth Fost reports that the book affected her husband almost as much as it affected her. "He began taking a more active role in child rearing (changing diapers, bathing, bedtime—most men did not do this in 1963)" and supported her decision to take a job. "I have enjoyed the bliss of parenting (now add grandparenting!) and working since 1963."

Fost acknowledged that Friedan's own "marriage (and many others) could not withstand the conflict that her liberating theories demanded. But somehow, my husband and I (it takes two to make this work) were able to choreograph our lives to be independent and interdependent— giving each other the room to do what we needed to do for ourselves, for each other and for our children to find happiness and fulfillment." It was *The Feminine Mystique*, she says, that launched them on this path.

Harry J. also believes that reading *The Feminine Mystique* improved his marriage. He and his wife were both raised strict Catholics. "We married in 1966 and approached married life just as our parents and society directed. We became breadwinner and homemaker without any second thoughts." But their marriage had some problems, and when he read Friedan's book in 1973, he found it "an eye-opener. My recollection is that it was a stunning description of the forces at work in our life." He adds that it "made me aware of my wife's need to someday escape this condition. I believe it prepared me to support her changing from homemaker to individual career woman."

Even reading the book in the 1990s, Trent Mauer came away with a clearer sense that marriage should be a true partnership. It made him resolve to improve his own domestic skills so that he "would never need to be with a woman because I didn't know how to cook or do laundry or care for children. I wanted to know that I would only be with her because I wanted to, and I wanted to make sure that she would never have to doubt why I was with her." Trent also vowed to make sure "that she would never have to go through the types of experiences that Friedan described."

SOME WOMEN WERE INTRODUCED TO FRIEDAN'S BOOK AS TEENAGERS BY their mother or an older female friend. Sunny M. read the book together with her mother when she was fifteen, three years after it was published. "My mother wanted me to have what she felt that she had not been allowed to have."

In a tribute to Friedan on the National Organization for Women web site, Linda Morse reported that a neighbor handed her the book when she was in her teens, saying, "Here, you read it, it's too late for me." Many of the women who wrote to Friedan soon after the book's publication expressed the same sense that it was too late for them but not for the next generation of women. One, describing herself as a college dropout and "victim of the Feminine Mystique," expressed her hope that her daughter could grow up without the "servile feeling" that had haunted her own life. Another declared, "It would be a crime to let another generation go as mine had," and prayed that her daughter could "avoid becoming a miserable housewife!"

Jessica T., now a nationally syndicated columnist, remembers: "I first heard of *The Feminine Mystique* when my mother, a stay-at-home farm wife who had dropped out of college to marry my father, began talking about it at the family dinner table. The culture of our rural farming community and our family was very patriarchal, and my sweet, self-effacing mother was not regarded by any of us as our father's equal.

"We loved and revered her," Jessica continues, "but Dad was definitely the boss. When Mom started talking about feeling 'trapped' like other housewives in the book, we all looked at her as if she had two heads." Jessica was about twelve at the time. The experience reinforced her resolve, already formed by seeing "how circumscribed" her mother's life was, "to chart a course as different from hers as I possibly could."

Marjorie Schmiege's daughter Cynthia said that her mother's discovery of the book not only relieved Marjorie's depression but also changed the goals she held for her children, opening opportunities for Cynthia that she might never have had were it not for Friedan's influence.

Other women came to the book on their own as teenagers or young women, and it helped them understand why they did not want to follow in their mothers' footsteps. Mary Rinato Berman vividly recalls reading the book in the park near her home in 1963, during the summer after she graduated from high school. Mary grew up in a six-story, forty-two-unit apartment building in New York, populated by a mix of Italian and Jewish families. Her Catholic parents had a "fairly balanced" marriage, but in a building where "everyone kept their doors open and we kids felt comfortable in all of the apartments," she had seen forty-one other marriages up close, and it wasn't pretty. She remembers "knowing of husbands with girlfriends living in the neighborhood, seeing women with bruises, hearing complaints when the women would get together."

The husband next door "regularly beat up his wife. He was also the biggest celebrator of Valentine's Day—armloads of flowers, chocolates, and the like. It definitely gave me a total dislike of the holiday.

"Then along came *The Feminine Mystique* and . . . I remember thinking that it didn't have to be that way."

Historian Ruth Rosen and sociologist Wini Breines have pointed out that many women who grew up in the 1950s and 1960s developed a deep suspicion of marriage and motherhood not by reading Friedan but by observing life in a "normal" family. These young women came to see their mothers as negative role models: the epitome of what they did not want to be. Friedan reinforced their determination not to repeat their mothers' lives.

One young woman wrote to Friedan that the book perfectly captured the story of her mother, who had stayed home for twenty-three years and raised four children: "The emptiness of her life appalls me: her helplessness and dependence on my father frightens me." As Linda Smolak put it decades later, reading Friedan "articulated what scared me to death about being a 'homemaker/housewife.'"

Many daughters raised by homemaker mothers had similar reactions to their mothers' lives even if they had not read Friedan. In an interview conducted by a researcher in the 1950s, one young woman commented, "I feel deathly afraid of devoting all my time and energy to being a wife and mother and then being nothing in middle age, because that's what happened to my own mother in her marriage."

Journalist and best-selling author Barbara Ehrenreich reports having the same fear. She was born in 1941 in Butte, Montana, into a working-class family supported by her father, a miner. By the time she was in her mid-teens, he had earned a degree from the Butte School of Mines and the family had risen into the middle class. Ehrenreich later told Ruth Rosen that in those days, "you had to steel yourself as a girl if you didn't want to follow a prescribed role. . . . Even at a young age, I could understand that the only good thing you could do as a woman was to be a housewife, but you would never have any respect that way. Because I don't think my father respected my mother. She was a full-time housewife, and that's what I did not want to be."

Some daughters grew up simmering with anger toward their mothers, whom they resented for trying to mold them into their own housewifely image. Polly J. says, "I felt nothing but contempt for [my mother] when I was in my teens. She never stood up to my dad. She never had an original idea, and she wasn't interested in anything my brothers and I were learning about, except the grades we were getting and if my homework looked neat.

"She was so sweet with the neighbors," Polly remembers, making a little face at the word "sweet," "but she sure bossed us around—especially me, because I was 'the girl' and my job was to keep the house picked up and never go downtown wearing pants. I hated all her petty rules and put-downs of my behavior. Only much later did it occur to me that her attitude might have come out of her own frustration or depression."

Judith Lorber recalls that her mother didn't like doing housework but explained that it was something a wife did for her husband. "She implied that the more you loved him, the less onerous housework was." The teenage Judith resented being required to help with the dishes and the cleaning while her brother did not have to do any work around the house. "My mother kept saying I had to be domesticated, and I said domestication was for cows! The end result was that I did everything I could to be the opposite of my homemaker mother."

Several women said that reading *The Feminine Mystique* allowed them to understand their mothers better and let go of their anger or resentment. "I had a lot of issues with my mother growing up, which I couldn't even begin to resolve until my late twenties," reports June Pulliam, now a college professor. When she was in her thirties, Pulliam assigned *The Feminine Mystique* in a class. "For the first time I understood the thwarted existence of my own mother and my father's sisters and the mothers of my friends. . . . It was as if someone had gone back and shown me a movie of my childhood with the director's commentary about my mother's grumbling discontent with her domestic role."

Kathy Heskin's mother graduated from college in 1930 "but was not allowed to work, either before or after her marriage. She was a woman who had great sadness and depression, and her mental illness progressed over the years, partly due to her frustration with life." When Kathy was sixteen and a counselor at summer camp, her mother wrote her a six-page letter about how deeply she had been affected by reading *The Feminine Mystique*. Her letter "was passionate and utterly bewildering," but "as sixteen-year-olds will, I forgot all about it until I was much older." Only then did she read the book herself. There were just two times, Kathy says, when she felt she understood her mother—"when I read the book of Job and when I read *The Feminine Mystique*."

Gary Gerst reports that reading *The Feminine Mystique* in 1968 or 1969 was just as transformative for him as a son—and as a future husband: "I gained a new sadness and empathy for my mom's squelched abilities." When he asked his mother about what he'd learned from the book, she admitted that she had actually read it much earlier but had never told her husband and family.

"I realized," recalls Gary, "that this was like a 'banned book' and she had to hide it from Dad." As she opened up to him about her musical and math talents and all the other interests she had put to one side for her marriage, Gary recognized for the first time how much of his mother's life "had been subverted or abandoned to 'be attractive to' or 'complement' a man." For Gary, "the problem with no name" meant that women "had been muffled, ignored, not even allowed to give voice to a truth or even able to describe it. How awful that such discontent by so many for so long was muted without even a term with which to understand it. . . . I know that from then on it also influenced what type of women I wished to date and eventually marry. I sought strong women who were not about to surrender their dreams or self to assigned servitude or silence."

6

〰〰〰

The Price of Privilege:
Middle-Class Women and
the Feminine Mystique

ONE MONTH AFTER *THE FEMININE MYSTIQUE* WAS PUBLISHED, FRIEDAN received a letter from Gerda Lerner, a civil rights activist with a background in left-wing politics who later became a pioneer in women's history. Lerner congratulated Friedan on a "splendid . . . job which desperately needed doing." But she expressed concern that Friedan had addressed herself "solely to the problems of middle class, college-educated women." Lerner reminded Friedan that "working women, especially Negro women, labor not only under the disadvantages imposed by the feminine mystique, but under the more pressing disadvantages of economic discrimination," and suggested that in addition to Friedan's proposals for expanding women's access to higher education, such women needed child care centers and maternity benefits.

Many critics have since gone further, dismissing *The Feminine Mystique* as written by a middle-class housewife who did not understand the needs of working women or minorities and who addressed problems unique to elite, educated readers. Even at the time of its publication, some people had the same reaction. Janice B., a sales clerk with two children in 1962, read the excerpt in the *Ladies' Home Journal* and couldn't understand what middle-class homemakers were making such a fuss about. "It wasn't that hard to go get a job," she recalls. "And having a job sure didn't solve all my problems as a wife and mother."

Vietta Helme, who read the book in the 1970s, recalls that Friedan's experiences were "utterly foreign to me as a working-class farm kid." Helme says that she could understand that it might have had "some value for over-privileged women," but "it was too far out of my demographic to have much meaning for me."

Lorraine G., an African-American woman who never read the book, wrote in an e-mail to me that she and her friends "were too busy struggling to achieve the American dream to be concerned with women who appeared to have it all." The summaries of Friedan's book she read while pursuing her doctorate in sociology led her to believe that the audience for *The Feminine Mystique* was "white women [who] had the luxury of being bored with their middle-class, full-time homemaker role, a role that most working women would cherish."

Larry R., a white man who read the book in 1966 after graduating from college, was similarly unimpressed, saying he couldn't understand why anyone would complain about being left in a large suburban home while someone else earned the money. "I don't have much patience with people who do not worry about food and shelter lamenting that they are bored."

Even middle-class women who remain grateful to Friedan for writing *The Feminine Mystique* often mention that, in retrospect, they are taken aback by how little Friedan seemed to know about the issues facing women who had to work out of necessity.

Friedan actively encouraged the belief that she was writing from her own middle-class experience, speaking to the largely apolitical, white, middle-class, suburban woman because she had been one herself. She too, she told her readers, had "lived according to the feminine mystique as a suburban housewife," only gradually coming to see that something was wrong with how she and other American women were being told to organize their lives. "I sensed it first as a question mark in my own life, as a wife and mother of three small children, half-guiltily and therefore half-heartedly, almost in spite of myself, using my abilities and education in work that took me away from home."

Her epiphany came in 1957, according to her account in an early chapter of the book, when she interviewed her college classmates fifteen years after their graduation from Smith College and found "a strange discrepancy between the reality of our lives as women and the image to which we were trying to conform, the image that I came to call the feminine mystique. I wondered if other women faced this schizophrenic split, and what it meant." And so, in her telling, she set out on a journey of discovery that culminated in *The Feminine Mystique.*

Friedan repeated this account in a 1973 *New York Times* reminiscence called "Up from the Kitchen Floor." "Until I started writing the book," she wrote, "I wasn't even conscious of the woman problem. . . . I, like other women, thought there was something wrong with *me* because I didn't have an orgasm waxing the kitchen floor."

Friedan's version of her own past was accepted as gospel until 1998, when historian Daniel Horowitz published—to Friedan's considerable chagrin—his meticulously researched (and very sympathetic) account of Friedan's intellectual and political history, which was much closer to that of activist Gerda Lerner than to the suburban housewives Friedan targeted in her book.

In 1943, four years before she married Carl Friedan, Betty Goldstein hadn't been thinking about orgasms when she wrote about kitchens. "Men, there's a revolution in your own kitchen," she had warned in an admiring review of Elizabeth Hawes's *Why Women Cry.* It was the revolt of "the forgotten female," she wrote, "finally waking up to the fact that she can produce other things besides babies."

Betty Goldstein's concerns about gender equality and her critical attitudes toward mainstream social scientists were forged long before she became Betty Friedan, the suburban housewife raising three children. At Smith College she had been an outstanding psychology student and a committed political activist, and after graduation, she wrote for union newspapers. Goldstein was familiar with the work of left-wing feminists such as Hawes, Eve Merriam, and Betty Millard, and wrote many articles about working women's struggles and needs.

After she married Carl Friedan, she continued this work, although she took a year off after having her first child. In 1952 she permanently lost or left—it is unclear which—her regular job with the United Electrical Workers union. From that point on, she struggled to establish herself as a self-employed writer.

In 1950, the Friedans moved to Parkway Village, a racially integrated development in Queens, among whose tenants were civil rights leader Roy Wilkins and several UN staff members. In her years there, Friedan was certainly not an isolated, apolitical housewife. She edited a community newsletter, participated in a babysitting cooperative, and in 1952 helped organize a rent strike. In a 1953 piece she wrote for the *UE News*, "Women Fight for a Better Life!" Friedan celebrated the struggles of immigrant, African-American, and union workers.

As the 1950s progressed, Friedan distanced herself, geographically as well as politically, from the leftist circles in which she had originally trained as a writer. In 1956 the Friedans moved to the suburbs of Rockland County, New York. She remained an engaged community activist but switched her focus to education, founding an "Intellectual Resources Pool" that offered adult education classes; brought in artists, scientists, and writers to enrich the school curriculum; and set up mentoring relationships between students and professionals. She forged a career as a freelance writer, gradually adapting her work to an audience of middle-class women rather than the union members for whom she had written during the previous decade.

Friedan's selective version of her own history has led many people to think that she didn't understand or sympathize with the obstacles facing working women and minorities. But in early drafts of *The Feminine Mystique,* she drew parallels between the prejudices against women and those against African Americans and Jews. Even in its final, watered-down version, *The Feminine Mystique* several times mentions Friedan's support for the civil rights movement and "for oppressed workers."

And only a few years after the book's appearance, as chair of the National Organization for Women, Friedan broadened her agenda to include many of the issues Lerner had suggested. Sociologist Cynthia Fuchs Epstein notes that most of the early legal cases NOW pursued were taken on behalf of working-class women, including African-American working women.

But there is no denying that *The Feminine Mystique* focused on the problems facing comparatively privileged white housewives, those who had more education than the three years of high school that George Gallup had found typical in his 1962 survey for the *Saturday Evening Post*. Although Friedan noted that "housewives of all educational levels" suffered from the feminine mystique, she assumed—not entirely without justification—that "the problem that has no name" was especially acute for women who had a middle-class standard of living and enough education that if they went back to work or school, they could find "meaningful" middle-class jobs.

Friedan's bias toward women from middle-class backgrounds, or married to middle-class husbands, was evident in her suggestion that women who wanted to work should hire housekeepers and nannies to take over their chores at home. Her book never discusses the issues facing the women who worked in those domestic jobs. In fact, several passages imply that such work, together with other types of service or clerical work, was beneath the talents of her readers. This elitist prejudice came from the same Betty Goldstein who as a student at Smith College had actively supported a drive to organize a union for maids in the campus dorms.

Despite its middle-class orientation, some uneducated and working-class women did embrace *The Feminine Mystique*. A postal clerk wrote to Friedan that it was "the most factual true book" she had ever read. Other letters praised the book but expressed a wish that the book could have been priced more affordably. One woman described herself as a housewife and mother of five with "a very poor education" and lamented that "if this is all there is for me to look forward to, I don't want to go on."

Still, the book was largely addressed to—and elicited the most heart-felt responses from—white women who had some higher education and whose husbands provided enough economic security that they could choose whether to work. This rapidly growing group of women faced new and distinctive dilemmas in postwar America.

The 1950s saw a remarkable increase in the number of Americans who achieved economic security. In the thirteen years between 1947 and 1960, the average worker's purchasing power increased by as much as it had during the previous fifty years. By 1960, nearly 60 percent of Americans had midrange incomes, about twice as many as in the prosperous years before the Great Depression.

One mark of this new prosperity was an explosion in the number of students in institutions of higher education. Men's enrollment in college grew faster than that of women, largely because of the benefits of the GI Bill, but between 1940 and 1960, the number of female college graduates increased from 1.4 million to 3.5 million. The number of women who had completed a few years of college grew even faster.

In the 1940s, the number of women who entered college each year was less than a third of those who graduated from high school. By 1958 it was 40 percent, and by 1963 it had reached 45 percent. And this increase occurred even as the percentage of female high school graduates was also rising sharply. In 1930, only 32 percent of seventeen-year-old girls had graduated from high school. By 1963, that number had increased to 73 percent.

The Feminine Mystique had its biggest impact on women in a generation caught between two worlds when it came to education. One world was that of their mothers and grandmothers, where any woman who aspired to go to college was consciously defying society's expectations of her role, and such a woman often continued to challenge societal norms after graduation. The other was the world their daughters and granddaughters would inherit, where the definition of appropriate female behavior would broaden to include not only getting an education but utilizing that education in paid work even after marriage.

In the early twentieth century, it still took audacity for a woman to attend college, and doing so was often a sign of unconventional aspirations. Women who entered college in the first two decades of the twentieth century tended to be fervent supporters of social causes such as votes for women, and most of them intended to make their mark after they graduated.

However, women who sought higher education in that era often felt they had to sacrifice family life. Up until 1900, more than half the graduates from women's colleges remained single, many of them carving out careers in new fields such as social work. Even as late as 1940, more than 30 percent of female college graduates ages forty to forty-nine were unmarried, compared to less than 13 percent of high school graduates and grade school graduates the same age.

When it came to graduate work, women were especially likely to feel they had to choose between getting a master's degree and a "Mrs. degree," and even when they did marry, a stunningly small percentage of highly educated women had children. An analysis of the marriage and motherhood patterns of women who attended graduate school at Columbia University found that only a quarter of the women born before World War I became mothers.

In the 1940s and 1950s, attending college became much more compatible with getting married and becoming a mother. Many women went for only a year or two, then dropped out to marry. But even women who graduated from college were more likely to marry and have children than their counterparts in the early decades of the century. Of the female Columbia University graduate students born between 1925 and 1929, almost 90 percent became mothers, compared to only 25 percent of the women born prior to 1914.

For many women of the 1950s, however, the growing likelihood that a woman would attend college and also embark relatively early on raising a family presented new dilemmas rather than new opportunities. By then, going to college was a statement of status, signifying that a family had achieved a secure middle-class standing in society. But becoming a full-time homemaker after marriage was also a statement of status. So the value of a college education played out differently for daughters and sons.

For men, going to college was the way to get a good job. For women, it was the way to get a good husband.

In the transitional world of the 1940s, 1950s, and early 1960s, it was now socially acceptable, even desirable, for a woman to attend some college before embarking on marriage and motherhood, but the aspirations that a college education sometimes encouraged were still frowned upon. Society strongly discouraged women who intended to marry and have children from setting their sights on a lifelong career, or even from taking their studies very seriously.

As early as 1953, in a thoughtful book on the dilemmas of educated women, sociologist Mirra Komarovsky noted that "technological and social changes over the past century and a half have disturbed an old equilibrium without as yet replacing it with another. As a result, our society is a veritable crazy quilt of contradictory practices and beliefs. . . . The old and the new moralities exist side by side dividing the heart against itself."

Komarovsky suggested that female students in the late 1940s and early 1950s were tempted by newer options and goals, but that they understood the likelihood of social censure if they pursued them. The reason so many came to espouse traditional roles "all the more passionately" during the 1950s, Komarovsky speculated, was that they were trying to silence or deny the other aspirations their education threatened to raise.

Whatever their motives, the vehemence with which postwar female college students insisted that marriage was their top priority was striking. Some young women stated in their college applications that their main goal in acquiring an education was to communicate better with their future husbands. One Vassar candidate wrote: "When I marry, I would like to converse with my husband's friends and business acquaintances with a mature and confident manner that can only come from a thorough education." Even when college students planned to work after graduation, they often attributed this to a desire to gain "some insight into the husband's world" or expressed the hope that a year or so of work might give them organizational skills they could use in the home.

Many educators encouraged this growing preoccupation, seeing it as a welcome shift from the "antifamily" tendencies of earlier generations of female college students. During the 1950s, the president of Radcliffe College, the women-only counterpart to Harvard, assured incoming students that their education would prepare them "to be splendid wives and mothers." If they were really lucky, they might even "marry Harvard men."

One 1952 advice book for teenage girls warned that studying could be a "dating handicap." Another advised young women to go far enough in school to be good companions to their husbands, but not so far as to compete with them. And a 1957 advice manual approvingly remarked on the "bright new trend" of women dropping out of college to help finance their husbands' more timely graduation. This gave a woman the "joy of being a part of her husband's preparation for a career" and of achieving her PhT, "Putting husband Through."

Coeds of the 1950s took this advice seriously. Komarovsky noted that 40 percent of them reported playing dumb on dates. And although a higher proportion of women entered college than in the early decades of the century, a lower proportion of women who entered college actually completed their degrees. In 1920 women composed 47 percent of all college students and earned fully half of all degrees, which meant they were *less* likely to drop out than men. In 1960, more than 60 percent of female college students dropped out before graduation, usually to get married.

Women who did graduate from college seemed less inclined to strive for excellence or aspire to nontraditional fields than in the prewar period. A study of female students at Vassar College at the end of the 1950s found that the percentage of physics and chemistry majors fell by more than half in the decade following World War II. Graduates became more likely to turn down a research job or forgo graduate work because it might hurt their marriage prospects.

A study of U.S. college seniors in 1961 found that almost 70 percent of the men who placed in the top 20 percent of their class planned to go on to graduate school, while only 36 percent of the equally high-achieving women had similar plans. A report funded by the Rockefeller Foundation pointed out that one in thirty of the highest-scoring male high school students went on to get a PhD, but only one in three hundred of the highest-scoring girls did. In 1920, women had earned 20 percent of all PhDs. That dropped to a low of 9 percent from 1950 to 1955, and had recovered to only 11 percent by 1963.

Some educators who remembered the commitment and drive of the earlier generation of female college students were appalled by the changes they saw in the postwar period and greeted *The Feminine Mystique* with tremendous enthusiasm. One woman, who had graduated in the first wave of women's education in the early twentieth century and then become a professor at the University of Illinois, wrote to Friedan that in the ten years before she retired in 1954, she had increasingly felt "that something had gone wrong with our younger women of college age." A Vassar professor expressed his frustration that female students "just won't let themselves get interested. They feel it will get in their way when they marry."

Even when young women did take their education seriously and wanted to pursue it further, many parents refused to support these aspirations. When anthropologist Sherry Ortner interviewed fellow female graduates of her 1958 high school class in Newark, New Jersey, several noted that their parents had steered them away from the better colleges where they sent their sons. One woman recalled that her parents had been willing to spend more on her brother's education than her own, even though she had been the better student. Another said that her father refused to help her attend graduate school because she would be "pricing herself out of the [marriage] market."

Parents also pressured their daughters to major in traditional women's fields such as teaching or nursing, even if their interests lay elsewhere. "They kept saying that 'if something happens to your husband, which God forbid,' I would need a 'respectable' occupation 'to fall back on,'" reports Rosalind F. "The assumption was that I wasn't going to work anyway, so why should I care what I majored in."

And women who harbored intellectual aspirations continued to fear that these were incompatible with a satisfying family life, except perhaps vicariously. When Peta Henderson, now a retired college professor, was a seventeen-year-old freshman at Swarthmore in the mid-1950s, she babysat to earn extra money. One evening she was working at the home of a humanities professor at her college. It wasn't a fancy home, and it certainly wasn't as well kept as the pictures of houses she had sometimes admired in women's magazines, but she found it tremendously appealing. After she put the children to bed, she walked through the house looking at all the books and papers, "and I distinctly remember saying to myself, 'I want to marry a college professor.'"

Six years later, still unmarried, she had completed bachelor's and master's degrees. But when her adviser praised her work and suggested that she go on to earn a PhD, Henderson grew anxious. "I can't get a PhD," she told her adviser. "I want to get married someday."

Another factor that may have dampened women's aspirations was the relative decline in their representation within colleges. Although women were entering colleges and universities in higher numbers than in the past, they were overwhelmed by the massive influx of male veterans. Even as the absolute numbers of women in college rose, their proportion decreased dramatically. Women were 47 percent of college students in 1920, and still a full 40 percent in 1944, but by the mid-1950s they were only a third.

In historian Linda Eisenmann's view, women became "increasingly incidental" on campus as administrators focused on meeting the needs of returning veterans. To accommodate the flood of male students, many schools limited the number of women they would admit. Some medical and engineering schools capped female admissions at 5 percent of their total enrollment.

Several political scientists have argued that the reason the women's movement of the 1960s appealed to white middle-class women, especially those with a college education, was that they experienced the most "relative deprivation" compared to the progress their male counterparts were making. The wage gap between men and women widened during the 1950s, and college-educated men gained more ground in the professions and other high-paying occupations than college-educated women. A survey of white women who graduated from college between 1946 and 1949 found that only half had been able to find the kind of work for which they had trained. Even at women's colleges, traditionally the largest employer of female academics, the proportion of women on the faculties declined substantially during the 1940s and 1950s.

The frustration and anger triggered by women's relative deprivation may have fueled the women's movement in the mid-1960s, but initially that relative decline merely discouraged many women from taking their education seriously. Women who went to college for the sake of ideas or to train for a career felt outnumbered, overshadowed, and to some extent silenced by the much larger group of coeds who harbored no such "unfeminine" ambitions. Many were intimidated by the cultural insistence— which grew even more shrill as its basis in reality eroded—that a normal woman would cheerfully sacrifice her intellectual and occupational aspirations for the more satisfying achievement of getting a husband and helping *him* to succeed.

The prevailing expectations of educated women in this era were epitomized in the commencement address delivered to the graduating class of Smith College in 1955 by Adlai Stevenson, two-time Democratic presidential candidate. Stevenson began by observing that the new technological economy hampered man's pursuit of larger ends, such as finding a greater meaning and purpose in life. The task of woman, said Stevenson, was to help her own particular man become "truly purposeful" and "to keep him whole." That, in his view, was how woman could play her "part in the unfolding drama of our free society."

Stevenson went on to explain to the Smith graduates the two main benefits of accepting this "assignment." First, "it is home work—you can do it in the living room with a baby in your lap or in the kitchen with a can opener in your hand." Second, it is "worthy" work, because by countering the male breadwinner's "contraction of mind and spirit," wives could help America defeat "totalitarian, authoritarian ideas" and "frustrate the evils of vocational specialization."

Like Friedan, Stevenson noted that the "mundane" nature of housework could be frustrating for women who had been exposed to "the great issues and stirring debates" fostered by higher education. "Once they read Baudelaire. Now it is the *Consumers' Guide*. Once they wrote poetry. Now it's the laundry list.

"Once they discussed art and philosophy until late in the night," Stevenson continued. "Now they are so tired they fall asleep as soon as the dishes are finished. There is, often, a sense of contraction, of closing horizons and lost opportunities. They had hoped to play their part in the crisis of the age. But what they do is wash the diapers."

Unlike Friedan, however, Stevenson called on women to embrace this "contraction" in their lives as "yet another instance of the emergence of individual freedom in our Western society." Across the world, "women 'never had it as good' as you do," Stevenson proclaimed. And regardless of whether you like the idea of becoming a housewife just now, he assured the graduates, once it happens, you *will* like it.

Many women who switched from Baudelaire to baking did like being full-time housewives. But those who failed to experience homemaking as the ultimate expression of their "individual freedom" were beset by feelings of self-doubt and guilt to a degree that is difficult for contemporary women to grasp—not despite their education but precisely because of it.

Women who attended college in the 1950s were especially likely to have been taught the "scientific" findings of Freudian psychiatrists and functionalist sociologists that any woman who wanted more meaning in life than she found in the kitchen and nursery suffered from psychological maladjustment. The magazines targeted to housewives of their race, income, and educational level promoted the views of Freudian psychiatrists and other human behavior "experts" about "healthy" and "unhealthy" gender roles more often and in more detail than did the periodicals aimed at white working-class or black middle-class women. The result was that educated housewives who did not feel what they knew they *should* be feeling experienced a special kind of self-doubt.

Certainly the pain of a frustrated stay-at-home housewife or a young middle-class woman contemplating her future as a homemaker was different than that of a low-paid clerk or a factory worker struggling to combine an exhausting job at work with an equally exhausting job at home. It was different from the stress facing a black woman in a marriage where even two incomes were not enough to raise the family out of poverty or protect her children from racial discrimination. But using the word "boredom" to describe the doubts and insecurities of these middle-class women unfairly trivializes their pain. While their distress may have been less rooted in material deprivation than that of working-class and minority women, it was in some ways more bewildering. And it was more frequently turned inward, because most of Friedan's readers recognized their privileges and acknowledged their own complicity in creating the life that was now making them unhappy. Many felt terrible because they *did* have the choice not to work and thought there was something wrong with themselves for not being properly grateful for that advantage.

Sharon V., who was thirty-four when she read *The Feminine Mystique* in 1964, explained the sense of unworthiness that had been haunting her: "There were Negroes being beaten in the South. There were children with bellies swollen from hunger in Appalachia. And here I was with comforts my mother would have given her eye-tooth for. What right did I have to be so miserable?" But telling herself that she had "no right" to these feelings didn't help. "I still had the feelings, but I felt guilty for having them, which made me feel even worse. Until I read *The Feminine Mystique*."

Julie Olin-Ammentorp's mother was another such woman, and Julie found that reading *The Feminine Mystique* helped her make sense of her mother's life. "She was of that generation of housewives that did not have much outlet for their intelligence, but also felt they couldn't complain because, generally speaking, they had it so good. . . . At the same time, *knowing* that you 'should' be happy because you had what all women were 'supposed' to want really didn't help."

This combination of insecurity in the face of experts and guilt about their discontent explains why so many of these comparatively privileged women gradually lost the self-confidence of their early years. In oral histories of and surveys from the 1950s, it is striking how frequently middle-class white women, especially those with some college education, expressed guilt, self-doubt, and inadequacy about their family behaviors.

Educated white middle-class women in the 1950s were more likely to feel guilty when they went to work—or even when they just *wanted* to work—than comparably educated black women or white working-class women with less education. And numerous sociological studies in the 1950s and early 1960s found that educated housewives, even those who enjoyed being homemakers, tended to devalue or second-guess their own child rearing more than working-class women did.

Constance Ahrons felt guilty about wanting to go back to school when all her friends were happy to stay home with their families. "I just assumed I'd be punished in some way," she told me. "That's what happens to women who are selfish. My friends said, 'You're so selfish.'"

Sandie Nisbett, a college graduate who was married with three children in the 1950s, loved her husband and kids immensely. "But I was totally wrapped up in that. I thought it was my responsibility to fix all the emotional issues in the household, and I gradually lost my sense that I could fix anything else." When Sandie finally decided she had to get out of the house, she felt "so insecure that I remember picking up a shorthand book at the library, thinking maybe I could be a secretary. It had nothing to do with my interests or my former training, but I couldn't imagine doing anything bigger. Women had jobs, not careers. The job would give me something to do, but I didn't dream higher."

Nisbett ended up teaching reintroduction classes for other women who had been housewives for years, "and you could see it every year. They came back with no self-confidence at all, even those who had been National Merit scholars."

Joyce Robinson, whose dreams included law school, didn't know what she "was more scared of—not being able to do it, or being able to do it and ruining my children's lives as a result." Robinson says that her self-confidence shot up as soon as she earned an A in her first class, "but the guilt didn't go away, even when my twenty-year-old daughter sat me down and read me a three-page letter about how much she loved and respected me."

Once women did go back to school or got jobs commensurate with their training—and many of them report that it was *The Feminine Mystique* that gave them the impetus to do so—they typically experienced a resurgence of self-confidence and self-esteem. Thanks to the book, "I got my mind back," one woman told me. "My depression fell off in layers, month after month, after I took her advice and went back to work the way I'd always wanted to but never quite dared," said another.

The difference that employment made in such women's lives is confirmed by a long-term study of women who graduated from Mills College in 1958 and 1960. The researchers found that between ages twenty-seven and forty-three, "large increases in independence and assertiveness" took place among all the women who went on to work outside the home, married and unmarried alike. The only women who did not experience such increases were the full-time homemakers.

A study of women who graduated from various colleges between 1945 and 1955 found that, decades later, women who took paid work, whether married or single, displayed higher self-esteem than those who became full-time homemakers. The married professional women even assessed their child care skills more positively than did the housewives. But these studies came too late to alleviate the guilt and anxiety many middle-class women felt at the time about their discontent with being a full-time homemaker.

The comparative lack of guilt expressed by working-class wives who worked or wanted to work did not mean that women in blue-collar families were more psychologically secure than middle-class women, or conversely, that middle-class women were more sensitive than their more impoverished counterparts. A twelve-year study of women married to blue-collar workers and living in blue-collar neighborhoods reveals much about the different patterns of pain and vulnerability working-class and middle-class wives experienced. The study, which came out in 1959, was commissioned by the publishers of *True Story*, a pulp magazine aimed at the wives of blue-collar wage earners. Its aim was to help advertisers and magazine editors better understand the distinctive values, motivations, and buying habits of working-class women.

The working women interviewed for this study experienced "pervasive anxiety," according to the researchers, but their anxiety was based on long-term physical hardship and material want rather than on the self-doubt and guilt recounted by so many middle-class housewives. When shown a picture and asked to construct a story about it, the two groups of housewives reacted very differently. One picture showed a girl with many hands pointing at her. The working-class women made up stories in which the girl was being shamed, ridiculed, accused, or bossed around by others. The middle-class women were "more likely to see the pointing hands as symbolic of the girl's inner state." One suggested she was having a bad dream because she had "something on her mind." Another speculated that she had "stolen something and the hands are her conscience eating at her."

Interviewers also showed the two groups a picture where a woman had her hands at the neck or head of another person. The middle-class women tended to interpret the picture as a woman helping another person who was ill or who had tripped. The working-class women were more likely to interpret it as a fight or an attack and to provide a lot of detail, often related to their own lives, about what provoked it and what might happen next.

The academics conducting the survey attributed the high degree of anxiety that ran through the blue-collar housewives' reactions to these simulated situations to an inability to manage strong feelings or see nuance in situations. "The volatility of the working class woman's emotions," they concluded, "contributes to her sense of the world as being chaotic." But a more reasonable interpretation is that these women were reacting to a world that was in fact more chaotic, insecure, and threatening than that of their middle-class counterparts.

The responses illustrate two very different sources of stress in these women's lives. The working-class women's experience with want and hardship directed their attention to the external world and other people as the main threats to their happiness and security. The pain of middle-class housewives arose out of the contradictions between what they were told they should be feeling and what they actually felt.

It is pointless to construct a hierarchy of who hurt more, and whether one kind of pain was more or less justified than another. And I say this as someone whose first reaction was to dismiss the pain of the middle-class housewives as less "real" than that of their working-class sisters. Early in my research for this book, I wrote to my literary agent, Susan Rabiner, expressing dismay at how few of the black and working-class women I interviewed had read Friedan. I was distressed that the book's appeal seemed to be concentrated among such a relatively privileged section of women.

Rabiner responded by describing her own experience of trying to get a job in advertising during the 1960s and being told that a woman could only be a secretary to a male copywriter, not a copywriter herself.

"To me it doesn't matter," Rabiner wrote, "that this group of women wasn't representative either in size or even aspirations of most American women of their time. It doesn't matter that they represented a small privileged slice of American women. It doesn't matter that there were other women who were working and not by choice. . . . What matters is that these women were being asked to deny what they were feeling."

Many of these women were privileged, Rabiner conceded. "They were lucky enough to be raised into families that considered it important to educate women and therefore let these women go to college. Then they were fortunate enough to be married to 'good earners,' men who could let them stay at home and become full-time mothers and actually preferred that they do so.

"But they were also like the farm boys from World War I who passed through New York City on the way to the killing fields of France and then, when the war was over, couldn't go back to the farm. We understood and accepted those soldiers who didn't return to the farm.

"But it took Friedan to help us understand that there were women who, through their education, saw glimpses of the world of work and then didn't want to go back to being housewives. Or they went back under enormous pressure from everyone, but spent the next years of their lives with their noses pressed against the proverbial glass—looking in at a world that they would never be part of."

7

African-American Women, Working-Class Women, and the Feminine Mystique

MANY PEOPLE BELIEVE THAT AFRICAN-AMERICAN AND WHITE WORKING-CLASS women did not relate to Friedan's arguments in *The Feminine Mystique* because most of them already worked outside the home due to economic necessity and would have preferred to be full-time housewives. But the differences between these groups are actually more complex.

It is true that a black woman had far less chance than a white woman of marrying a man who earned enough to support a family. Black men earned, on average, 60 percent of white men's wages throughout the 1950s, and the poverty rate of black families was close to 50 percent, making a male breadwinner–female homemaker marriage impossible for many black families, regardless of their preferences.

Even when African-American men earned a middle-income wage, they were typically much less economically secure than their white counterparts. Black families with the same annual income as whites had, on average, only one-tenth as many assets, and they were far less likely to receive the kind of government aid that subsidized upward mobility for white families during the 1950s. In his study of the fight to integrate the Levittown suburbs of New York and Pennsylvania, David Kushner points out that of the $120 billion in new housing underwritten by the federal government between 1934 and 1960, less than 2 percent went to minorities. By the latter date, fewer than 40 percent of black families owned their own homes, compared to more than 60 percent of whites, and on average their homes were worth much less.

In 1963, a white male high school graduate earned more than a female college graduate, white or black. A woman who married a white high school graduate could generally raise her children on his income alone, and she could almost certainly do so if she married a white college graduate. Such upward mobility through marriage was far less likely in the African-American community. Black male college graduates also earned less than white male high school graduates.

So even a college-educated African-American woman who expected to marry a man with equal education might well need, like her less-educated sisters, to work after marriage. As a result, black college women were less likely than their white counterparts to feel there was a contradiction between the professional roles they were being trained for in college and the future roles they would assume as wives.

In a study of 5,000 white college women in the 1950s, fewer than 40 percent reported that they were attending college to train for a future career. Most said they were in college to expand their cultural literacy, enjoy the social life, or acquire the prestige attached to a college degree. A study of white female freshmen and sophomores found that the majority viewed their college education not as a ticket to lifelong work but as something to fall back on in an emergency.

Black female college students, by contrast, saw education as a step toward establishing a future career. A 1956 study of black female college graduates found that nearly 90 percent reported having gone to college to prepare for a vocation.

Black women's expectations of working outside the home were not simply a reluctant capitulation to financial necessity. The African-American women polled in 1956 were not interested in education solely as a way to earn money. They were more likely than the white college students to say that college should also train women to be "useful citizens," concerned about matters beyond their immediate family.

Such attitudes reflected African-American women's long-standing tradition of engagement outside the home. Historian Linda Gordon, studying female activists at the end of the nineteenth century, found that while only 34 percent of the white activists had combined marriage with life as a public figure, 85 percent of black female activists had found marriage compatible with their activism.

It was black activists, not white feminists, who first referred to women and men as "co-breadwinners" and advocated that women make a "three-fold commitment"—to family, career, and social movements. Long before Betty Friedan insisted that meaningful work would not only fulfill women as individuals but also strengthen their marriages, many African-American women shared the views of Sadie T. Alexander, an influential political leader in Philadelphia, who argued in 1930 that working for wages gave women the "peace and happiness" essential to a good home life.

This is not to say that black women were sheltered from the problems and prejudices facing women who tried to combine work with marriage. A study of African-American women who graduated from college in the 1930s found that many expressed anxiety about their relationships with men. Like their white counterparts, these women were concerned that their education might make them less attractive to potential mates. They worried about whether holding down a job would leave enough time for their family, although, far more often than white women, they also expressed concern about whether they would be able to devote enough attention to religious, cultural, and community affairs while managing both a job and a family.

As in the white community, many African-American men wanted to reserve the upper ranks of work and politics for their own sex. Black women were the backbone of the civil rights movement, but they were seldom its public representatives. Rosa Parks's lawyer once told her that he believed women's proper place was in the kitchen. Ella Baker ran the voter registration drives for the Southern Christian Leadership Council in the 1950s but was never considered for its most prestigious position, which was always held by a male. During the 1960s, as the Black Power movement gathered steam, Baker complained that some leaders were urging black women to step back to "bolster the ego of the male."

Nor were black women exempt from the attacks of Freudians and social scientists who argued that female independence was bad for husbands, children, and the community at large. Psychologist John Dollard, sociologist E. Franklin Frazier, and psychoanalyst/anthropologist Abram Kardiner insisted that black men had been doubly emasculated—first by slavery and later by the economic independence of their women.

Frazier, a black sociologist, acknowledged that the female-centered kin networks of the rural South had helped protect black communities in the past. But he claimed that in the urban North, black women's economic dominance and sexual aggressiveness had resulted in disorganized families and impoverished communities. And, like his white counterparts in sociology and psychiatry, he saw no contradiction in simultaneously attacking middle-class homemakers. "The life of many a 'wealthy' Negro doctor," he wrote in 1962, "is shortened by the struggle to provide diamonds, minks, and an expensive home for his wife."

In August 1960, *Ebony* magazine published an article by Lerone Bennett Jr. on "the problems and possibilities" inherent in black women's traditional "independence and self-reliance." Bennett noted that black women had played an important role in the fight for freedom but argued that their independence had not been "an unmixed blessing." Reflecting the influence of Freudianism, he reported that many researchers believed that the traditional self-sufficiency of the Negro woman had placed her "more in conflict with her innate biological role than the white woman." The black woman has "proved that women are people," he concluded, but she "now faces a greater task. In an age when Negroes and whites, men and women, are confused about the meaning of femininity, she must prove that women are also women."

Still, articles in *Ebony* from the 1950s and 1960s were less likely to interpret family behaviors through the lens of Freudianism than were articles in the middle-class white magazines of the period, and more likely to assume that black women would work outside the home and take an active role in community affairs.

Bennett's 1960 article, which was reprinted in the September 1965 issue, described several successful marriages where husband and wife both worked. He quoted an African-American researcher, Dr. Angella Ferguson, who argued that black women should have the opportunity to pursue a "career outside the home" and that even wives and mothers who didn't want paid work "should participate in some civic or community activity in order that they may continue to grow throughout their married life." The article also featured a sidebar by E. Franklin Frazier, who in this particular piece praised the "self-assertion" of black women and the egalitarian nature of modern African-American marriages.

Several black women I interviewed for this book said that in the 1950s and 1960s, they knew no families in which mothers dropped out of the labor force for more than a year or two at a time. White women raised in the 1950s often reported that their mothers and grandmothers criticized them when they later chose to combine motherhood with paid employment. But black women raised in that era often faced the opposite reaction when they or their friends considered becoming stay-at-home mothers in later decades. Their mothers and grandmothers made disapproving comments such as "I didn't raise you to be dependent" or "You'll never get any respect by just staying home."

In 1960, almost 60 percent of black middle-class families were two-earner households, compared to less than 40 percent of white middle-class families. And a much higher proportion of black middle-class moms with children of preschool age were in the labor force than their white counterparts. Furthermore, sociologist Bart Landry points out, the black women most likely to work outside the home in this period were those *least* likely to need to do so.

In the 1950s and 1960s, white, college-educated, middle-class wives were already more likely to hold a job than the less-educated wives of blue-collar men, though such women rarely worked while their children were young. But those in the upper middle class were the least likely of all white mothers to work outside the home.

By contrast, upper-middle-class black mothers were the *most* likely among black mothers to hold outside jobs. Sixty-four percent of black upper middle-class mothers had jobs in 1960, compared to only 27 percent of white upper-middle-class mothers and 35 percent of white lower middle-class mothers.

Landry's contention that black middle-class wives, not white feminists, were the true pioneers of modern family patterns is supported by his finding that black wives were less willing than white wives to let their husbands decide whether they would work. Among white middle-class families, when the husband expressed a preference for the wife to stay home, 89 percent of the wives did so, but this was true for only 56 percent of black wives whose husbands disapproved of their working.

In ignoring the experience of African-American women in *The Feminine Mystique*, Friedan missed an opportunity to prove that women could indeed combine family commitments with involvement beyond the home. Friedan could have used their example to show that women need not feel guilty for engaging in work or community activism outside the home, even if they had the financial means to be full-time homemakers, and that working mothers could maintain strong family ties, inspiring both love and respect in their children.

Some black women did read *The Feminine Mystique* back in the 1960s and got something positive from it. Three African-American professionals e-mailed me to say that Friedan had been important to them as they struggled against male prejudices in graduate school or medical school. Gloria Hull, a black feminist scholar and poet, has written elsewhere that Friedan's work affected her deeply when she read it in 1970 and that even today she remains "struck by its clear passion and radical persuasion."

However, the content of *The Feminine Mystique* and the marketing strategy that Friedan and her publishers devised for it ignored black women's positive examples of Friedan's argument. So it is not surprising that *The Feminine Mystique* got little attention in the black community. Nor is it surprising that the black women who did read the book seldom responded as enthusiastically as did her white readers. African-American women had less need for outside reassurance to view themselves as strong and independent, and they felt less guilt about working outside the home. Their self-image as mothers coincided rather than conflicted with their identity as providers for the family.

Furthermore, black women were less likely than white women to have access to employment Friedan defined as fulfilling and creative. In 1950, 41 percent of all employed black women worked in private homes, almost invariably as domestic laborers. An additional 19 percent worked as cleaners or maids in offices, hotels, and restaurants. Working-class African-American women began to make their way out of domestic labor and into white-collar or manufacturing jobs in the 1950s, but given the low wages of African Americans in this era, few black women would have related easily to Friedan's advice that women should hire a house-keeper or nanny to take over their household chores. And given her own experience—or her mother's—any black working woman who read the book through to page 255 probably would have been offended by the sug-gestion that housework was especially suited to the "feeble-minded."

Finally, many black women considered the struggle for racial equality more urgent than the struggle for male-female equality. They might resent the antifemale prejudices they encountered in the black community, but they did not feel the same sense of relative deprivation as white women. "Our menfolk weren't doing all that well either," Donna G. told me. "We didn't feel much envy for their options. And most of the time—not all, but most—it felt like the racial stereotypes we faced were causing more immediate harm than the gender ones."

THE ARGUMENT THAT MANY WOMEN WOULD HAVE ENVIED THE PROBLEMS of middle-class wives who felt trapped in suburban homes may apply in part to white working-class women. White working-class wives were not only less likely to work outside the home than college-educated women, but they also expressed more satisfaction with housework and more agree-ment with prevailing notions of women's roles.

When sociologist Mirra Komarovsky interviewed working-class women in 1958 and 1959 for her book, *Blue Collar Marriage*, she found that the lower the educational level of the homemaker, the more likely she was to identify herself in terms of her family role and the less likely she was to disparage housework. College-educated housewives had the most unfavorable attitudes toward housework, and high-school-educated house-wives came next. Women who had not completed high school expressed the least disrespect for the job.

A 1959 study of women married to blue-collar workers found that working-class wives were more likely than middle-class wives to accept their husband's dominance and to express fear of his disapproval. They expressed fewer expectations of intimacy and equality in their marriages.

But this acceptance of inequality meant that in some important ways femininity was less of a mystique for working-class than for middle-class wives. These women acquiesced to masculine privilege with a clear-eyed sense of their economic dependence. They had little illusion that embracing their "feminine role" would produce inner fulfillment and were therefore less likely to feel bewildered when it did not. Unlike middle-class housewives, most had no qualms about saying they found domestic chores monotonous.

The working-class women interviewed by 1950s sociologists saw the home as a place where women worked, not as a place where they might satisfy creative or intellectual needs. Market researchers discovered that working-class women and middle-class women had very different wish lists for the perfect home. Middle-class women wanted distinctive architecture and aesthetically pleasing designs that would express their individual tastes, making the home a place of self-realization. Working-class women wanted modern appliances that would save time and make their work easier.

Working-class housewives also had less exposure than middle-class housewives to Freudian prescriptions for marital relationships and parenting. They expressed fewer worries about whether their own feelings were normal or their child rearing practices up to date. When Komarovsky interviewed working-class wives who did work outside the home, she found that they felt much less guilt than middle-class mothers who did so.

Komarovsky commented that speaking with working-class wives transported her back to a "pre-Freudian" world where a woman did what she had to do without constantly examining her motives or second-guessing her choices. "The self-doubts raised by the spread of psychoanalytic theory

('What is wrong with me that motherhood and homemaking do not suffice?') do not plague our respondents," reported Komarovsky. Blue-collar housewives who worked or wished to work at a paying job admitted their desire to "get out of the house" or away from the kids "without any embarrassment or defensiveness."

The 1959 marketing study also found that the stay-at-home wives of blue-collar men were quite open about their full range of motives when they wanted to take a paying job. "I wish I was working," one homemaker told the interviewers. "When you're out working you make friends and it's more fun. I hate housework." Another volunteered: "I would like to get to work, and quit this housekeeping. This is monotonous." A woman who had left a part-time job in a real estate office complained that at home all day, "I feel like I'm no use to anyone." Not one expressed any guilt or ambivalence about wanting a job.

When working-class homemakers expressed a preference for staying home, it was often not because they didn't want to work but because they recognized that few husbands in those days were willing to step up and share the housework. After the publication of *The Feminine Mystique*, one woman wrote to Friedan to say, "Most working women don't have careers. We have jobs, just like men. . . . If we're lucky, we like our jobs, and find some satisfaction in doing them." But as long as husbands refused to help around the house, she continued, most of us would be willing to "chuck the wage earning back in our husbands' laps."

She proceeded to explain why: "We don't really like to throw the last load of clothes in the washer at 11:30 P.M., and set the alarm for 6:00 so we can iron a blouse for a school age daughter, fix breakfast and school lunches all at the same time, do as much housework as possible before bolting to the office, and face the rest of it, and the grocery shopping and preparing dinner when we get home. This isn't our idea of fulfillment."

Another woman wrote that she had held several jobs on and off since her marriage but the burden of a job plus caring for three children and a husband was too much. "It's no fun to come home and see the sweet, dear, lazy bum asleep on the couch after being on my feet all day." She added that he "thinks he would lose some of his masculinity if anyone saw him hanging out the wash, or washing dishes." So she was determined to stay home "until men get some of their Victorian ideas out of their heads" and become "willing to help with the housework."

Many critics have since argued that Friedan oversold the benefits of employment in *The Feminine Mystique,* waxing eloquent about its role in building women's self-esteem while ignoring the fact that few jobs available to women involved creative and satisfying work. But I believe the book suffers from the opposite flaw. Friedan did not appreciate the intangible rewards, such as a sense of self-confidence or independence, that women could gain from work she dismissed as unskilled or menial.

Friedan insisted that the only way for a woman "to find herself, to know herself as a person," was to embark on "work of her own," but she was also adamant that "a job, any job, is not the answer—in fact, it can be part of the trap." Friedan discouraged her readers from expecting any satisfaction from the jobs that were then employing most female entrants into the labor market, such as retail sales and clerical work. "Women who do not look for jobs equal to their actual capacity, who do not let themselves develop the lifetime interests and goals which require serious education and training" are condemning themselves "to a nonexistent future."

Contrary to the claims of some critics, Friedan did not urge women to place the pursuit of money, fame, or power above all else. If faced with a choice between "serious volunteering" in connection with some "lifelong commitment" and taking a moneymaking job that was not part of a larger life plan, Friedan advised her readers to opt for volunteering.

But Friedan did not recognize that many women found a sense of satisfaction and confidence even in jobs that she assumed her readers would look down on. One woman who worked in a cafeteria told Komarovsky, "I'm strong and I do a good job. They like the way I put food on the plates without slopping it over. . . . They tell me I help digestion because I make cracks and laugh, and they like it." Another said she liked being able to bring home stories from the job to tell her husband.

In interviews conducted in Greensboro, North Carolina, and the Champaign-Urbana area of Illinois in the late 1950s, nearly 90 percent of working women said they valued the opportunity to interact with other people and the recognition they received for doing their work well. Other surveys found that even women whose primary reason for working was economic often mentioned the sense of independence and accomplishment they achieved as reasons they stayed on the job.

Marie B. describes working as a typist after graduating from high school in 1959. Despite her parents' and in-laws' disapproval, she kept her job after she married her high school boyfriend in 1961. "There wasn't any 'job ladder,'" she recalls, "except for moving out of the typing pool and becoming someone's private secretary. Or marrying the boss, I guess. So it might sound funny to you professionals, but I really liked my job. It gave me a sense that I was 'someone,' more than being just a wife gave me. But my mother-in-law was always making catty comments about working. So I began to think there was something wrong with me for liking it and especially for not wanting to quit when I got pregnant. Not that I had a choice. As soon as I began to show, my boss 'suggested' I resign."

Myra Marx Ferree has devoted most of her professional life to studying working-class women. Raised in the 1950s and 1960s by a mother who worked as a sales clerk in the lingerie section of a department store, she became the only one of seven children to graduate from college. She read *The Feminine Mystique* in graduate school and remembers thinking that "Friedan misrepresented my mother's life and that of other working class women I knew. She seemed to think that women could only feel oppressed if they already had a college education that they were 'wasting.'"

Ferree felt that all women, not just those with college educations, were subjugated by the idea "they weren't people with aspirations and a sense of adventure or desire to make some sort of mark on the world, or that if they were, they had to renounce that self . . . when they got married." It bothered her that Friedan "seemed to think that only some women wanted or needed meaningful work and that most jobs for non-college-educated women were ipso facto not meaningful."

For her dissertation, Ferree interviewed 115 working-class women in Somerville, Massachusetts, and the experience reinforced her reservations about *The Feminine Mystique*. The women told her that working outside the home gave them a sense of self-reliance and worth, even when the job itself was far from ideal. "I will never forget the woman who worked in a mayonnaise factory, often in water up to her ankles in a refrigerated room," Ferree recalls. "I expected her to say she would prefer not to be working." Instead, the woman made a distinction between her specific job and her self-identity as a worker. "I sure would like to quit THIS job," the woman told Ferree, "but I can't imagine not working."

In later studies Ferree found that working-class women who held jobs were more satisfied with their lives than those who stayed home. They had a greater sense of competence and self-esteem, and higher feelings of social connectedness and personal autonomy. Other surveys over the years have shown that women who earn an income also feel more entitled to a voice in family decisions.

Like Komarovsky, Ferree did find that less-educated housewives were happier staying home than educated housewives. But they were still less happy than women of the same education who had jobs. Whatever their degree of education, women who worked outside the home were more likely to be satisfied than comparable women who did not. Part-time workers were the most satisfied of all, perhaps because they had the benefits of employment without as much conflict between the time demands of work and family.

Another problem with the claim that *The Feminine Mystique* was irrelevant to working-class women, historian Ruth Rosen points out, is that many of the young college women attracted to the women's movement in the 1960s "were raised by blue collar parents who wanted their daughters to be the first in their family to attend college. Higher education is what transformed these working-class adolescents into middle-class women." As late as 1966, according to a Higher Education Research Institute Study, fewer than 30 percent of entering freshmen came from a family where the father had completed college, and only 20 percent had a mother who was a college graduate.

Rosen told me that in researching her book, *The World Split Open*, she was struck by how many such daughters, whose mothers *had* worked outside the home while they were growing up, were terrified that they themselves might become housewives. "The dominant image was that even if your mom was working, the right 'step up' into the middle class was to become a housewife. Only they didn't want to." For many of these upwardly mobile women, *The Feminine Mystique* provided welcome reinforcement for their desire to build a career rather than retire into full-time homemaking.

Jennifer Glass, now a sociology professor, reports that in their working-class neighborhood of Dallas, her mother was the only woman employed outside the home, "and she held it against my father, even though he worked two jobs." For as long as Glass can remember, "my mother complained about having to work, probably because she got stuck with the second shift and was very tired all the time."

But because the other neighborhood mothers often picked up a little extra cash by babysitting Jennifer, she "really got to know the other mothers on our block, watched their soap operas with them, and saw how their husbands treated them and how diminished their own lives were. It did not seem like a life I wanted to live, so I just discounted all my mother's griping and complaining."

Kathleen D. was the first in her family to go to college, and her working-class Irish grandparents were "already planning the wedding I was going to have and the house I was going to live in as soon as I met a nice college boy who would marry me and rescue me from the life that my mother had had to live. But I didn't want to be rescued. I wanted a better job than she or my dad had, but becoming a full-time housewife was not the sort of occupational mobility I had in mind."

Brigit O'Farrell, who came from a white working-class family in Ohio, was a college sorority girl when she read *The Feminine Mystique* in 1965. "The general expectation [in my family] was that I would be a teacher or work for the telephone company, then marry and have a family," she recalls. Reading *The Feminine Mystique* "made me question the whole idea that the most important thing in life was to find the right man." After college she found a job at the newly created Equal Employment Opportunity Commission and devoted her entire career to battling sex discrimination, especially that faced by blue-collar and union women.

Elaine Ingalli, raised in a blue-collar Catholic family, was fascinated by biographies of famous women as early as the third grade. "Almost my whole childhood I wanted to be one of two things: an airline stew or president." She read *The Feminine Mystique* "some time between 1970–74, as a newlywed, newly minted college grad. . . . About all I remember from the first reading of Friedan was the idea that housework expanded to fill the time/space one had for it—and that stayed with me for years."

Maddy G., whose father was a blue-collar worker, reported that her mom, who had worked as a secretary for several years, had become depressed after quitting her job when her third child was born. She did not want to end up the same way, and reading Friedan in the late 1960s bolstered her resolve. "I became doubly determined not to let housework and marriage take over my life."

Someone loaned Friedan's book to Shirley Sandage when she was "a working-class young mother . . . with one son and another on the way." Her immediate reaction was, "My God, she's talking about me." Sandage later founded the Migrant Action Program in northern Iowa in the 1960s and held down a variety of important government jobs. In 2008, at age eighty, she was still helping other women "understand their possibilities in this modern world." She credits *The Feminine Mystique* for helping set her on this path.

Sherry Fisher's father and mother, both factory workers, scrimped and saved to send her to college. "I was the first from my neighborhood to go to college, and I was so excited by the new possibilities in front of me. I could be a nurse, an accountant, a journalist. And then it dawned on me that even though my parents were really proud that I had been at the top of my class all through high school, now that I'd 'made it' into college, they wanted to marry me off to a man who could take care of me so I could stay home for the rest of my life. *The Feminine Mystique* gave me the arguments I needed to resist their pressure. I carried it around with me like a shield."

THE MAJORITY OF YOUNG WOMEN FROM WORKING-CLASS FAMILIES IN THE late 1950s and early 1960s did not go to college. They took a job before marriage and expected to quit work soon after they wed. The ranks of such women swelled in this period, with growing numbers of young women heading out to work in the new "help wanted—female" jobs opening up in urban America.

In 1958, *The Best of Everything*, Rona Jaffe's novel about work, sex, romance, and disappointment in the lives of these young women, hit the *New York Times* best-seller list and remained there for five months. It was soon made into a hit movie.

"You see them every morning at a quarter to nine," the opening paragraph of the novel began, "rushing out of the maw of the subway tunnel, filing out of Grand Central Station, crossing Lexington and Park and Madison and Fifth avenues, the hundreds and hundreds of girls. Some of them look eager and some resentful, and some of them look as if they haven't left their beds yet. . . . Some of them are wearing pink or chartreuse fuzzy overcoats and five-year-old ankle-strap shoes and have their hair up in pin curls underneath kerchiefs. Some of them are wearing chic black suits (maybe last year's but who can tell?) and kid gloves and are carrying their lunches in violet-sprigged Bonwit Teller paper bags. None of them has enough money."

Jaffe's novel mixed erotic tension with cautionary tales about the dangers of "giving in" to predatory men. But however unconvincing some of her plot lines sounded to highbrow critics, Jaffe was describing a real sociological phenomenon: the explosion of white-collar jobs that brought huge numbers of young women into the workforce. Many, perhaps most, aspired to marry a man who would support them, but along the way they were exposed to the pleasures and risks of personal independence, as well as the growing prevalence, even emerging acceptability, of premarital sex.

Historian Elaine Tyler May argues that in the course of the 1950s, sexual repression gave way to "sexual brinksmanship." As the *Ladies' Home Journal* put it at the time, "sex suggestiveness" was now part of "the nicest girls'" repertoire. But it was still the woman's responsibility to "draw the line." The balancing act this required created new sources of private guilt and public humiliation for women.

When *The Best of Everything* was reissued in 2005, Jaffe recalled: "Back then, people didn't talk about not being a virgin. They didn't talk about going out with married men. They didn't talk about abortion. They didn't talk about sexual harassment, which had no name in those days. . . . I thought that if I could help one young woman sitting in her tiny apartment thinking she was all alone and a bad girl, then the book would be worthwhile."

In 1962 Helen Gurley Brown, later editor of *Cosmopolitan*, published an even more phenomenal best seller. Written in a style that was far more accessible for women without a college education than Friedan's book, Brown's *Sex and the Single Girl* advanced the provocative idea that women should not see marriage as "the best years of your life." Rather, wrote Brown, marriage "is insurance for the *worst* years of your life. During your best years you don't need a husband. You do need a man of course every step of the way and they are often cheaper emotionally and a lot more fun by the bunch."

Brown insisted that women had the same sexual desires as men and the same right to satisfy them. She also thought women needed a job. "While you're waiting to marry, or if you never marry, a job can be your love, your happy pill, your means of finding out who you are and what you can do, your playpen, your family, your entrée to a good social life, men and money." She advised women to try for "some kind of work that brings recognition. That can build more self-esteem than any psychiatrist, self-help book, or lecture."

Like Jaffe, Brown recognized that working girls seldom earned enough money to live the good life she espoused. Since men made more money, women could use their sex appeal to even things up while getting their own sexual pleasure along the way. Brown encouraged them to make sure their sexual fun came with material perks. The single girl, she advised, should insist that the man pay for all dates, all trips, and all alcohol (even if it was consumed at her apartment). Periodically he should throw in some expensive gifts, or even cash.

Sex and the Single Girl was an even bigger publishing sensation than *The Feminine Mystique*, selling more than 2 million copies in three weeks. Brown received so much fan mail that the post office told her they could not continue to deliver it and she would have to pick it up herself.

Jennifer Scanlon, a professor at Bowdoin College, argues that Brown was "a feminist trailblazer" who did for young white working-class women what Friedan did for middle-class suburban wives. Brown did identify as a feminist, even writing to Friedan to praise *The Feminine Mystique*. She vigorously supported the Equal Rights Amendment and the struggle to legalize abortion. And her rejection of the prevailing cant about virginity and female sexual passivity struck a chord with many young women.

Still, Brown's advice to women was double-edged. She suggested that women use their femininity at work to get promotions and after hours to get treats and luxuries they could not otherwise afford. But although manipulating gender and sexual stereotypes to one's own advantage may be satisfying, even empowering, to individual women, it can set back equality for other women by reinforcing those stereotypes. Brown's strategy ultimately pitted working women against one another in competition for the favor of men rather than uniting them for collective goals.

Throughout the postwar era, however, some working-class women did come together to combat sexual discrimination. During the 1940s and 1950s, female workers in auto factories, the meatpacking industry, electrical plants, and other industrial jobs began challenging sex discrimination by employers as well as by fellow unionists. They campaigned for after-school programs and low-cost nurseries, along with tax exemptions for child care expenses. In the late 1950s, flight attendants began their campaign against being treated like sex objects.

Well before pay discrimination was made illegal in the 1960s, writes historian Alice Kessler Harris, working women were flooding government agencies with complaints about the practice. It was on their behalf that the National Organization for Women, which Friedan helped to found in 1966, mounted its first legal actions and legislative campaigns.

So despite its silence about the specific needs of working-class and minority women, and despite its occasional lapses into elitism, *The Feminine*

Mystique's assault on stereotypes about femininity and its defense of women's right to work were certainly in the interests of working women, black and white. And the prominence Friedan achieved as a result of the book helped make her a leader of a movement that improved the status of working-class as well as middle-class women. The relationship of *The Feminine Mystique* to the origins and evolution of the feminist movement, however, is more complex than many of the book's fans or critics realize.

8

∿∿∿∿∿

Demystifying *The Feminine Mystique*

A NUMBER OF MYTHS ABOUT THE ORIGINS AND IMPACT OF *THE FEMININE Mystique* have been perpetuated over the years, some by Friedan herself. One myth widely repeated in feminist circles is that the book awakened women to their discontent, igniting the contemporary women's movement. The antifeminist version claims that until *The Feminine Mystique* came along, women were "living in peace in what they considered to be a normal, traditional" life. Friedan's book "wrenched" them from their homes.

But Friedan did not "discover" what so many 1950s housewives were feeling, nor did her book launch the movement that eventually transformed women's place in American society. These two processes were separated by several years, and giving the book or its author too much credit for these developments ignores the rich history of female resistance that Friedan herself portrayed in her chapter on the struggle for suffrage, "The Passionate Journey." It also discounts the massive societal shifts already eroding the traditional boundaries of a woman's place by the time of the book's publication and disregards the multiple sources of the movement that erupted in the late 1960s and early 1970s.

In describing how she came to write *The Feminine Mystique*, Betty Friedan portrayed herself as just another unhappy housewife who stumbled upon her subject almost by accident. To the extent that she acknowledged having been anything but a homemaker, it was to accuse herself of having perpetuated the feminine mystique as a freelance writer for women's magazines. "I helped create this image," Friedan declared in her chapter about "The Happy Housewife Heroine." "I have watched

American women for fifteen years try to conform to it. But I can no longer deny my own knowledge of its terrible implications."

In her 1976 book, *It Changed My Life,* Friedan wrote that as she examined her sources for *The Feminine Mystique* in 1962, "I sensed the inescapable implications of the trail of evidence I had followed—that if I was right, the very assumptions on which I and other women were basing our lives and on which the experts were advising us were wrong. I thought, I must be crazy. . . . But all along I also felt this calm, strange sureness, as if in tune with something much larger, more important than myself that had to be taken seriously. At first I seemed alone in that awareness."

A compelling story, but untrue. Daniel Horowitz's exhaustive study of Friedan's political background shows that Friedan's critique of women's place in American society can be traced back to her left-wing activism in the 1930s and 1940s. In 1951, reporting on a meeting of rank-and-file women organized by the United Electrical, Radio and Machine Workers, Friedan paid tribute to working women's determination to no longer "be paid or treated as some inferior species by their bosses, or by any male workers who have swallowed the bosses' thinking."

As Friedan attempted to reach a new audience of middle-class readers in the mid-1950s, she downplayed her ties to the labor movement and to the Left, in part because she had seen firsthand how the climate of guilt by association during the Red Scare of the 1950s had derailed careers. Her boyfriend at Berkeley, physicist David Bohm, had been called before the House Un-American Activities Committee (HUAC) and accused of espionage. Although he was acquitted at a subsequent trial, his academic career in the United States was destroyed.

Bohm's case was only one of many. In 1950 Senator Joseph McCarthy charged Dorothy Kenyon, the U.S. representative to the UN Commission on the Status of Women, with being a "fellow traveler"—someone who worked with the Communist Party without being an official member. A Senate investigating committee cleared Kenyon, but her political career was ruined. The same year, Richard Nixon used similar red-baiting tactics to defeat Congresswoman Helen Gahagan Douglas in a Senate race.

Civil rights activist and feminist pioneer Pauli Murray has described in her autobiography how insidious the atmosphere at that time was. The onus was placed on individuals to prove they were *not* subversive, rather than on the government or employers to prove they were. Murray, an African-American woman who had been denied admission to Harvard Law School because of her sex, went on to study at the University of California at Berkeley and at Yale, becoming a well-respected attorney and later an ordained Episcopal priest. She was rigorously vetted for her loyalty when she applied to practice law in New York State, but when she pursued a position in a Cornell University program that was helping Liberia codify its laws, she was turned down. The hiring officer told her that although they had no evidence whatsoever of wrongdoing on her part, the university needed "one hundred percent protection" from any insinuations of disloyalty, and her past associations might be suspect in "the troublous times in which we live."

In those "troublous" political times, many individuals and groups turned on—and turned in—past associates to prove their loyalty and save their own jobs. Hollywood celebrities went before HUAC to name acquaintances they had seen at left-wing political meetings or had heard make statements that could be construed as sympathetic to communism. Many political groups required prospective members to take loyalty oaths before they could join.

The NAACP and the National Council of Negro Women instructed their members to "prove our patriotism" by refusing to work with any individuals or groups suspected of being subversive. Some Americans dissociated themselves entirely from civil rights activists because while equal rights might be fine in principle, "communists were trying to stir the Negroes up."

Friedan never issued the anticommunist denunciations that were a staple of public writing at the time, but she was determined not to be blacklisted or discredited because of her prior associations. That meant glossing over a large part of her life. Friedan's secretary Pat Aleskovsky had worked many weekends typing Friedan's manuscript, even leaving dinner parties to take Friedan's dictation over the phone. But Friedan told Aleskovsky that she could not mention her in the acknowledgments for fear of exposing the book to red-baiting smears, because Pat's husband had once been named as a suspected communist at a public HUAC hearing.

When Friedan learned that Daniel Horowitz was exploring her radical past for his book, *Betty Friedan and the Making of* The Feminine Mystique, she denied him permission to quote anything from her unpublished papers, told confidantes that he was attacking her, and threatened to sue him. She viewed his research as an extension of the McCarthyism she had seen so many others subjected to. And just as Friedan feared, even almost forty years after her book's publication, some social commentators used Horowitz's findings about Friedan's background to argue that feminism had been part of a communist plot.

Friedan's ability to portray herself as an apolitical suburban housewife allowed her book to reach many women who shared her dissatisfactions but might never have bought the book had they known of her previous political associations. One woman wrote to tell Friedan that it had inspired her to become a Republican activist. Another wanted to start an Ayn Rand–Betty Friedan club, which goaded Friedan into replying that she had no desire to be associated with Rand's views. (Rand was an ardent proponent of free market capitalism.) A woman who was reading the book with her minister husband reported that it had been recommended by the president of the Baptist Women's Mission Society. Another noted that the book reinforced ideas she was already teaching in her church group for Mormon teens.

While Friedan's silence about her left-wing associations during the 1940s might be understandable in the repressive political atmosphere in which she was writing, her refusal to fully acknowledge her intellectual and personal debts is more difficult to justify. Friedan had a pattern of building up her own achievements by downplaying aid from others and by exaggerating the hostility or disinterest with which her ideas were initially received. Although she usually cited her primary sources—interviews she had done, studies she had read—Friedan was less conscientious about secondary sources. For example, Friedan's chapter on motivational research and "The Sexual Sell" is hugely indebted to Vance Packard's 1957 book, *The Hidden Persuaders*, but that chapter credits only the staff of the Institute for Motivational Research, a group she undoubtedly learned of from Packard.

In her book's preface, Friedan argued, with considerable exaggeration, that feminism had died out completely after World War II, leaving the ideology of "the happy housewife" unchallenged. Therefore, in Friedan's account, she was forced to "hunt down" the origins of the mystique and its effect on women. She "found a few pieces of the puzzle in previous studies of women," she conceded, "but not many," for previous writers had accepted the feminine mystique and used its tenets to analyze women. She acknowledged in passing that reading "Simone de Beauvoir's insights into French women" and the work of American sociologist Mirra Komarovsky had been "provocative" for her. But this brief reference minimized the tremendous debt Friedan and her book owed to both those thinkers.

De Beauvoir's 1949 book, *The Second Sex*, which appeared in translation in America in 1953, rigorously analyzed the consequences of a woman's enforced domesticity, exploring how it deformed her individual personality and the institution of marriage itself. But more than a decade passed before Friedan acknowledged that she, "who had helped start women on the new road," had herself been "started on that road by de Beauvoir." Even then, Friedan claimed that she had been influenced by the book's existentialism rather than by its feminism, which she dismissed as "depressing." *The Second Sex*, she said, "just made me want to crawl in bed and pull the covers over my head. It did not lead to any action to change the lot of women, which somehow *The Feminine Mystique* did."

Because de Beauvoir was a prominent left-wing French intellectual, she did not get much of a hearing in the mainstream press of 1950s America. Even the liberal magazine *The Nation* warned its readers that de Beauvoir had "certain political leanings." So perhaps Friedan's reluctance to admit the influence of *The Second Sex* was part of her desire to establish her political respectability.

But 1953 was also the year that Mirra Komarovsky, a thoroughly respectable academic, published *Women in the Modern World: Their Education and Their Dilemmas*. While more cautious in her conclusions than Friedan, Komarovsky pioneered the use of intensive life histories and interviews to explore the anxieties of modern housewives, especially those who had gone to college before marriage. She then proceeded to dismantle the arguments against women's education by Freudian psychoanalysts and some family-life professionals.

Friedan never mentioned these aspects of Komarovsky's work. Later in *The Feminine Mystique* she referred to Komarovsky's "brilliant" analysis of how girls learn to play the womanly roles expected of them, but otherwise Friedan lumped Komarovsky with the antifeminists, unfairly charging her with "virtually endorsing the continued *infantalizing* of American women."

Friedan also failed to acknowledge the work of Elizabeth Hawes, whom she had reviewed in the 1940s, or that of Eve Merriam, a poet and leftist activist who wrote a 1959 article "The Myth of the Necessary Housewife," arguing that no society in history had wasted the talents of half its adult population the way America was doing. Merriam was known at the time to be at work on a book critiquing the ideology of domesticity. This came out in 1964 under the title *When Nora Slammed the Door*.

As *The Feminine Mystique* neared publication, Friedan and her publisher worried that it would be eclipsed by the many other books on women's issues that were already out or scheduled to appear around the same time. A vice president at Norton, soliciting a cover blurb from bestselling author and American icon Pearl S. Buck, wrote: "One of our main problems is that much is being written these days about the plight (or whatever it is) of the educated American woman; therefore this one will have to fight its way out of a thicket."

In a review in the August 1963 issue of *Marriage and Family Living*, prominent sociologist Jessie Bernard mentioned that *The Feminine Mystique* had arrived on her desk just one day after she had sent off her own manuscript discussing educated women's retreat into the home. But, she said generously, Friedan has analyzed the same topic "in far greater detail and far more passionately."

Several women wrote to tell Friedan that they had been planning to write a book on the same topic. Said one: "It is amusing to think that the title of my proposed book was 'Somebody spit on the stove.' Now, Miss Friedan has!" Another woman mused that "I ought to have hated that book and you," because she had proposed a book on the same topic six years earlier and had never written it, even though several publishers had expressed interest. "But I *don't* hate either the book or you because you've done an infinitely better and more important job than I would have."

It in no way disparages Friedan's accomplishments to point out that *The Feminine Mystique* was not ahead of its time. Books don't become best sellers because they are ahead of their time. They become best sellers when they tap into concerns that people are already mulling over, pull together ideas and data that have not yet spread beyond specialists and experts, and bring these all together in a way that is easy to understand and explain to others.

The Feminine Mystique synthesized a wide range of scholarly research and contemporary social criticism. It translated important sociological and psychological findings into accessible language and personalized such research by combining it with the stories of individual housewives. Friedan also produced a dramatic journalistic exposé of the advertisers who tried to sell to women, the psychiatric community that tried to pacify them, and the educators who patronized them. The resulting account melded riveting personal stories with challenging intellectual criticism. And the title was brilliant in its own right, a striking catchphrase that provided a simple summary of how women were constrained by prevailing social expectations.

In *THE FEMININE MYSTIQUE* AND IN HER LATER AUTOBIOGRAPHICAL WRITING, Friedan claimed that the book's origins lay in the hostile reception she received from women's magazines when she first argued that women's frustration was caused by the narrow roles they were forced into rather than by exposure to an education that diverted them from their proper feminine aspirations. Friedan reported that when she used the questionnaire for her 1957 survey of her Smith College classmates as the basis of an article titled "Are Women Wasting Their Time in College?" *McCall's* rejected it, the *Ladies' Home Journal* rewrote it to say the opposite of what she intended, and the editor of *Redbook* declared that Friedan had "gone off her rocker."

In her 2000 book, *Life So Far*, Friedan stated that these adamant rejections made her realize that her article "would never get printed in one of those big women's magazines," because it "threatened the whole firmament they stood on . . . the whole amorphous, vague, invisible miasma around 'the role of women,' 'feminine fulfillment' as it was then defined by men and psychological followers of Freud, and taken for granted by everyone as true." That day, she recounted, she phoned her agent "and told her not to send that article to any more magazines. I was going to write a book."

Once again, Friedan's narrative is gripping but does not accord with the evidence. When I examined Friedan's papers at the Schlesinger Library and the records of her publisher, the W. W. Norton Company, at Columbia University, I found no independent confirmation of Friedan's claims that editors had reacted with outrage to this article. A letter by Friedan herself noted that after the *Ladies' Home Journal* decided not to publish the article, several other women's magazines had expressed interest but wanted it to be more broad than the Smith survey. Friedan wrote that this interest was what made her begin "to realize there was a book here."

Actually, Friedan had no lack of supporters in the women's magazines. The public affairs editor of the *Ladies' Home Journal* in the 1950s and 1960s was Margaret Hickey, a longtime feminist, daughter of a suffragist, and, starting in 1961, member of the President's Commission on the Status of Women. And Friedan's correspondence shows that several editors were sympathetic to her views.

Of course, some editors vehemently opposed Friedan's arguments, and others agreed with her but were reluctant to publish anything that might offend advertisers who used the feminine mystique to pitch their wares. In some cases, Horowitz shows, various women's magazines seem to have pressured Friedan to revise articles she wrote during the 1950s, toning down points that might be considered feminist. In at least one case, they removed favorable references to struggles against religious and racial prejudice.

Still, as early as 1955, *Charm* accepted the article "I Went Back to Work," about Friedan's own experience returning to paid employment after having a child. She had done so, she told readers, "both from economic necessity and from personal choice." In the next few years, Friedan was able to publish several laudatory articles about women who successfully combined marriage and careers, and by 1959 she had a book contract for what became *The Feminine Mystique.*

On December 18, 1959, her editor, George Brockwell, wrote to *Reader's Digest* that "Good Housekeeping has just signed up one Betty Friedan to do the leading article in their anniversary issue next May. This article will be on women's search for identity . . . and will be so good that your magazine people may be tempted. I know it will be good, for it will in effect be an abridgement of the prospectus of the book Mrs. Friedan is doing for us. We are very high on this project and expect it to be a big one. I therefore hope that your magazine people can be persuaded to wait for the book rather than jumping at the Good Housekeeping article."

In 1960, *Good Housekeeping* duly published that abridgement, titled "Women Are People Too." In May 1961, *Mademoiselle* published a Friedan piece that became "The Crisis in Women's Identity" in the final version of her book. And in 1962, Friedan's publisher pushed back the publication date by a month to allow both the *Ladies' Home Journal* and *McCall's* to publish excerpts before the book was in stores.

As Norton's prepublicity memos enthused, it was unprecedented for two competing mass-circulation magazines to excerpt the same book. Having these appear in the two largest English-language magazines in the world gave *The Feminine Mystique* a huge boost and partially offset the bad luck that the book came out during a 114-day strike of all the

New York newspapers, which made it impossible to get reviews or place ads in that important market during the critical first months.

For the rest of her life, Friedan insisted that her publisher had done nothing to promote the book until she browbeat him into hiring an independent publicist. But by the end of 1962, Norton had already sold the book club rights to Book Find for $5,000 (the equivalent of more than $36,000 in 2010 dollars), collected endorsements from many prominent individuals, and was projecting that *The Feminine Mystique* would be a best seller backed by "national advertising and other promotions."

The newspaper strike was a huge blow to publicity plans for the book's launch, but by the time Friedan's new publicist came onboard in April, supposedly to rescue the book from oblivion, it was already in its fifth printing, and Norton had taken out ads in several major newspapers. In a note to Norton about plans for West Coast promotions, the publicist pointed out that Friedan had already made about twenty television and radio appearances before she took on the campaign. *The Feminine Mystique* sold approximately 60,000 copies in hardback, a large amount even nowadays, and nearly 1.5 million copies in paperback.

Friedan was a lively and sought-after lecturer, with a knack for fanning controversy and stimulating buzz. Even her ferocious ego helped get the book talked about. Once, while on the television show *Girl Talk*, Friedan warned host Virginia Graham during the break that if she wasn't given more time to make her points, she would chant the word "orgasm" ten times.

Some of Friedan's more outrageous or acerbic statements to the press made her sound like the 1960s counterpart of the incendiary Ann Coulter, only with less leg and more brain. But unlike Coulter, Friedan did more than pander to her audience's prejudices. *The Feminine Mystique* challenged its readers to expand their horizons intellectually as well as emotionally and to channel the indignation that her argument produced into constructive change in their own lives.

The book did not, however, transform women's societal role. In 1965, women's legal status still had more in common with the 1920s than the 1970s, and the political agenda of women's rights activists remained extremely modest. Almost no one was raising the demands that would become central to the women's movement in the late 1960s and early 1970s—establishment of preschool and child care centers; the right to contraception and abortion; criminalization of sexual harassment and marital rape; protection against domestic abuse or sexual violence; abolition of laws penalizing unwed mothers or reinforcing a husband's authority over his wife. It was even hard to find anyone suggesting that husbands share child care and housework.

The specific agenda Friedan presented in *The Feminine Mystique* broke no new ground in this regard. She mentioned that the work of the President's Commission might mitigate discrimination and made a passing reference to the need for maternity leave and child care, but most of her concluding chapter focused on women's need to get an education and to make sure their life plan included developing the capacity to engage in creative work. She did not advocate that women organize to oppose the multitude of laws and practices that relegated women to second-class citizenship, restricted their access to many jobs, and gave husbands the final say over family decisions and finances. When such a movement did emerge, it was not as a direct result of *The Feminine Mystique*, although that book brought Friedan the fame that allowed her to play a major leadership role.

SOME THREE YEARS AFTER SHE PUBLISHED *THE FEMININE MYSTIQUE*, Friedan was instrumental in founding the National Organization for Women. She became its first president, a position she held until 1970. The immensely successful Women's Strike for Equality in 1970 was Friedan's idea, and she helped organize the Women's Political Caucus in 1971. She was a towering figure in the second wave of the women's movement. But here, too, Friedan is often given—and sometimes claimed for herself—too much individual credit.

In Friedan's account, after she gained national attention with *The Feminine Mystique*, she was approached by an "underground" group of women who shared her ideas but couldn't risk their jobs or reputations by seeming too militant. They begged her to put aside the new book she was writing and build a new women's movement. The decisive moment, she explained to a *New York Times* reporter in 1970, came when a female attorney who worked for the recently formed Equal Employment Opportunity Commission pulled Friedan into her office.

Closing her door and breaking down in tears, the woman begged the writer to do something: "'Mrs. Friedan,' she said, 'You're the only one who can do it. You have to start an NAACP for women.'" Such incidents, Friedan told the reporter, made her realize that "women needed a movement. So, I guess I started it."

Since then, many accounts of Friedan's life have claimed that the feminist movement was moribund in the early 1960s and that Friedan "single-handedly" revived it. In fact, however, a core group of activists had been building feminist networks during the previous two decades, and by the early 1960s they had been joined by significant numbers of female government appointees who were chafing at the slow pace of change and already discussing the possibility of building an independent women's rights movement.

It is certainly true that when Friedan was honing her ideas in the 1950s and early 1960s, the National Woman's Party and the National Federation of Business and Professional Women's Clubs were nothing like the powerful movement that had organized to win women the vote in the first two decades of the twentieth century. But feminists were networking behind the scenes and had achieved some successes. In 1956, President Dwight D. Eisenhower, responding to their pressure, urged Congress to pass a measure requiring equal pay for equal work, pointing out that women had cast a majority of ballots in the previous election. Congress did not act on his request, but Eisenhower did appoint more women to government posts.

John F. Kennedy was elected president in 1960 by a very narrow margin, and like Eisenhower, he recognized the importance of securing women's support. In 1961, on the advice of Esther Peterson, head of the Women's Bureau and assistant secretary of labor, Kennedy created the President's Commission on the Status of Women, to "develop plans for fostering the full partnership of men and women in our national life." In 1962, the National Federation of Business and Professional Women began a campaign, with the president's approval, to get similar state commissions established across America. Such commissions were a key precursor to NOW, because they brought together women activists who had not been in regular touch, allowing them to compare notes, develop collective strategies, and often broaden their goals.

Another important development was the gradual abating of the sharp conflicts that had divided feminists since the 1920s over whether to press for an Equal Rights Amendment or try to preserve and expand protective legislation. In 1961, Eleanor Roosevelt remarked that the spread of unionization had extended many needed work protections to men as well as women, so that special protective legislation was becoming less necessary and the ERA might soon become a desirable goal. Esther Peterson and most of the members of the President's Commission continued to oppose the ERA, but the commission's Committee on Civil and Political Rights was co-chaired by an ERA proponent, and Pauli Murray, by then a noted civil rights lawyer, proposed a way to move beyond the debate. She suggested that sex-based discrimination be attacked, just as was being done with racial discrimination, as a violation of the Fourteenth Amendment.

There was progress on other fronts as well. In July 1962, Kennedy ordered all federal agencies to disregard gender in hiring, training, and promoting employees. A year later, Congress passed the Equal Pay Act. In October 1963 the President's Commission on the Status of Women issued its final report, documenting the extent of sex discrimination and recommending reforms such as making marriage an economic partnership in which property was seen as belonging to both spouses. In addition to proposing this new protection for housewives, the committee also called for paid maternity leave for working women and for making child care available to families.

Although the report was published eight months after Friedan's book, she knew it was in the works and referred to it in her book as an encouraging sign of the potential for change. Within a year the commission had distributed more than 80,000 copies of the report, which was also translated into Swedish, Italian, and Japanese. In 1965, the report was published as a commercial book, edited by Margaret Mead, and sold extremely well.

Clearly a new movement to expand women's rights was already on the horizon by 1963. In addition to the core group of feminists who had long been working behind the scenes, economic and political trends had gradually been undermining some of the opposition to incorporating women more fully into America's economic and political life. Indeed, Robert Jackson has argued that women were by this time, as his book title claims, *Destined for Equality*.

As the booming postwar economy created a growing demand for new workers, especially in the expanding service and retail sectors, industry increasingly put out the welcome mat for women, despite objections from some male workers and pundits who decried the "feminization" of the workplace. The Cold War and the Korean War also raised fears that the United States might lose out to the Soviet Union unless it trained women in needed defense fields such as engineering. By the beginning of the 1960s, politicians and employers agreed that both the economy and the political system needed more "woman power."

Most of the opinion-makers who supported expanding women's participation in the economy expected that men would continue to organize and direct that woman power. Few envisioned an equal partnership at work or in government, much less at home. But the trend toward assigning status based on individual merit and educational achievement was eroding the assumption that one group, be it whites or men, was automatically entitled to monopolize positions of power and prestige. And these economic and social changes were encouraging many young women, even without reading Friedan, to direct more attention to getting an education or preparing themselves for a career.

IN THE FIRST HALF OF THE 1960S, HOWEVER, MOST MASS ORGANIZATION and public debate continued to focus on the civil rights movement. There were no actions by women comparable to the sit-ins in the South or the picket lines in the North, much less anything on the scale of the 1963 March on Washington. In fact, the wedge that feminists would later use to organize their own movement was an almost accidental by-product of struggles between southern segregationists and civil rights leaders.

Federal officials had initially been reluctant to enforce integration. But the pressure of almost ten years of demonstrations for equal rights, combined with dramatic television coverage of white southerners' violent resistance, created a powerful sentiment for justice in the United States and put America under intense pressure abroad. Finally, in 1963, President Kennedy introduced the Civil Rights Bill. After Kennedy's assassination later that year, the new president, Lyndon B. Johnson, urged Congress to enact a more comprehensive law to protect blacks' voting rights; ban racial discrimination in jobs, housing, and schools; and put the Justice Department on the side of plaintiffs who argued that their rights were being violated. Title VII of the bill outlawed discrimination in employment on the basis of race, color, religion, or national origin.

The bill faced strong resistance, especially from southern members of Congress. Adding sex to the list of categories of prohibited discrimination was part of the convoluted maneuvering that surrounded this battle, which produced what historian Ruth Rosen calls "a bizarre coalition" of southern congressmen and supporters of women's rights.

It began when a few members of the National Woman's Party approached Congressman Howard Smith, the southern chairman of the House Rules Committee, and pointed out that if the bill passed in its present form, black men would have protections that were denied to white women. They urged him to present an amendment adding "sex" to the bill. Smith agreed, although he later admitted that his main motive had been to stir up trouble in the bill's supporters, many of whom opposed women's rights and might therefore join the southerners in voting against the bill.

The amendment delighted most of the female members of the House of Representatives but worried many supporters of civil rights. Esther

Peterson of the President's Commission on the Status of Women declared that she "was not willing to risk advancing the rights of all women at the expense of the redress due black men and women." Representative Edith Green decided to vote against the amendment, which she supported in principle, because she feared that linking the two issues would jeopardize the chance of winning this important piece of legislation for racial equality. Some male politicians voted *for* the sex amendment for the same reason, hoping its inclusion would kill the entire bill.

The amendment to add the category of sex to Title VII passed the House by a vote of 168–133. Two days later, the entire bill passed the House by a vote of 290–130.

Next the bill went to the Senate, where southern senators immediately began a filibuster that brought everything else to a halt for fifty-four days. Behind the scenes, several senators talked about amending Title VII to strike the word "sex." At this point feminist legislators such as Representative Martha Griffiths and Senator Margaret Chase Smith, both supporters of the entire bill, mobilized their networks to oppose dropping the sex discrimination clause. Ultimately the White House, fearing the loss of even one sincere women's rights supporter in the Senate in what might be a very close vote, threw its support behind the bill as it had passed the House, and the Senate finally voted 73–27 in its favor.

The inclusion of a woman's plank in such a sweeping piece of democratic legislation in the absence of an organized women's movement, points out historian Cynthia Harrison, was an anomaly. It resulted more from the tremendous sense of urgency produced by the civil rights struggle than from any grassroots pressure that women's rights advocates were able to mobilize. But getting the ban on sex discrimination enforced in the absence of a mass movement was another matter.

Almost immediately, working women began to deluge the commission with complaints of discrimination, but the agency set up to enforce the new law, the Equal Employment Opportunity Commission (EEOC), refused to outlaw sex segregation in employment ads. After all, said the director of the EEOC dismissively, the sex clause in Title VII was "a fluke . . . conceived out of wedlock."

Many in the media agreed that the clause should not be taken seriously. "Why," demanded a writer in the *New Republic*, "should the mischievous joke perpetrated on the floor of the House of Representatives" be treated seriously by responsible administrators?

If businesses could no longer designate some jobs by sex, pundits asked, would Playboy Clubs, for example, be forced to employ male bunnies to serve drinks and show off their bodies? The *Wall Street Journal* enjoined its readers to picture "a shapeless, knobby-kneed male 'bunny' serving drinks to a group of stunned businessmen in a Playboy Club" and raised the hilarious prospect of "a matronly vice-president" chasing a male secretary around her desk. The manager of an electronics company that employed only women told a journalist that if opponents of sex segregation got their way, "we'll have to advertise for people with small, nimble fingers and hire the first male midget with unusual dexterity [who] shows up."

A *New York Times* editorial warned that if employers were not allowed to specify that only men could apply for certain jobs there would be "no more milkman, iceman, serviceman, foreman or pressman. . . . The Rockettes may become bi-sexual, and a pity too. . . . Bunny problem indeed! This is revolution, chaos. You can't even safely advertise for a wife any more." And the personnel officer of a major airline raised the horrifying prospect of what might happen "when a gal walks into our office, demands a job as an airline pilot and has the credentials to qualify."

The EEOC's blatant disregard of the new law angered feminists in government service, who had thought until then that their patient work through official channels was paying off. In October 1965, at the usually placid conference of the National Council of Women of the United States, Pauli Murray publicly chastised the EEOC chair, saying that the committee's policy of permitting sex-segregated ads violated Title VII. "If it becomes necessary to march on Washington to assure equal job opportunities for all," said Murray, "I hope women will not flinch from the thought."

After reading newspaper accounts of these comments, Betty Friedan sought out Murray, who had done some typing for her several years earlier, and Murray in turn introduced her to what Friedan later called "the feminist underground" in government circles. Many of these women were already convinced that women needed an independent national civil rights organization, comparable to the NAACP. In fact, the original idea has been variously credited to Addie Wyatt, Aileen Hernandez, Pauli Murray, Muriel Fox, Dollie Lowther Robinson, Richard Graham, and Friedan herself, which suggests that many individuals were coming to a similar conclusion.

Whoever came up with the idea, the government feminists saw Friedan as someone who could be especially effective in pressing the issue forward, both because of her high profile since the publication of *The Feminine Mystique* and because she was not a government employee who could be fired if she alienated higher-up administrators. They took pains to include Friedan in their discussions, urging her to get involved in political organizing.

They also invited her to attend the third national meeting of state women's commissions in June 1966, which many hoped would compel the EEOC to start enforcing the law. Shortly before that conference, Representative Martha Griffiths lambasted the EEOC on the floor of Congress for its "arbitrary arrogance, disregard of law, and . . . flat hostility to the human rights of women." Catherine East of the Women's Bureau of the Department of Labor arranged to get copies of Griffiths's speech to all the conference delegates. A showdown was brewing.

At the conference, Friedan participated in behind-the scenes discussions with fifteen to twenty women who were determined to move beyond the polite lobbying tactics of their superiors. Her room was the site of a late-night meeting where they heatedly debated the next step in pushing forward their grievances.

The following day, when they were told they could not offer resolutions critical of the Johnson administration, the women decided it was time to step outside government channels and start a new women's association—the National Organization for Women. Friedan came up with the name, writing it on a napkin at the table where the dissidents huddled. The women agreed with Friedan that this should not be an organization "of" women, but one "for" women, welcoming sympathetic men as well.

Friedan played a central role in founding NOW and, with Pauli Murray, helped develop a statement of purpose that addressed a far wider constituency and range of issues than had *The Feminine Mystique*. Of special note, given later claims that NOW dealt only with white middleclass concerns, the statement pointed out that black women were "victims of the double discrimination of race and sex" and pledged "active support to the common cause of equal rights for all those who suffer discrimination and deprivation."

Under Friedan's leadership, NOW established task forces on equalizing employment opportunities, education, and political rights; improving the image of women; and fighting female poverty. Friedan quickly became a national leader, working energetically to publicize and expand the movement's reach. *The Feminine Mystique* continued to sell well, and in combination with Friedan's activities in NOW, she was in great demand as a speaker and lecturer around the country.

Things did not always run smoothly in the new organization. Initially, Friedan tried to exclude lesbians from public roles and vehemently opposed addressing their concerns. Even after this issue was resolved, her criticisms of other feminist leaders were sometimes divisive. But she continued to win recruits to the cause, and her audacious call for a National Strike for Equality in 1970, when the movement had begun to flag, was a brilliant move that helped unite the more mainstream NOW leaders with younger women who had been independently exploring feminist issues and forming what they called "women's liberation" groups throughout the country.

Many of these young women came to their views by very different routes than either the traditional feminists or the women influenced by *The Feminine Mystique*. For the younger women who energized the early 1970s women's movement, *The Feminine Mystique* was less likely to provide a "click" moment than it was for the slightly older group of women who first discovered it. Some read Friedan's book after they became activists, seeking validation for their views, but others skipped right over Friedan's book to read the more radical pamphlets and books being published by the early 1970s.

Some young women had already turned against the prevailing gender ideology of the 1950s and early 1960s simply by seeing the damage that ideology had done to their mothers. Noted author and columnist Anna Quindlen comments that for many young women who had observed the lives of their mother's generation, motherhood appeared to be "a kind of cage. . . . You stayed home and felt your mind turn to the stuff that you put in little bowls and tried to spoon into little mouths and eventually wound up wiping off of little floors."

In fact, many mothers had already encouraged their daughters to make different choices than they had made. Studying the archives of the Institute for Human Development from the 1950s, historian Jessica Weiss found women expressing new hopes for their daughters long before *The Feminine Mystique*. "I sure don't want [them] to turn out to be just a housewife like myself" (a 1957 interview). "I want them to have something, to be more independent than I was" (1958). "I'd like to see them make a living so the house isn't the end of all things" (1959). So some young activists of the 1960s were not rebelling against their mothers but simply taking their mothers' advice a little further than their moms had perhaps anticipated.

Other young women had so fully absorbed the postwar rhetoric about equality and self-fulfillment that they reacted with shock and indignation when they discovered there were unspoken exceptions when it came to women. As a girl, Sherry Bogartz grew up playing baseball with her brothers in an old cow pasture by her parents' chicken farm. She was furious when she found out they could join Little League but she could not. As a college freshman in 1963, never having heard of feminism or *The Feminine Mystique*, Bogartz circulated a petition demanding an end to special curfews and dress codes for female students. She later became a leader of the women's liberation movement in San Diego, then moved to New York to work for the Women's National Abortion Action Coalition.

Many other women of Bogartz's age group reported developing, on their own, a powerful sense that it was unfair of society to bar women from so many new opportunities. "I totally believed the propaganda that

America was the shining light of 'the free world,'" said Jolene J. "So I was totally angry when those freedoms were denied to me."

A large group of young women had their gender consciousness raised by their experiences in the civil rights movement, something that, unbeknownst to them, had also happened to their foremothers in the nineteenth-century women's rights movement. In the 1840s and 1850s, idealistic women had flocked to the abolitionist cause, outraged by the horrors of slavery, but they often became frustrated when men refused to allow them to speak at meetings or vote on important strategy decisions, and some eventually began to organize on behalf of women's rights as well.

When Angelina Grimke's future husband, also an abolitionist, suggested that she focus on the antislavery cause rather than dividing her energies between that and women's rights, she responded: "Can you not see that woman could do, and would do, a hundred times more for the slave if she were not fettered?" Abolitionist and feminist Abby Kelley remarked that women "have good cause to be grateful to the slave for the benefits we have received to *ourselves*, in working for *him*. In striving to strike his irons off, we found most surely, that *we* were manacled *ourselves*."

In the 1960s, some women in the Student Nonviolent Coordinating Committee, the youth section of the southern civil rights movement, underwent a similar evolution. In 1964, Mary King and Casey Hayden, two white women who had spent many nights discussing Simone de Beauvoir's *The Second Sex* and Doris Lessing's 1962 novel about women's struggle for independence, *The Golden Notebook*, circulated an anonymous paper pointing out that "much talent and experience are being wasted by this movement when women are not given jobs commensurate with their ability." In 1965, they signed their names to a more extensive article, "Sex and Caste: A Kind of a Memo," arguing that the movement needed to improve women's status.

Some young people came to believe that racism, war, and social inequality were deeply embedded in America's fundamental political and economic institutions. Many of them joined various groups of the New

Left, where male chauvinism was in some ways more blatant than in places where it was still disguised as a chivalrous concern for women's delicate nature. Young men in this movement rejected middle-class conventions about the sanctity of premarital chastity, marriage, and the male-breadwinner role, but in repudiating traditional forms of male obligation, they did not renounce male entitlement. And when they talked about sexual liberation, they often meant that a woman had the duty to say yes rather than the right to say yes or no.

Leaders of organizations such as Students for a Democratic Society often cultivated an aggressive style that turned contemptuous if their female comrades challenged them. Women who attempted to raise the issue of male-female equality in these groups were sometimes shouted down and sexually insulted at raucous meetings. Disillusioned and angry, many came to embrace a far more militant version of feminism than Friedan espoused.

For women from these different backgrounds, *The Feminine Mystique* was less often a revelation than a welcome vindication of decisions they had already reached. Lorraine Dusky recalls reading the book in 1964, as a college senior. "Heated arguments with my Midwestern, middle-class parents over my career choice had given way to their grudging acceptance. . . . I was a journalism major and managing editor of Wayne State University's *Daily Collegian*, hell-bent on a career to rival Brenda Starr's with or without the Mystery Man." The book, she remembers, "pumped high octane gas into my resolve."

But by the time others read it, they felt they had already gone beyond the issues Friedan addressed. Judith Lorber, who became a professor of sociology and women's studies in 1972, notes that although she still has her paperback copy of *The Feminine Mystique*, there is no underlining in it and she did not write anything in the margins because she "was not a homemaker and had been determined since the age of fourteen never to be 'just a housewife.'" Lorber's underlining and enthusiasm were saved for Shulamith Firestone's *The Dialectic of Sex: The Case for Feminist Revolution* and Kate Millett's *Sexual Politics*.

Like Lorber, younger women were often more influenced by books that raised a sharper critique of male privilege than was found in *The Feminine Mystique*. Such women often cite Simone de Beauvoir, as well as the works of Firestone, Millett, Germaine Greer, Juliet Mitchell, Robin Morgan, and Marilyn French as their inspiration.

THE WOMEN'S MOVEMENT CERTAINLY WOULD HAVE TAKEN OFF WITHOUT Friedan's book, but acknowledging this only makes what the book *did* achieve all the more powerful and moving. *The Feminine Mystique* electrified a layer of women "in between," women who might otherwise have been lost entirely, to themselves and to the women's movement.

This generation of women was just beginning to be caught up in the societal sea change that was drawing more women into the workplace, increasing the economic and cultural importance of education, making the labor of a full-time housewife less essential to families, and raising aspirations for personal growth and equal opportunity. They longed, however inarticulately, to participate in these social changes, but they had few resources to help them resist the cultural insistence that their longings were unnatural and illegitimate.

Having little or no access to the support systems and alternative messages about women's capabilities the suffrage struggle had spawned and that would return to the fore in the late 1960s, these women reacted with self-doubt and guilt rather than outrage to the frustrations they were experiencing. Isolated as they were in their individual families, they might well have wasted their lives mired in depression—or even, some believe, lost their very sanity—if Friedan had not reached into their homes, using the same language as the women's magazines that were their main sources of information, in a way that encouraged them to embrace rather than repudiate their aspirations for a life beyond the home. Many of them were inspired to do exactly what Friedan urged—use their education and talents in meaningful work that served a higher purpose.

Lifting so many women out of such deep self-doubt and despair was a tremendous accomplishment. And even after the revival of the women's movement, *The Feminine Mystique* remained especially powerful for women whose families or communities had kept them isolated from new ideas and possibilities. I talked to women—and some men—who, long after the 1950s, had been raised to follow that decade's patterns in their values and lives—people in small communities in Utah, Idaho, California, and Georgia who found themselves just as miserable in the 1980s or 1990s as the women who had embraced Friedan in 1963. They described stumbling upon the book almost accidentally—in one case having a librarian whisper that she might want to read it—and finding it as much a revelation as did Friedan's original readers.

One unexpected testimony to the book's continued power to reach people trapped in personal dependence came from a prominent gay historian I interviewed. In the 1990s he had a stay-at-home boyfriend "who suffered from the same anxieties as the housewives Friedan profiled." At his advice, his partner read the book, taking comfort from the idea that the depression he had at first experienced as a personal inadequacy was an understandable reaction to the lack of independent meaning in his life.

A few years later, the historian picked up Friedan's book himself and was "astounded" by its power. "Her diatribes against homosexuals were repellent. I was shocked to see that she reflected uncritically the biases of the 1950s. . . . But the book still spoke to me, a gay man of the twenty-first century."

AFTER STRIPPING AWAY THE GRANDIOSE CLAIMS ABOUT THE IMPACT OF *THE Feminine Mystique*, its achievements are still impressive. The book was a journalistic tour de force, combining scholarship, investigative reporting, and a compelling personal voice. And for an important layer of women, reading the book was a life-changing experience.

Friedan exposed her readers to a rigorous criticism of mainstream psychiatry and social sciences, introducing them to the progressive ideas embedded in the new humanistic psychology. To modern readers, Friedan's acceptance of many 1950s shibboleths about controlling mothers, weak men, and the "ominous" growth of homosexuality seems particularly dated, but at the time, Friedan was highly effective in exposing the contradictions in this ideology. As historian James Gilbert points out, she repeated the Freudians' indictment of mom-ism "only to sabotage their arguments, turning them upside down to plea for the liberation of women from cultural stereotypes." If you want men to be free of controlling wives and mothers, she argued, you must free women from the compulsion to focus all their energy on marriage and motherhood.

For an older generation of educators who already disliked the anti-intellectual trends in women's education, Friedan's book was a godsend. "I assigned it to every class I could get away with," one midwestern professor told me. "And it really helped my female students understand the need to take their education seriously."

Linda Barker read *The Feminine Mystique* in 1963, at age eighteen, when the book was chosen as the summer reading for the entire incoming freshman class at Connecticut College for Women. She did not experience the wave of relief reported by so many housewives who read the book in the early 1960s, but she believes Friedan's arguments helped inoculate her against going down the same path. She remembers, "We certainly had more choices with all the new conveniences" of modern society. But "what was I going to do with those choices? I didn't want to expand housewifery to the full time available."

Rebecca Adams recalls that during her senior year in college, all the women were required to attend an evening meeting on *The Feminine Mystique* hosted by the dean of women. The discussion had little impact on her at the time. She and her friends went back to their dorm and spent more time making fun of the dean than talking about Friedan's ideas. Adams graduated, married, and went to work as a social welfare caseworker. In her eighth month of pregnancy, she quit her job to stay home. But a few years later, having just finished playing with her daughter, she began to vacuum the carpet. "All of a sudden, I heard this voice that said, 'there's more to life than this,' and that meeting with the dean of women popped into my mind along with Betty Friedan and *The Feminine Mystique*." Soon afterward she began taking classes at a nearby university.

Even before these young women began to act on ideas that they got from the book, the older women Friedan had inspired to go back to school or seek meaningful work were swelling the ranks of profeminist educators and mentors. They founded domestic violence shelters, inaugurated classes for displaced homemakers, and started women's centers. A disproportionate number of the early women's studies programs and women's centers in America were established by women who entered this line of work after reading Friedan and going back to school.

The Feminine Mystique also built personal and political bridges between the generations: an older woman who sent the book to her young niece; a housewife who got it from her teenage babysitter; daughters who belatedly learned to sympathize with their mothers' depression or anger by reading the book.

Heather Booth's mother read the book shortly after it was published, when Heather was still in her teens. "She thought it was very important and tried to engage me in a conversation about women's role," Booth reports, but Heather couldn't really understand the "problem without a name." Like many other socially aware young people, Booth was more concerned about the civil rights struggle. She worked with the Congress of Racial Equality and with the Student Nonviolent Coordinating Committee and went to Mississippi to organize during the summer of 1964.

Only after she returned did Booth get drawn into the discussions of women's roles that were beginning to take place on campuses in 1965 and 1966. She helped conduct a study that revealed the tremendous disparity in how male and female students were treated in class, and she read Friedan for herself about the same time. "It was a bolt of lightning—there is a problem and we need to name it and address it. And the people who have the problem need to lead that fight to correct the problem."

The very title of Friedan's book made an enormous contribution to the movement, capturing and concentrating many women's feeling that they were being sold a bill of goods. The genius of the phrase was that it could stand in for many types of discontent in many facets of women's lives. Melinda Rice, who never read the book, "used the phrase all the time. But to me it didn't have anything to do with the problems of house-wives. It was the laws and social customs that kept women second-class citizens and discriminated against us in pay and promotions. Later I came to call those laws and customs 'sexist.' But at first, 'the feminine mys-tique' was the only phrase I had to explain what I hated without reciting a whole litany of grievances."

Later, the phrase also became a way to acknowledge, in Terry M.'s words, that "even those of us who strongly believed in the principles of gender equality had internalized a pattern of deferring to men and doubt-ing our own capacities." The phrase captured the two-sided nature of the struggle that unfolded in the late 1960s and early 1970s: against the external barriers that kept women from achieving their goals and realizing their potential, and against the internal voices that led women to doubt that potential and pre-shrink their aspirations.

Whatever the limits of Friedan's book for today's readers, her insis-tence on the need to break down prevailing assumptions about women, work, and family and to look for the societal origins of dilemmas that are often experienced as purely personal remains extremely relevant. This is especially true when it comes to figuring out how to balance the need for meaningful work and meaningful relationships, for creative fulfillment and for love.

9
〰〰〰〰

Women, Men, Marriage, and Work Today: Is the Feminine Mystique Dead?

ALTHOUGH MANY PEOPLE BELIEVE *THE FEMININE MYSTIQUE* WAS HOSTILE toward marriage and that Friedan herself was a "man hater," nothing could be further from the truth. Friedan may have disdained the mundane details of housework, but she was consistently, almost romantically, optimistic about heterosexual love and marriage in a world where women were men's equals. She was, after all, a woman who once suggested that her tombstone read: "She helped make women feel better about being women and therefore better able to freely and fully love men."

The final paragraphs of *The Feminine Mystique* look forward to a day when "women's intelligence . . . can be nourished without denying love." When women do not need to find their meaning in life solely through their mates' achievements, Friedan predicted, wives will be less "destructive to their husbands," men will no longer need to "fear the love and strength of women," and girls, seeing their mothers' fulfillment, will be even more "sure that they want to be women."

Who knows what possibilities may exist for love, Friedan asked, when men and women "can finally see each other as they are" and when they can share "not only children, home, and garden . . . but the responsibilities and passions" of creative work?

Friedan's optimism that expanding educational and professional opportunities for women would improve marriage seemed crazy to marriage experts of her day. Sociologists were convinced that marital stability depended upon men specializing in earning income and women specializing in caring for home and children, with husband and wife exchanging their own distinctive products and services.

Conventional wisdom held that marital harmony would be threatened if a woman acquired educational and economic resources of her own. As one early-twentieth-century marriage expert put it, women who succeeded in school or work acquired "a self-assertive, independent character, which renders it impossible to love, honor, and obey." Right up to the 1980s, sociologists and economists such as Gary Becker insisted that a woman with her own resources had less incentive to marry and was less attractive as a potential mate. If such a woman did marry, she was more likely to divorce than other females because she had the resources to walk away if she was dissatisfied. This was called the "independence effect."

For generations, the independence effect seemed like a law of nature. Female college graduates and career women were considerably less likely to marry than women with less education. If a married woman took a job, the couple was in fact more likely to divorce. And just as the independence effect predicted, divorce rates soared as women poured into the labor force in the late 1960s and 1970s. By 1980, when Becker was sending his *Treatise on the Family* to press, half of all American marriages were ending in divorce.

But a few years later, this seemingly eternal economic principle unraveled. History has shown that in the long run, Betty Friedan came closer to the truth than did her critics. Although initially divorce rates rose as more wives went to work, that trend reversed after the mid-1980s. As working wives became more common and the momentum of the women's movement continued to overturn old inequities at home and on the job, the divorce rate began to fall. The divorce rate dropped from a peak of 22.8 per 1,000 couples in 1979 to 16.7 per 1,000 couples by 2005. Today divorce rates tend to be lowest in states where more than 70 percent of married women work outside the home.

Women no longer need to choose between completing their education and having a family. The difference between marriage rates for female college graduates and women with less education has almost disappeared. Earning a master's degree is now perfectly compatible with becoming both a Mrs. and a mom.

Educated women tend to marry and have children later than other women, but unlike during the 1960s, marrying later is now associated with a lower-than-average chance of divorce. In fact, divorce rates for educated women have fallen so much that such women are now *more* likely to be married at age thirty-five and forty than their less-educated counterparts. Educated couples, especially those with egalitarian gender views, also report the highest marital quality.

And fewer educated women than in the past are forgoing motherhood. As late as 1992–1994, 30 percent of forty- to forty-four-year-old women with a master's degree and 34 percent of women with a PhD were childless. As of 2006–2008, that was true of only 25 percent of forty- to forty-four-year-old women with a master's degree and only 23 percent of such women with a PhD.

High-earning women have also experienced a marked change in marriage prospects. Analyzing Current Population Surveys from the early twenty-first century, economist Heather Boushey found that women between twenty-eight and thirty-five who worked full-time and earned more than $55,000 a year were just as likely to be married as other working women of the same age. According to sociologist Christine Whelan, 88 percent of women thirty to forty-four earning more than $100,000 per year are married, compared to 82 percent of other women. Mate selection surveys reveal that men now find educated women and career women much more attractive as marriage partners than in the past, and are far less likely to feel threatened by a woman who earns as much or more than they.

The specialization into separate gender roles that supposedly stabilized marriages in the 1950s and 1960s actually raises the risk of divorce today.

As late as 1980, a wife's employment was associated with higher marital conflict. But by 2000, marriages in which wives were employed outside the home had less conflict and fewer marital problems than male-breadwinner marriages. Marriages in which one partner earns all the income and the other does all the housework are now more likely to split up than marriages in which husbands and wives each do some bread-winning and homemaking.

The independence effect has also benefited women who choose not to marry (or are not allowed to do so under current law). Unmarried heterosexual women and lesbians have many more options than they did half a century ago. Women who have left abusive or unloving husbands report being much happier than did divorced women in the 1950s. And unwed and divorced women face much less social stigma and discrimination than in the past.

Even stay-at-home wives benefit from the independence effect. It was working wives who first pressed husbands to take on more responsibilities at home, and the longer a wife works outside the home, the more housework her husband tends to do. But these new norms have trickled down to male-breadwinner families as well, with the result that men in all families now perform significantly more housework and child care than in the past. Comparative studies of Western nations find that the higher the proportion of women in a country's workforce, the more housework men do, even when their own spouse is not employed.

In the United States in 1980, fully 29 percent of wives reported that their husbands did no housework. Twenty years later that figure had fallen to 16 percent, while one-third of American wives reported that their husbands did half or more of the housework and/or the child care.

It should come as no surprise that when one spouse does substantially more housework than the other, that spouse reports lower marital quality than the one who does less work. But husbands and wives who share the housework more equitably report above-average levels of marital happiness. Couples who share housework also spend more leisure time together, which is another plus for marital satisfaction.

When a man is not sure whether he is doing his fair share of housework, he might want to be "better safe than sorry." Two big predictors of a man's marital happiness are how little criticism he gets and how much sex he gets. Several studies confirm that a wife who feels the division of housework is fair is less likely to feel critical toward her husband and more likely to feel sexually attracted to him. A 2006 survey conducted by Neil Chetnik found that the happier a woman was with the division of household chores, the happier her husband was with his sex life. A fifteen-year study by the National Institute of Child Health and Human Development concluded in 2006 that wives also feel more "marital intimacy" when husbands perform more child care. (But when husbands and wives work split shifts to maximize parental time with children, this lowers each spouse's reports of love for the other.)

Fatigue is the biggest cause of decreased sexual desire for both homemakers and employed women, but surprisingly, employed women do not report fatigue at a higher rate than homemakers. Whether a woman is a homemaker or works a paid job—part-time, full-time, or even more than full-time—does not affect the couple's sexual satisfaction or the frequency of sex. But job satisfaction does. Couples in which both husband and wife feel they have rewarding jobs report the greatest sexual satisfaction.

Another counterintuitive finding is that couples who spend more time at paid work and more time on housework have *more* sex than couples who supposedly have more time on their hands. It appears that women and men who work hard together and have fun at it also tend to play hard together and have fun at that too.

The increased participation of wives in paid work has had its downside. Dual-earner couples raising children, especially young children, report that they almost always feel rushed and that the constant multitasking they must engage in is stressful. Employed married mothers have nine fewer hours of free time per week, and get three hours less sleep, than stay-at-home married moms. And when wives work above-average weeks of forty-five hours or more, marital quality tends to fall.

Marital quality also suffers when wives who do not want to work are forced into employment. People are generally happier—and they make those around them happier—when they are doing something they want to do. Women who want to work and men who approve of their wives working have higher marital quality than couples where one or both are unhappy about the wife's working.

Unfortunately, men and women often don't get their first choice when it comes to family-work arrangements. In 2000, 25 percent of the wives who worked full-time said they would prefer to be homemakers. On the other hand, 40 percent of all wives without paying jobs said they would rather be employed. Forty percent of employed women and a third of employed men would like to reduce their work hours.

Couples in which the wife works solely because of financial constraints but would rather stay at home, or where the husband wants to be the sole provider but cannot achieve that goal, have experienced declining marital satisfaction since 1980, even as couples with secure middle-class jobs have reported increased marital satisfaction. Lower marital quality is especially likely among couples where the man refuses to help out at home when his wife goes to work. And whatever their education or income level, when wives hold high standards for equality of housework and their husbands do not meet their expectations, they report worse-than-average marital satisfaction.

Still, Friedan's claim that, on average, independence is good for women and good for their partners holds up across the board. Women who work outside the home have higher self-esteem and lower lifetime rates of depression than full-time homemakers. And married mothers with high-prestige jobs report greater well-being than any other group of women.

Men have also benefited from the increased flexibility that female independence gives families. Men who entered the workforce in the 1950s and 1960s often had to spend their whole life at jobs they disliked because of the pressure to be the sole provider, and they almost invariably report feeling regret for the time they missed with their children and envy for the greater intimacy their sons or grandsons have with their own kids.

DO ALL THESE CHANGES MEAN THAT WOMEN ARE "FREE TO BE THEMSELVES" today? Have we reached the point that men and women can, as Friedan predicted, "finally see each other as they are," rather than through the distorted lens of gender stereotypes?

Societal attitudes toward women—and women's attitudes toward themselves—have been revolutionized in the decades since Friedan's book hit the stores. The mass media now regularly portray women as capable, gutsy, powerful, and smart. And in real life, Hillary Clinton nearly won the nomination for president in 2008, while Sarah Palin ran for vice president, drawing little criticism for taking on such a demanding task while the mother of five children, one of them an infant with Down syndrome.

In her book *When Everything Changed*, Gail Collins describes the new territory that opened up during each decade of the "amazing journey" American women undertook between 1960 and the early twenty-first century. In 1970, Collins reports, the dean of the University of Texas dental school limited females to 2 percent of all admissions, because "girls aren't strong enough to pull teeth." But by the turn of the twenty-first century, perhaps buffed up by their exploding participation in sports over the previous three decades, women made up 40 percent of dental school graduates. Today women receive a majority of bachelor's and master's degrees, and in 2007 they pulled even with men as new recipients of PhDs.

Women's academic achievement is no longer confined to traditional "women's" fields such as literature or social work. On July 25, 2008—sixteen years after the talking Barbie doll chirped "math class is tough"—*Science* magazine reported that the long-standing gap between high school boys and girls on standardized math tests had disappeared. Today high school girls take as many advanced math classes as the boys, and women now earn the majority of bachelor's degrees in chemistry and in the biological and agricultural sciences.

As late as 1970, less than 8 percent of physicians were female. Today women are a full quarter of all practicing physicians and compose nearly half the enrollment in medical schools. In 1972, women were only 3 percent of all licensed attorneys; by 2008, nearly one-third of all lawyers in the United States were female. As of 2009, women accounted for 51.4 percent of managerial and professional jobs. We have had two consecutive female secretaries of state, and currently three women sit on the Supreme Court.

But the glass ceiling is not yet shattered. A March 2010 study by the American Association of University Women found that among post-doctoral applicants, women had to publish three more papers in the most prestigious journals, or twenty more in the less prestigious ones, to be considered as productive as male applicants. Female legislators compose less than 20 percent of the U.S. House of Representatives. In the television news industry, two-thirds of the news producers, but only 20 percent of the news directors, are female.

Men make up more than three-quarters of all workers earning more than $100,000 a year, and as of 2010, women ran only 3 percent of Fortune 500 companies. At the other end of the wage spectrum, women remain disproportionately concentrated in the low-wage retail and service sectors of the economy.

Women are still plagued by many of the same mixed messages that prevailed in the 1950s and 1960s. Catalyst, an organization formed in 1962 to help women enter the workforce, surveyed more than 1,200 senior executives in the United States and Europe and titled its 2007 report "Damned If You Do, Damned If You Don't." The organization found that when women "act assertively, focus on work tasks, display ambition," or engage in other behaviors that receive high praise when done by men, they are perceived as "too tough" and "unfeminine." But when women pay attention to work relationships and express "concern for other people's perspective," they are considered less competent than men.

Housewives and stay-at-home mothers don't get a free pass either. Although they are seldom portrayed as the smothering matriarchal figures described in postwar diatribes, polls and surveys show that other Americans consistently rate housewives low in competence, often classing them with other stigmatized groups, such as the disabled and elderly.

Many women still internalize a self-effacing definition of femininity that reinforces second-class status. Young women are four times less likely than young men to negotiate their first salary to a higher level, and econ-omists estimate that this unwillingness to assert their own monetary worth ends up costing women $500,000 in earnings by the time they reach age sixty.

Nevertheless, the feminine mystique may now be less of a barrier to gender equality than the "masculine mystique." A recent study of middle school students in a southeastern American city found that the feminine stereotypes that prevailed in the 1950s and 1960s were virtually dead. Not one girl interviewed by researchers Barbara Risman and Elizabeth Searle thought she had to play dumb or act "feminine" around boys. Girls aspired to be strong and smart, and they admired girls who were. None of them felt it would be inappropriate for a girl to do things that used to be called masculine, whether physical or academic.

But attitudes about masculinity had not moved all that far. If a boy participated in activities or expressed feelings traditionally viewed as fem-inine, he was teased, bullied, or ostracized. The boys harshly policed one another to make sure no one was "acting like a girl" and they were quick to label boys who did not conform to the "manliness" code as "gay." The girls did not normally initiate such bullying or teasing, but they usually acquiesced to it.

Even as adults, some men still see masculinity as a zero-sum game where gains in female achievements or power take something away from their own identity. These men provide a ready audience for the shock jocks, TV shows, and video games that celebrate male violence and sex-ually objectify women even more crassly than was deemed acceptable in the past.

In historical perspective, however, the change in attitudes about gen-der has been enormous. One reason *The Feminine Mystique* seems dated today is that most of the belittling claims about women's nature that Friedan rebuts have dropped out of mainstream culture. Few people today believe—or at least admit believing—that "being feminine means being submissive," that the normal woman "renounces all active goals of her own . . . to identify and fulfill herself through the activities and goals of her husband, or son," or that femininity can be "destroyed by education."

The idea that females are naturally passive or that their highest fulfillment comes from being a "happy housewife" is viewed as hopelessly retro.

And despite the raunchy, antifemale rhetoric that pervades so much of popular culture, most men have improved their attitudes and behavior considerably. Sexual assaults by young men against young women have dropped dramatically in the past two decades. Domestic violence rates have also fallen sharply. And men in families perform much more child care and housework than at any time in the past hundred years.

But two *new* feminine mystiques stand in the way of the equality and harmony Friedan envisioned. The first—the hottie mystique—reaches its height during the teen years and the early twenties, before most young women are thinking seriously about marriage and motherhood. The second—the supermom mystique—kicks in not at marriage, as did the happy housewife ideology, but at childbirth.

The middle school girls Risman and Searle interviewed had rejected the old behavioral norms for femininity. They did not feel there was anything they *must do* or *could not do* because they were female. But they held strong beliefs about how they *must* or *must not look*. Appearing "hot" was mandatory, although looking "slutty"—a distinction clearer to the girls than to their parents—threatened a girl's social standing. The interviewers were astonished by how preoccupied the girls were with the "right" display of their sexuality—through clothes, makeup, hairstyle, and even how they walked and talked.

Such pressure to look sexy starts even before middle school. The Barbie doll, whose large, pointy breasts made 1950s parents nervous about buying one for preteens, is now a toy that most marketers—and children themselves—feel is appropriate for the three- to six-year-old crowd. By 2006, Margaret Talbot reported in the *New Yorker*, girls in the age range that used to buy Barbie dolls were clamoring for Bratz dolls, whose facial features and revealing clothes made them resemble *Girls Gone Wild* participants. Barbie's marketers responded to the challenge with "My Bling Bling Barbie," described on the Web site as wearing "an ultra hot halter top and sassy skirt *sooo* scorchin'."

Sexuality researchers find that most young girls don't associate the sexy clothes they want with sex itself. They just think it's cool to look like a big girl. But so much emphasis on looks can be dangerous. By age nine, half of all girls report having been on a diet, and by the eighth grade, 80 percent of girls say they are dieting. According to a February 19, 2007, report by the American Psychological Association's Task Force on the Sexualization of Girls, an early emphasis on being sexy can not only push a girl into initiating sex before she is emotionally ready but can also stunt the full development of her other interests and competencies.

What Betty Friedan labeled "The Sexual Sell" in one chapter of *The Feminine Mystique* may be more pervasive and powerful than ever. Even though the students to whom I assigned Friedan's book found most of it irrelevant to their contemporary concerns, they responded viscerally to that chapter and to another called "The Sex Seekers." Almost all testified to the pressures they felt not only to buy consumer goods but to present themselves as objects to be consumed. In Friedan's day, commented one, "women were supposed to accessorize and display their homes. Now women—and increasingly men too—are supposed to accessorize and display our bodies." Many suggested that *Sex and the City* was simply an updated version of the marketing myth Friedan exposed back in 1963, falsely promising women they will be empowered by buying more things and having more orgasms.

Yet while the hottie mystique may hold many teens and young women in its thrall, by their late twenties or early thirties most contemporary women have learned to integrate their search for sexual or romantic fulfillment with a range of aspirations and interests far broader than those available to women in the past. Although their options are still constrained by inequalities connected to race and class, young women know they have more choices than ever before. If they marry, they are far less likely to enter unequal and constricting relationships than did their grandmothers. If they do not marry, they can still have satisfying and productive lives.

Once a woman becomes a mother, however, her options tend to narrow. New limits, mystiques, and mixed messages come into play. Motherhood may in fact have replaced gender as the primary factor constraining women's choices.

Young childless women have made dramatic gains in the workplace, in part because of their growing educational advantage over men. Today in a number of major urban centers, including New York, Dallas, Boston, Chicago, Minneapolis, and Los Angeles, women between twenty-one and thirty earn more than men the same age. Nationwide, females in this age group earn almost 90 percent of what their male peers of the same age make, a much smaller wage gap than exists between older men and women. In addition, a growing proportion of wives outearn their husbands.

Perhaps these young women are the leading edge of a new wave of females who will be able to work alongside men on equal terms. But as things now stand, these same women are likely to fall behind their male peers once they have children. Many women who become mothers temporarily drop to part-time work or leave the workforce for a period of time. This creates a wage gap that continues to widen over the years, even after they return to full-time work, costing women hundreds of thousands of dollars over the course of their lives.

Meanwhile, women who stay on the job after they become mothers face new prejudices, along with outright discrimination. Employers and coworkers often assume they will be less committed and less effective at work, and many professional working women describe having had important projects or clients handed over to others after they had a child, even though they did not decrease their work hours.

In 2007, researchers at Stanford University constructed fake résumés that were identical in all respects except gender and parental status and asked college students to evaluate and rank them. The students consistently rated the supposed mothers as less competent than the nonmothers. Applicants identified as mothers were 79 percent less likely to be offered jobs, and when hired, they were offered an average of $11,000 a year less in salary. The students also held the mothers to higher standards of performance and punctuality than women with identical résumés but no children, and were much less likely to recommend them for promotion.

When the researchers sent out similar résumés in response to more than six hundred actual job advertisements, applicants identified as childless received twice as many callbacks as the supposed mothers.

These penalties for motherhood may help to explain why, although almost 90 percent of women who earn $100,000 or more per year are married, half of them have not had children by age forty.

AMERICANS GREATLY VALUE THE IDEAL OF MOTHERHOOD, AND WE ALSO greatly value the work ethic. But we often find it difficult to value both at once. For impoverished women with children, society comes down firmly on the side of work. Poor women get no social kudos if they try to stay home with their infants. Instead they are pressured to find any job that gets them off public assistance, even one that pays less than poverty-level wages or requires them to leave their kids in inadequate child care and unsafe neighborhoods for ten hours a day. Yet many Americans simultaneously believe that the gold standard for middle-class women is stay-at-home mothering and that good mothering—the kind that middle-class children deserve—is incompatible with work outside the home.

Most people do not realize this, but contemporary mothers and fathers now spend more time with their children than parents did in 1965—and much more time than parents did in the first four decades of the early twentieth century. In fact, although employed mothers today spend less time in primary child-care activities than stay-at-home mothers do, they spend more time than stay-at-home mothers did at the time that *The Feminine Mystique* was published—the heyday of the male breadwinner–female homemaker family. Furthermore, husbands of employed mothers do more child care than husbands of full-time homemakers, and they have greater knowledge of their children's interests, activities, and social networks.

Nevertheless, a new ideology of hands-on motherhood has taken root in some middle-class and affluent circles, one that requires a really good mother to devote herself to organizing a constant round of playdates, sports activities, enrichment experiences, and teachable moments for her children. In her book *Perfect Madness*, Judith Warner describes this ideology at its most extreme as the "mommy mystique"—an all-consuming search for perfection in child rearing, accompanied by an equally consuming anxiety that Mommy may have overlooked something.

While Friedan's housewives were often haunted by the sense that they were not doing anything meaningful, the mothers Warner interviewed were convinced that every decision they made and every detail they controlled was incredibly meaningful, both for their children's future and their own standing as good mothers. If 1950s housewives obsessed about the cleanliness of their kitchen and the whiteness of their laundry, these women obsessed over what snacks to take to school, where to hold a child's birthday party, and what clothes and toys to buy for their children.

Still, the kind of obsessive mothering Warner describes is confined to a minority of mothers. And although the presence of even one such mom in a classroom or play circle can trigger immediate guilt in the rest of the mothers, there are signs of a growing reaction against overparenting.

A more insidious problem facing American women today is the tendency to pit stay-at-home moms against working moms as if the two groups had incompatible values and priorities—the "mommy-wars mystique." Its premise is that mothers who stay home and mothers who work for pay are divided into two hostile camps, and we must take sides about which group is "right."

Some pundits encourage women to opt out of the workforce to raise their children. Others, in the titles of two recent books, urge mothers to "Get to Work," warning that if they quit work or downgrade their hours they are falling prey to "the Feminine Mistake." But arguing about what choices a mother should make to resolve the caregiving crisis in contemporary America disregards the shared dilemmas all mothers face. It also misses the opportunity to make common cause with fathers on an issue that concerns them as well.

The mommy-wars mystique ignores the women who don't have a choice either way. Some would like to opt out or cut back on work hours but cannot, either because their families need the money, or because in the United States the long-term financial and career penalties for part-time work are prohibitively large—often far out of proportion to the actual reduction in hours. Other women, whose families need the money even more, would like to get a job but cannot opt in because they don't have access to affordable child care or cannot earn a wage that would cover their child care and transportation.

Paradoxically, the only group in which stay-at-home mothers outnumber those who combine paid work with parenting is women married to the most poorly paid men in the country. Of the women whose husbands' earnings are in the bottom 25 percent of the income distribution, 52 percent are outside the paid labor force.

The second highest percentage of stay-at-home moms is found in families where the husband is in the top 5 percent of earners, making more than $120,000 a year. But even in this group, 60 percent of mothers work outside the home. Among wives whose husbands' earnings are in the middle range, 80 percent work outside the home.

Another misconception promoted by the mommy-wars mystique is that educated professional mothers are abandoning work to stay home with their kids. In fact, highly educated women are more likely to combine work with motherhood than less-educated women, and less likely to take extended time off after childbirth. And such women are *less* likely to drop out of work after becoming mothers today than were their counterparts back in the 1960s and 1970s.

But educated women are the most likely to read the newspapers and magazines that repeat the myth that educated mothers like themselves are leaving the labor force in droves. This creates the impression that there is something deviant in their decision to continue working, which can make them, like their middle-class counterparts in the 1950s, feel guiltier about their choice to work than their working-class sisters.

The biggest problem with the mommy-wars mystique is that most women want the same basic things from work and family life. Only a minority of moms who work outside the home really want to return to full-time schedules as soon as they have exhausted their maternity leave, and an even smaller percentage of so-called opt-out mothers really want to leave paid employment completely.

For many working mothers who end up leaving their jobs, a more accurate description of their actions is that they were *pushed* out, says Joan Williams, director of work/life law at the University of California's Hastings Law School. Williams's claim is supported by sociologist Pamela Stone's in-depth interviews with educated, professional women who quit work to stay home with their children. Stone found that in most cases, beneath the wistful assurance that this was "my choice," the decision to quit work was usually taken as a last resort, after a woman's employer rejected her request for more flexible hours or part-time work, or after her husband refused to adjust his own work schedule and household commitments so she could continue to work. Only 16 percent of the women Stone interviewed reported that their first preference had been to stay home with the children full-time.

The rigid work policies and practices that push some women out of their jobs when they become mothers also penalize women who freely leave work because they want to be with their children full-time. Most women who leave their jobs for family reasons plan to return to work within a few years. But in one recent study, more than a quarter of mothers who wanted to reenter the workforce were unable to do so, and many others had to take part-time jobs even though they wanted to work full-time.

Mothers pay a high price for whatever choices they make—or are forced to make. Working mothers find it hard to negotiate flex time or are looked down upon for doing so, and often run themselves ragged trying to juggle competing demands on their time. Women who temporarily opt out discover that their work as mothers counts for nothing when they try to find a new job. And full-time homemakers may find themselves dismissed by people they meet at parties or other events as "just a housewife." Meanwhile, their husbands often put in longer work hours to make up for the loss of two incomes, cutting into the shared parenting time most modern couples hoped for when the baby was on the way.

These problems all have a common source. Despite the rhetorical reverence our society accords motherhood and fatherhood, in reality the everyday work of parenting garners little social respect and even less practical support.

Mirra Komarovsky pointed to this contradiction back in 1953, at the height of the feminine mystique, commenting on the oft-repeated assurance that motherhood was the most important and difficult job in the world. If society actually believed this, she remarked, "a nursery school teacher would rate a salary at least equal to the beginning salary of a street cleaner, and the curtailment of social services to children would not be the first economies that politicians feel safe to propose in a period of retrenchment." Not much has changed since then in America's real, rather than rhetorical, social priorities.

The devaluation of motherhood and fatherhood is part of what may be the biggest contemporary mystique of all: what sociologists Phyllis Moen and Patricia Roehling label the "career mystique." This is the idea that a successful career requires people to commit all their time and energy throughout their prime years to their jobs, delegating all caregiving responsibilities to someone else.

The feminine mystique defined the ideal wife as having no interests or obligations outside the home. The career mystique defines the ideal employee—male or female—as having no familial or caregiving obligations that compete with work.

The career mystique is not the inevitable or the only way to organize work and family. Through most of history, workers didn't balance work and family. They combined the two, integrating responsibilities rather than juggling them. Men and women worked together on farms and in household businesses where the rhythms of labor had to take into account the rhythms of birth, child rearing, illness, death, and neighborly obligations. Even during the early period of industrialization, workers often labored alongside other family members or lived close enough to work to come home for lunch.

When middle-class careers first developed in the last third of the nineteenth century, what made them more desirable than working-class occupations was not just their larger salaries but their shorter hours. A hundred years ago, the most prestigious and remunerative careers were those that required the least amount of time away from home. In those days, blue-collar workers envied the "bankers' hours" that allowed managers and professionals to arrive at work later and leave earlier than less-well-paid employees.

The middle-class career mystique developed hand in hand with the middle-class feminine mystique over the course of the twentieth century. Both were based on new assumptions about the nature of work and the nature of the family.

The assumption about work was that if a man displayed company loyalty, he could earn a wage adequate to support a family, steadily move up the job ladder, and eventually retire with a pension. The assumption about family was that each ideal employee came with a wife who would take care of the house, do the shopping, raise the children, care for ill family members, and have dinner waiting when he came home.

But the assumptions of the career mystique are out of touch with the further evolution of both family life and work life. Today few workers have the luxury of a full-time caregiver at home, even though obligations to children last longer than in the past and many have responsibilities to aging parents as well. Seventy percent of American children live in households where every adult is employed.

And few workers have the security of a lifetime job or guaranteed pension plan any longer. For all families except those in the top quarter of the income distribution, male wages have stagnated over the past twenty-five years, so that most families have been able to achieve upward income mobility only by adding a second income. The young male high school graduates who made the most dramatic earnings gains in the 1950s have experienced the greatest losses in real wages and job security.

Meanwhile, employees who *do* earn enough to support a family, especially professionals and managers, are often forced to work more hours than they really need or want and to be almost constantly available by e-mail or cell phone even while at home. For example, in the legal profession a forty-hour workweek is widely viewed as part-time, and a person who drops back to that level often takes a pay cut of 20 percent per hour, magnifying the income loss associated with reducing one's hours.

This too-much-or-nothing approach to hours and income is a peculiarly American phenomenon. Almost one-quarter of all American men spend fifty hours or more on the job each week, compared to only 7.3 percent of Swedish men and 3.5 percent of men in the Netherlands. U.S. workers also get less vacation time than Europeans, who typically get three to six paid weeks per year. The United States, unlike 134 other countries, has no laws limiting the maximum length of the workweek. And the United States stands nearly alone among the major industrial powers in not mandating subsidized parental leaves. Only about half of all American workers qualify for the twelve weeks of unpaid parental leave provided for by the Family Medical Leave Act.

We are beginning to see a wave of dissatisfaction with the career mystique, much as we did against the feminine mystique in the 1950s. And this dissatisfaction is now widely felt by men as well as women.

The Families and Work Institute first began measuring workers' reports of work-family conflict in 1977, when 41 percent of mothers and 35 percent of fathers in dual-earner households with children under eighteen reported either some or a lot of work-family conflict. By 2008, there had been a slight rise in the percentage of mothers reporting such conflict, from 41 percent to 45 percent, but the number of fathers complaining about it had soared to 59 percent.

As men's dissatisfaction with the demands of the career mystique has grown, so has their willingness to challenge it. In 1977, only 12 percent of fathers in dual-earner couples reported having taken time off from work to care for their child. Today almost one-third of fathers say they have done so, even though they recognize that supervisors typically view fathers who take parental leave as less committed workers.

Of the men who work more than fifty hours a week, 80 percent say they would prefer shorter hours. Even hard-charging executives are changing their priorities. In a *Fortune* poll of male executives, 64 percent said they would choose more free time over money and 71 percent said they would choose time over advancement. Such sentiments are even stronger among younger male workers.

Men's growing discontent is a positive thing. As so many women who read Betty Friedan's book in the 1960s can attest, people can begin to change their lives only after they identify their discontent and recognize its causes. So we must get beyond the notion that resolving work-family tensions is a women's issue, a notion that threatens to perpetuate or even revive the old feminine mystique. As long as women continue to make all the compromises needed for families to coexist with the career mystique, we deny children the benefits of involved fathers, we deny men the rewards of shared parenting, we reinforce gender inequalities in pay and work opportunities that have been largely eliminated for childless women, and we risk once more forcing women to choose between love and work.

Oscar Wilde once remarked that it's a sorry map of the world that contains no island of Utopia. And it's a sorry map of our human relationships that cannot envision a better way to meet our work and caregiving commitments than by continuing to accommodate the false choices the career mystique imposes on us.

Betty Friedan asked us to imagine a world where men and women can both find meaningful, socially useful work and also participate in the essential activities of love and caregiving for children, partners, parents, friends, and neighbors. Today that goal is even more relevant than when she wrote *The Feminine Mystique*.

Acknowledgments

IT IS IMPOSSIBLE TO WRITE A BOOK COVERING SUCH AN IMPORTANT ERA IN the history of women and families without relying heavily on the work of many other researchers. I list the most important books and articles in my bibliography, but I owe a special thank-you to Daniel Horowitz, whose work on Betty Friedan's political and intellectual history is a must-read, and who also offered me advice in personal conversations and commented on an early draft of Chapter 8. I also want to acknowledge the hundreds of other researchers, both professionals and amateurs, who have worked since the 1960s to uncover women's long-hidden history, and the tremendous contributions of women's studies departments, teachers, and centers around the nation—many of them inspired directly by Friedan's ideas.

My biggest debt is to the 188 women and men who responded to my surveys about *The Feminine Mystique* and then, in many cases, shared details of their lives with me in extended follow-up interviews. I also thank the scores of students who over the years have taken oral histories of their own families and neighbors as part of their work with me. I am particularly grateful to the students in my 2006 program, "What's Love Got to Do with It?" who read and participated in many lengthy seminar discussions of *The Feminine Mystique* and also interviewed older family members about whether they had read the book when it was first published. I hope they will recognize the many ways their comments and questions in class enriched my thinking.

I am very grateful to Ellen Shea and the librarians at the Schlesinger Library on the History of Women in America, Radcliffe Institute, Harvard University, for helping me navigate the Betty Friedan Papers. Thanks also to Nancy Cott for facilitating my research visit there, as well as for her inspiring and voluminous work on the history of women and family life.

Tara C. Craig, the reference services supervisor at the Rare Book & Manuscript Library at Columbia University's Butler Library (and also an Evergreen alum), helped me locate the relevant parts of the W. W. Norton Collection for my research into the publishing history of *The Feminine Mystique*. Lorraine Glennon and Diane Salvatore, then at the *Ladies' Home Journal*, took time from their busy schedules to discuss the history of that magazine with me, and Jill Jerabek, Lorraine's research assistant, tracked down an enormous number of hard-to-find back issues for me.

Portions of Chapter 9 first appeared in my article "Sharing the Load" in a joint report of the Center for American Progress and the Maria Shriver Foundation: Heather Boushey and Ann O'Leary, eds., *The Shriver Report: A Woman's Nation Changes Everything* (Washington, DC: Center for American Progress, 2009). Thanks to the Center for American Progress and Maria Shriver for giving me permission to use these.

I would like to thank Ruth Rosen both for the wonderful historical work she has done on the history of American women and for her advice and encouragement on this project. Although we had never met in person, she responded warmly and at length to my questions. Elizabeth Long's intelligent observations and questions about the publishing history of *The Feminine Mystique* first stimulated me to do the research on that topic. Betsey Stevenson, Justin Wolfers, and Heather Boushey provided invaluable information about contemporary trends in marriage, divorce, and women's work patterns. I stand in awe of their research skills and appreciate their willingness to answer my sometimes naive questions about data.

The library staff at The Evergreen State College has always gone way beyond that extra mile for me. Reference librarians Paul McMillan, Liza Rognas, Sarah Pedersen, Randy Stilson, Sara Huntington, Jules Unsel, and Jenny DeHaas, and government documents librarian Carlos Diaz, were always there to help. Equally vital to my work have been the patience and kindness of the circulation staff: Mindy Muzatko, Jason Mock, Joel Wippich, and Jean Fenske. Thanks also to my successive research assistants, Alex Bertolucci and Valerie Adrian, for tracking down sources and hard-to-find magazine articles. I am grateful to the deans and provost at The Evergreen State College, who allowed me extra leaves of absence, despite the inconvenience to their curriculum scheduling, when this book took much longer than I'd originally estimated. I would also like to thank my program secretaries at TESC, Sherri Willoughby, Marcia Zitzelman, and Sheila Sawyer.

My colleagues at the Council on Contemporary Families have been extremely helpful with their time and resources. I especially thank Paula England for suggesting sources, providing data, and allowing me to pester her with questions and ideas. Virginia Rutter was unfailingly generous with ideas, sources, and encouragement, as were Barbara Risman, Mignon Moore, Steven Mintz, and Joshua Coleman. The briefing papers and press releases on the council's Web site, www.contemporaryfamilies.org, are an excellent source for new research on trends in gender relations and family life. Andrew Cherlin, Arloc Sherman, Suzanne Bianchi, and John Schmitt were also especially gracious in providing references and answering queries.

JoAnn Miller of Basic Books first suggested I take on this project, and although there were times in the early stages of research and writing when I regretted saying yes, I am now immensely grateful for the learning opportunities she opened up for me. Lara Heimert shepherded the book through its actual writing, making astute suggestions for changes but gracefully allowing me to make my own mistakes when I got bullheaded about some of my passages. Thank you, Lara. Finally my agent, Susan Rabiner, is one of the most incisive and insightful critics I could ever have hoped for, and a supportive friend as well.

Lastly, I thank my husband, Will Reissner, who helped me sift through 1960s newspaper ads and magazines, tracked down sources, edited every chapter, and made my work easier and my life happier in so many other ways.

Selected Bibliography

FOR THE QUOTATIONS FROM *THE FEMININE MYSTIQUE* IN THIS BOOK, I RELIED on the 2001 Norton edition, which includes an eloquent introduction with personal testimony about the book's impact by Anna Quindlen (New York: Norton, 2001). The single most important biography of Friedan and her work is Daniel Horowitz, *Betty Friedan and the Making of* The Feminine Mystique (Amherst: University of Massachusetts Press, 1998).

Other sources on Friedan and *The Feminine Mystique* include: Judith Adler Hennessee, *Betty Friedan: Her Life* (New York: Random House, 1999); Jannan Sherman, ed., *Interviews with Betty Friedan* (Jackson: University Press of Mississippi, 2002); Rachel Bowlby, "'The Problem with No Name': Rereading Friedan's *The Feminine Mystique*," *Feminist Review* 27 (September 1987): 61–75; Sandra Dijkstra, "Simone de Beauvoir and Betty Friedan: The Politics of Omission," *Feminist Studies* 6 (Summer 1980): 290–303; Susan Oliver, *Betty Friedan: The Personal Is Political* (New York: Pearson Longman, 2008); Betty Friedan, *"It Changed My Life": Writings on the Women's Movement* (1976; New York: Dell Publishing, 1991); Justine Blau, *Betty Friedan: Feminist* (New York: Chelsea House Publishers, 1990).

On the impact and reception of Friedan's book, see Elizabeth Long, "Mobilizing Texts: A Consideration of *Silent Spring* and *The Feminine Mystique*," keynote address, "Beyond the Book" Conference, Birmingham, UK, September 1, 2007, and Patricia Bradley, *Mass Media and the Shaping of American Feminism, 1963–1975* (Jackson: University Press of Mississippi, 2003). For a comparison of *The Feminine Mystique* and modern self-help books, see Wendy Simonds, *Women and Self-Help Culture* (New Brunswick, NJ: Rutgers University Press, 1992). For an analysis of the hostile responses Friedan received from readers of *McCall's*, see Jessica

Weiss, "'Fraud of Femininity': Domesticity, Selflessness, and Individualism in Responses to Betty Friedan," in *Liberty and Justice for All?: Rethinking Politics in Cold War America 1945–1965*, ed. Kathleen G. Donohue (Amherst: University of Massachusetts Press, forthcoming).

On how the mass media has misread the central tenets of *The Feminine Mystique*, see Kathryn Cady, "Labor and Women's Liberation: Popular Readings of *The Feminine Mystique*," in *Women's Studies in Communication* 32 (2009): 348–379. For an article celebrating Friedan's contributions after her death, see Marlene Sanders and Lorraine Dusky, "Betty Friedan Woke Women from Mystique of Sleep," *Women's E-News*, February 7, 2006, www.womensenews.org/article.cfm/dyn/aid/2628, retrieved March 15, 2008. For conservative assessments of Friedan, see: Kate O'Beirne, *Women Who Made the World Worse* (New York: Sentinel, 2006); Betty Steele, *The Feminist Takeover: Patriarchy to Matriarchy in Two Decades* (Gaithersburg, MD: Human Life International, 1987), p. 3; Jane Crain, "The Feminine Mistake," *Chronicles*, March 1990, p. 36; Christina Hoff Sommers, "Reconsiderations: Betty Friedan's 'The Feminine Mystique,'" *New York Sun*, September 17, 2008.

The most important primary sources I use in this book come from the 188 interviews I did with women and men who read *The Feminine Mystique* shortly after its publication, the oral histories my students and I have taken over the years, and the letters and personal papers in the Friedan archives in the Schlesinger Library. All references to letters received by Friedan and written by her, unless otherwise noted, come from the Betty Friedan Papers, Schlesinger Library, Radcliffe Institute, Harvard University. Information about the book's publishing history came from the W. W. Norton and Co. Inc. papers; Rare Book and Manuscript Library, Columbia University; and from back issues of *Publishers Weekly*.

Aside from the 1959 classic study of the women's suffrage struggle, Gerda Lerner, *Century of Struggle* (1959; Cambridge, MA: Belknap Press of Harvard University Press, 1975), most of the sources for my historical discussion of women are drawn from the rich and extensive literature on women's history and gender issues that has blossomed since the mid-

1960s, much of it written by women who were inspired by Friedan. Among the many useful overviews of U.S. women's and family history are: Nancy Cott and Elizabeth Pleck, eds., *A Heritage of Her Own* (New York: Simon & Schuster, 1979); Nancy Cott, ed., *No Small Courage: A History of Women in the United States* (New York: Oxford University Press, 2000); S. Jay Kleinberg, Eileen Boris, and Vicki Ruiz, eds., *The Practice of U.S. Women's History* (New Brunswick, NJ: Rutgers University Press, 2007); Nancy Woloch, *Women and the American Experience* (New York: McGraw-Hill, 1984); John Modell, *Into One's Own* (Berkeley: University of California Press, 1989); Claudia Goldin, *Understanding the Gender Gap: An Economic History of American Women* (New York: Oxford University Press, 1990); Jordan Stanger-Ross, Christina Collins, and Mark Stern, "Falling Far from the Tree: Transitions to Adulthood and the Social History of Twentieth-Century America," *Social Science History* 29 (2005): 625–648; Francesca Cancian, *Love in America: Gender and Self-Development* (New York: Cambridge University Press, 1987); Glenna Matthews, *"Just a Housewife": The Rise and Fall of Domesticity in America* (New York: Oxford University Press, 1987); Mary Ryan, *Mysteries of Sex: Tracing Women and Men Through American History* (Chapel Hill: University of North Carolina Press, 2006). More references are available in the endnotes of three of my own works: *The Social Origins of Private Life: A History of American Families* (London: Verso, 1988); *The Way We Never Were: American Families and the Nostalgia Trap* (New York: Basic Books, 1992); and *Marriage, a History: How Love Conquered Marriage* (New York: Viking Press, 2005).

For the history of women from the suffrage struggle though World War II, see Nancy Cott, *The Grounding of Modern Feminism* (New Haven, CT: Yale University Press, 1987); Lois Banner, *Women in Modern America* (New York: Harcourt, Brace, Jovanovich, 1974); Susan Ware, *Holding Their Own: American Women in the 1930s* (Boston: Twayne, 1982); Glen Elder, *Children of the Great Depression* (Chicago: University of Chicago Press, 1974); Susan Hartmann, *The Home Front and Beyond: American Women in the 1940s* (Boston: Twayne, 1982); Karen Anderson, *Wartime*

Women: Sex Roles, Family Relations, and the Status of Women During World War II (Westport, CT: Greenwood Press, 1981).

Jessie Bernard, *American Family Behavior* (New York: Harper and Brothers, 1942), was a useful source into the sociological thinking of the early 1940s, while William Graebner's *The Age of Doubt: American Thought and Culture in the 1940s* (Boston: Twayne, 1990), provided excellent background on the cultural changes that occurred during and after the war. For a little-known feminist polemic from the 1940s, a book that Friedan knew but never cited, see Elizabeth Hawes, *Why Women Cry, or Wenches with Wrenches* (Cornwall, NY: Reynal & Hitchcock, 1943).

The literature on postwar culture and gender roles is immense. For a fascinating year-by-year study of a family whose history and dynamics illustrate many of the wartime and postwar trends described in this book, see Donald Katz's five-decade saga of the Gordon Family, *Home Fires* (New York: HarperCollins, 1992). The now-classic critique of Friedan's characterization of the postwar era as uniformly quiescent is found in Joanne Meyerowitz, ed., *Not June Cleaver: Women and Gender in Postwar America* (Philadelphia: Temple University Press, 1994). See also Kate Weigand, *Red Feminism: American Communism and the Making of Women's Liberation* (Baltimore: Johns Hopkins University Press, 2001), and the many sources I cite below on the history of labor-union women.

Other sources on postwar America that I found especially useful for this book include: Elaine Tyler May, *Homeward Bound: American Families in the Cold War Era* (New York: Basic Books, 1988); Lizabeth Cohen, *A Consumers' Republic: The Politics of Mass Consumption in Postwar America* (New York: Knopf, 2003); William Chafe and Harvard Sitkoff, eds., *A History of Our Time: Readings on Postwar America* (New York: Oxford University Press, 1995); Michael Gambone, *The Greatest Generation Comes Home* (College Station: Texas A&M University Press, 2005); Shelley Nickles, "More Is Better: Mass Consumption, Gender, and Class Identity in Postwar America," *American Quarterly* 54 (2002): 582–622; Daniel Horowitz, *The Anxieties of Affluence: Critiques of American Consumer*

Culture, 1939–1979 (Amherst: University of Massachusetts Press, 2004); Andrea Tone, *The Age of Anxiety* (New York: Basic Books, 2009). I received Rebecca Jo Plant's *Mom: The Transformation of Motherhood in Modern America* (Chicago: University of Chicago Press, 2010), too late to fully incorporate it into my account, but her perceptive analysis of anti-maternalist thought in the United States is worth seeking out.

For the views and influence of psychoanalysis in the postwar era and on into the 1960s, see Mari Jo Buhle, *Feminism and Its Discontents: A Century of Struggle with Psychoanalysis* (Cambridge, MA: Harvard University Press, 1998); Ellen Herman, *The Romance of American Psychology: Political Culture in the Age of Experts* (Berkeley: University of California Press, 1995); Kyle Cuordileone, *Manhood and Political Culture in the Cold War* (New York: Routledge, 2005); Lisa Appignanesi, *Mad, Bad and Sad: Women and the Mind Doctors* (New York: Norton, 2008); Carol Warren, *Madwives: Schizophrenic Women in the 1950s* (New Brunswick, NJ: Rutgers University Press, 1987); Richard Levinson, "Sexism in Medicine," *American Journal of Nursing* 76 (1976): 426–431; Herbert Modlin, "Psychodynamics and Paranoid States in Women," cited in Robert Roth and Judith Lerner, "Sex-Based Discrimination in the Mental Institutionalization of Women," *California Law Review* 62 (1974): 789–815.

Primary sources for this section of the book include Philip Wylie, *Generation of Vipers* (New York: Rinehard, 1955); Ferdinand Lundberg and Marynia Farnham, *Modern Woman: The Lost Sex* (New York: Harper and Brothers, 1947); Edward Strecker, *Their Mother's Sons: The Psychiatrist Examines an American Problem* (Philadelphia: Lippincott, 1946); and Margaret Mead, *Male and Female: A Study of the Sexes in a Changing World* (New York: William Morrow, 1949), along with the many popular magazines I cite.

Kristin Celello discusses the advice that twentieth-century "marriage experts," most of them influenced by psychoanalysis, offered husbands and wives, in *Making Marriage Work* (Chapel Hill: University of North Carolina Press, 2009). Rebecca Davis reveals how psychoanalysts reinforced the feminine mystique during and after World War II, but also how in the late 1960s and 1970s, the clients of marital counselors challenged therapists' assumptions, gradually forcing them to recognize problems such as domestic violence, in *More Perfect Unions: The American Search for Marital Bliss* (Cambridge, MA: Harvard University Press, 2010).

For more insight into the 1950s in particular, see: Jessica Weiss, *To Have and to Hold: Marriage, the Baby Boom and Social Change* (Chicago: University of Chicago Press, 2000); Sherry Ortner, *New Jersey Dreaming: Capital, Culture, and the Class of '58* (Durham, NC: Duke University Press, 2003); Ralph LaRossa, "The Culture of Fatherhood in the Fifties," *Journal of Family History* 29 (2004): 47–70; James Gilbert, *Men in the Middle: Searching for Masculinity in the 1950s* (Chicago: University of Chicago Press, 2005); David Kushner, *Levittown: Two Families, One Tycoon, and the Fight for Civil Rights in a Legendary Suburb* (New York: Walker and Co., 2008); Ira Katznelson, *When Affirmative Action Was White: An Untold History of Racial Inequality in Twentieth-Century America* (New York: Norton, 2005); Peter Biskind, *Seeing Is Believing: How Hollywood Taught Us to Stop Worrying and Love the Fifties* (New York: Henry Holt and Co., 2000); Brett Harvey, *The Fifties: A Women's Oral History* (New York: HarperCollins, 1993); Wini Breines, *Young, White, and Miserable: Growing Up Female in the Fifties* (Boston: Beacon, 1992); Lary May, *Recasting America: Culture and Politics in the Age of Cold War* (Chicago: University of Chicago Press, 1989); Ann Fessler, *The Girls Who Went Away* (New York: Penguin Press, 2006); Brandon French, *On the Verge of Revolt: Women in American Films of the Fifties* (New York: Frederick Ungar Publishing, 1978); Abigail Stewart, "The Women's Movement and Women's Lives," in *Exploring Identity and Gender*, ed. Amelia Lieblich and Ruthellen Josselson (Thousand Oaks, CA: Sage, 1994); Andrea Tone, *The Age of Anxiety* (New York: Basic Books, 2009). Many of these works discuss McCarthyism, but see also Elizabeth Pontikes, Giacomo Negro, and Hayagreeva Rao, "Stained Red: A Study of Stigma by Association to Blacklisted Artists During the 'Red Scare' in Hollywood, 1945–1960," *American Sociological Review* 75 (2010): 456–478.

An interesting sample of primary sources, illustrating the complexity and contradictions of that decade, would include: Mirra Komarovsky,

Women in the Modern World: Their Education and Their Dilemmas (Boston: Little, Brown and Co., 1953); Rona Jaffe, *The Best of Everything* (1958; New York: Penguin, 2005); Lena Levine, *The Modern Book of Marriage* (New York: Bartholomew House, 1957); John Keats, *The Crack in the Picture Window* (Boston: Houghton Mifflin, 1956); Alva Myrdal and Viola Klein, *Women's Two Roles: Home and Work* (London: Routledge and Kegan Paul, 1956); Vance Packard, *The Hidden Persuaders* (New York: D. McKay Co., 1957); Eve Merriam, "Are Housewives Necessary?" *The Nation*, January 31, 1959.

I also read extensively in the *Ladies' Home Journal, Redbook, McCall's, Ebony, Life,* the *Saturday Evening Post, Reader's Digest,* and *Good Housekeeping.* When I quote specific issues I give the date in the text. The Gallup poll article that opens Chapter 2 is George Gallup and Evan Hill, "The American Woman: Her Attitudes on Family, Sex, Religion and Society," *Saturday Evening Post*, December 22, 1962. My quotations from Adlai Stevenson come from the reprint of his commencement address, "A Purpose for Modern Women," *Women's Home Companion*, September 1955.

A good guide to the women's magazines of the era can be found in Nancy Walker, ed., *Women's Magazines, 1940–1960: Gender Roles and the Popular Press* (Boston: Bedford/St. Martin's, 1998). See also Kathleen L. Endres and Therese L. Lueck, *Women's Periodicals in the United States: Consumer Magazines* (Westport, CT: Greenwood Press, 1995). The readership figures for women's magazines come from Politz Research, *Main Report: 1964 Politz Magazine Study; the Audiences of Eleven Magazines, Advertising Page Exposure of Five Magazines* (New York: Alfred Politz Media Studies, 1965).

Many of the polls I cite can be found in George Gallup, *The Gallup Poll: Public Opinion, 1935–1971* (New York: Random House, 1972), and Joseph Veroff, Elizabeth Douvan, and Richard Kulka, *The Inner American: A Self-Portrait from 1957 to 1976* (New York: Basic Books, 1981).

On the social and legal climate of the 1960s, see Margaret Mead and Frances Kaplan, eds., *American Women: The Report of the President's Commission on the Status of Women* (1963; New York: Charles Scribner's

Sons, 1965); Nancy MacLean, *The American Women's Movement, 1945–2000: A Brief History with Documents* (Boston: Bedford/St. Martin's, 2009); Elizabeth Pleck, *Domestic Tyranny: The Making of Social Policy Against Family Violence from Colonial Times to the Present* (New York: Oxford University Press, 1987); Linda Gordon, *Woman's Body, Woman's Right: A Social History of Birth Control in America* (Urbana: University of Illinois Press, 2002); Susan Douglas, *Where the Girls Are: Growing Up Female with the Mass Media* (New York: Times Books, 1994); Leo Kanowitz, *Women and the Law: The Unfinished Revolution* (Albuquerque: University of New Mexico Press, 1969); Lynne Olson, *Freedom's Daughters* (New York: Scribner's, 2001); Joan Hoff-Wilson, *Law, Gender and Injustice: A Legal History of U.S. Women* (New York: New York University Press, 1991); Nancy Polikoff, *Beyond (Straight and Gay) Marriage: Valuing All Families Under the Law* (Boston: Beacon, 2008); Lis Wiehl, *The 51% Minority* (New York: Ballantine Books, 2007); Victor Brooks, *Boomers: The Cold War Generation Grows Up* (Chicago: Ivan R. Dee, 2009); Lorraine Dusky, *Still Unequal: The Shameful Truth About Women and Justice in America* (New York: Crown Publishers, 1996); Jack Demarest and Jeanette Garner, "The Representation of Women's Roles in Women's Magazines over the Past 30 Years," *Journal of Psychology* 126 (1992): 357–369; Jennifer Scanlon, *Bad Girls Go Everywhere: The Life of Helen Gurley Brown* (New York: Oxford University Press, 2009). The Chicago Women's Liberation Union Herstory Web site has good information on discrimination against women in the 1960s: www.cwluherstory.com. See also http://feminist.org/research/chronicles.

Primary sources from the 1960s that illustrate the continued prevalence of what are sometimes thought of as "1950s" ideas about gender include: Edna Rostow, "The Best of Both Worlds: Feminism and Femininity," *Yale Review*, March 1962; Editorial, "Some Gentle Observations About Women," *Saturday Evening Post*, March 17, 1962; Helen Andelin, *Fascinating Womanhood* (New York: Bantam, 1965); Helen Gurley Brown, *Sex and the Single Girl* (New York: Random House, 1962). My discussion of the Ridgely Hunt case in Chapter 2 is based on "The Masculine Mystique," *Chicago Tribune*, July 28, 1963, and Nancy Hunt, *Mirror Image: The Odyssey of a Male-to-Female Transsexual* (New York: Holt, Rinehart, and Winston, 1978). Due to a misleading set of dates on the copyright page of Eve Merriam, *After Nora Slammed the Door: American Women in the 1960s* (Cleveland: World Publishing Co., 1964), this feminist book is often said to have preceded *The Feminine Mystique*. Merriam's book did not appear until a year after Friedan's, although it drew on three of Merriam's previously published articles, of which Friedan was probably aware.

For a lively and wonderfully informative account of how much has changed since the 1960s, see Gail Collins, *When Everything Changed: The Amazing Journey of American Women from 1960 to the Present* (New York: Little, Brown and Co., 2009).

My discussion of women's educational trends and experiences was informed by: Linda Eisenmann, *Higher Education for Women in Postwar America, 1945–1965* (Baltimore: Johns Hopkins University Press, 2006); Mabel Newcomer, *A Century of Higher Education for American Women* (New York: Harper, 1959); U.S. Department of Labor, Women's Bureau, *Trends in Educational Attainment of Women* (Washington, DC: Government Printing Office, 1969); Jessie Bernard, *Academic Women* (University Park: Pennsylvania State University Press, 1964); William Chafe, "The Challenge of Sex Equality," in *The Challenge of Change: Perspectives on Family, Work and Education*, eds. Matina Horner, Carol Nadelson, and Malkah Notman (New York: Plenum Press, 1983); James Davis, *Great Aspirations: The Graduate School Plans of American College Seniors* (Chicago: Aldine, 1961); Eli Ginzberg and Associates, *Educated American Women: Life Styles and Self-Portraits* (New York: Columbia University Press, 1966); Mabel Newcomer, *A Century of Higher Education for Women* (New York: Harper, 1959); Barbara Solomon, *In the Company of Educated Women* (New Haven, CT: Yale University Press, 1985); Marion Cuthbert, *Education and Marginality: A Study of the Negro Woman College Graduate* (1942; New York: Garland, 1987); Jeanne Noble, *The Negro Woman's College Education* (New York: Teachers College, Columbia

University, 1956); Mirra Komarovsky, *Women in the Modern World: Their Education and Their Dilemmas* (Boston: Little, Brown and Co., 1953); Abigail Stewart and Joseph Healy Jr., "Linking Individual Development and Social Changes," *American Psychologist* 44 (1989): 30–42; Kathleen Hulbert and Diane Schuster, *Women's Lives Through Time: Educated American Women of the Twentieth Century* (San Francisco: Jossey-Bass Publishers, 1993); Ravenna Helson, "The Mills Classes of 1958 and 1960," in Hulbert and Schuster, *Women's Lives Through Time*; *Trends in the Educational Attainment of Women*, U.S. Department of Labor, Women's Bureau, January 1965; and Lynn Peril, *College Girls: Bluestockings, Sex Kittens, and Coeds, Then and Now* (New York: Norton, 2006). The figures on the educational attainment of parents of entering freshmen came from Alexander Astin, et al., *The American Freshman: Thirty-Five-Year Trends, 1966–2001* (Los Angeles: Higher Education Research Institute, University of California, 2002).

Scores of wonderful books have been written on the origins and history of the "second wave" of the women's movement. If you have to choose just one, you can't go wrong with Ruth Rosen, *The World Split Open* (New York: Penguin Books, 2000). But I found many others useful for this book: Toni Carabillo, *Feminist Chronicles, 1953–1993* (Los Angeles: Women's Graphic, 1993); Rachel Blau DuPlessos and Ann Snitow, eds., *The Feminist Memoir Project: Voices from Women's Liberation* (New York: Three Rivers Press, 1998); Sara Evans, *Born for Liberty: A History of Women in America* (New York: Free Press, 1989); Jo Freeman, *The Politics of Women's Liberation* (New York: David McKay, 1975); Estelle Freedman, *No Turning Back: The History of Feminism and the Future of Women* (New York: Ballantine Books, 2002); Judith Hole and Ellen Levine, *Rebirth of Feminism* (New York: Quadrangle, 1971); Robert Jackson, *Destined for Equality: The Inevitable Rise of Women's Status* (Cambridge, MA: Harvard University Press, 1998); Cynthia Harrison, *On Account of Sex: The Politics of Women's Issues, 1945–1968* (Berkeley: University of California Press, 1988); Georgia Duerst-Lahti, "The Government's Role in Building the Women's Movement," *Political Science Quarterly* 104 (1989): 249–268;

Sara Evans, *Personal Politics: The Roots of Women's Liberation in the Civil Rights Movement and the New Left* (New York: Knopf, 1979); Pauli Murray, *Song in a Weary Throat* (New York: Harper & Row, 1987); Gael Graham, *Young Activists: American High School Students in the Age of Protest* (DeKalb: Northern Illinois University Press, 2006); Flora Davis, *Moving the Mountain: The Women's Movement in America Since 1960* (New York: Simon & Schuster, 1991); Marcia Cohen, *The Sisterhood: The True Story of the Women Who Changed the World* (New York: Simon & Schuster, 1988); Gerda Lerner, "Midwestern Leaders of the Modern Women's Movement: An Oral History Project," *Wisconsin Academy Review* 41 (1994): 11–15; Susan Hartmann, *From Margin to Mainstream: American Women and Politics Since 1960* (New York: Knopf, 1989); Blanche Linden Ward and Carol Green, *American Women in the 1960s: Changing the Future* (New York: Twayne, 1993); Barbara Ryan, *Feminism and the Women's Movement* (New York: Routledge, 1992); Sheila Tobias, *Faces of Feminism: An Activist's Reflections on the Women's Movement* (Boulder, CO: Westview, 1997); Lisa Baldez and Celeste Montoya Kirk, "Gendered Opportunities: The Formation of Women's Movements in the United States and Chile," in *The U.S. Women's Movement in Global Perspective*, ed. Lee Ann Banaszak (Lanham, MD: Rowman & Littlefield, 2006); Susan Brownmiller, *In Our Time: Memoir of a Revolution* (New York: Dell, 1999); Mary King, *Freedom Song: A Personal Story of the 1960s Civil Rights Movement* (New York: William Morrow, 1987); Sara Evans, "Sons, Daughters, and Patriarchy: Gender and the 1968 Generation," *American Historical Review* (April 2009): 332–347; Anne Costain, *Inviting Women's Rebellion: A Political Process Interpretation of the Women's Movement* (Baltimore: Johns Hopkins University Press, 1992); Leila Rupp, *Survival in the Doldrums: The American Women's Rights Movement, 1945 to the 1960s* (New York: Oxford University Press, 1987); Beth Bailey, *Sex in the Heartland* (Cambridge, MA: Harvard University Press, 1999); Maurice Isserman and Michael Kazin, *America Divided: The Civil War of the 1960s* (New York: Oxford University Press, 2008); Judith Lorber, "Beyond Gender: The Feminine Mystique," *Signs* 26 (2000): 328; Linda Kerber, Alice

Kessler-Harris, and Kathryn Kish Sklar, eds., *U.S. History as Women's History: New Feminist Essays* (Chapel Hill: University of North Carolina Press, 1995); Dorothy Shawhan and Martha Swain, *Lucy Somerville Howorth: New Deal Lawyer, Politician, and Feminist from the South* (Baton Rouge: Louisiana University Press, 2006); Judith Ezekiel, *Feminism in the Heartland* (Columbus: Ohio State University Press, 2002); Beth Bailey, *Sex in the Heartland* (Cambridge, MA: Harvard University Press, 1999); Linda Gordon, *The Moral Property of Women: A History of Birth Control Politics in America* (Urbana: University of Illinois Press, 2002).

On the controversy over whether NOW would recognize lesbians as a legitimate part of the women's movement, see Lillian Faderman, *Odd Girls and Twilight Lovers: A History of Lesbian Life in Twentieth-Century America* (New York: Columbia University Press, 1991).

Readers of my chapter on African-American women and white working-class women will recognize my immense debt to Bart Landry, *Black Working Wives: Pioneers of the American Family Revolution* (Berkeley: University of California Press, 2000). Primary sources on educated African-American women in the 1940s and 1950s include Marion Cuthbert, *Education and Marginality: A Study of the Negro Woman College Graduate* (1942; New York: Garland, 1987), and Jeanne Noble, *The Negro Woman's College Education* (New York: Teachers College, Columbia University, 1956).

Many of the books on women's history and the women's movement cited above pay attention to diversity among women by race, ethnicity, and class, but for more detailed studies of African-American women and other racial-ethnic groups, see: Vicki Ruiz and Ellen Carol Debois, eds., *Unequal Sisters*, 4th ed. (New York: Routledge, 2008); Vicki Karen Anderson, *Changing Woman: A History of Racial Ethnic Women in Modern America* (New York: Oxford University Press, 1996); Benita Roth, *Separate Roads to Feminism: Black, Chicana, and White Feminist Movements in America's Second Wave* (New York: Cambridge University Press, 2004); Winifred Breines, *The Trouble Between Us: An Uneasy History of White and Black Women in the Feminist Movement* (New York: Oxford University

Press, 2006); Ann Valk, *Radical Sisters: Second Wave Feminism and Black Liberation in Washington, DC* (Urbana: University of Illinois Press, 2008); Bruce Fehn, "African-American Women and the Struggle for Equality in the Meatpacking Industry, 1940–1960," *Journal of Women's History* 10 (1998): 45–69; Ruth Feldstein, *Motherhood in Black and White: Race and Sex in American Liberalism, 1930–65* (Ithaca, NY: Cornell University Press, 2000); Becky Thompson, "Multiracial Feminism: Recasting the Chronology of Second Wave Feminism," *Feminist Studies* 28 (2002): 337–360; Jane Dabel, *A Respectable Woman: The Public Roles of African American Women in 19th-Century New York* (New York: New York University Press, 2008); Denise Segura, "Working at Motherhood: Chicana and Mexican Immigrant Mothers and Employment," in *Mothering: Ideology, Experience, and Agency*, ed. Evelyn Nakano Glenn, Grace Chang, and Linda Rennie Forcey (New York: Routledge, 1994); bell hooks, *Ain't I a Woman: Black Women and Feminism* (Boston: South End Press, 1981); Elizabeth Spelman, *Inessential Woman: Problems of Exclusion in Feminist Thought* (Boston: Beacon, 1988); Gloria T. Hull, "History/My History," in *Changing Subjects: The Making of Feminist Literary Criticism*, ed. Gayle Greene and Coppelia Kahn (New York: Routledge, 1993); Gloria Hull, Patricia Bell Scott, and Barbara Smith, eds., *All the Women Are White, All the Blacks Are Men, But Some of Us Are Brave* (Old Westbury, NY: Feminist Press, 1982); Paula Giddings, *When and Where I Enter: The Impact of Black Women on Race and Sex in America* (New York: William Morrow, 1984); Riché Jeneen Daniel Barnes, "Black Women Have Always Worked," in *The Changing Landscape of Work and Family in the American Middle Class*, ed. Elizabeth Rudd and Lara Descartes (Lanham, MD: Lexington Books, 2008); Stephanie Gilmore, *Feminist Coalitions: Historical Perspectives on Second Wave Feminism in the United States* (Urbana: University of Illinois Press, 2008); Vicki Ruiz, *From Out of the Shadows: Mexican Women in Twentieth-Century America* (New York: Oxford University Press, 1998); Donna Franklin, "African Americans and the Birth of Modern Marriage," in *Families as They Really Are*, ed. Barbara Risman (New York: Norton, 2010).

For a review of trends in African-American inequality, see Michael Katz, Mark Stern, and Jamie Fader, "The New African American Inequality," *Journal of American History* (June 2005): 75–108.

The detailed surveys of wives of blue-collar workers in the 1950s appear in Lee Rainwater, Richard Coleman, and Gerald Handel, *Workingman's Wife: Her Personality, World and Life Style* (New York: Oceana Publications, 1959).

Works dealing with the history of working-class women, both whites and minorities, and their role in the struggle for gender equality, include: Dorothy Sue Cobble, *The Other Women's Movement: Workplace Justice and Social Rights in Modern America* (Princeton, NJ: Princeton University Press, 2004); Mirra Komarovsky, *Blue Collar Marriage* (New York: Vintage Books, 1962); Alice Kessler-Harris, *Out to Work: A History of Wage-Earning Women in the United States* (New York: Oxford University Press, 1982); Cynthia Fuchs Epstein, "The Major Myth of the Women's Movement," *Dissent* (Fall 1999): 83–86; Dennis Deslippe, *Rights, Not Roses: Unions and the Rise of Working-Class Feminism, 1945–1980* (Urbana: University of Illinois Press, 2000); Myra Marx Ferree, "Working-Class Jobs: Paid Work and Housework as Sources of Satisfaction," *Social Problems* 23 (1976): 431–444; Nancy Gabin, *Feminism in the Labor Movement: Women and the United Auto Workers, 1935–1975* (Ithaca, NY: Cornell University Press, 1990); Ruth Milkman, *Gender at Work: The Dynamics of Job Segregation by Sex During World War II* (Urbana: University of Illinois Press, 1987); Annelise Orleck, *Common Sense and a Little Fire: Women and Working-Class Politics in the United States, 1900–1965* (Chapel Hill: University of North Carolina Press, 1995).

Portions of Chapter 9 appeared previously in my article "Sharing the Load," in *The Shriver Report: A Woman's Nation Changes Everything*, ed. Heather Boushey and Ann O'Leary (Washington, DC: Center for American Progress, 2009). For the classic arguments favoring specialization within marriage and warning of the dangers of "the independence effect" see: Gary Becker, *A Treatise on the Family* (Cambridge, MA: Harvard University Press, 1981); Gary Becker, "Human Capital, Effort, and the Sexual

Division of Labor," *Journal of Labor Economics* 3 (1985): S33–S58; and Talcott Parsons, "Age and Sex in the Social Structure of the United States," *American Sociological Review* 7 (1942): 604–616.

For current trends in marriage dynamics and marital satisfaction, see: Betsey Stevenson and Justin Wolfers, "Marriage and Divorce: Changes and Their Driving Forces," *Journal of Economic Perspectives* 21 (2007): 27–52; Zvika Neeman, Andrew Newman, and Claudia Olivetti, "Are Career Women Good for Marriage?" Institute for Economic Development Discussion Paper 167, April 2007; Adam Isen and Betsey Stevenson, "Women's Education and Family Behavior: Trends in Marriage, Divorce and Fertility," November 24, 2008, http://bpp.wharton.upenn.edu/betseys/papers/Marriage-divorce-education.pdf; Heather Boushey, "Baby Panic Book Skews Data," *Women's E-News*, July 3, 2002, www.womensenews.org/story/commentary/020703/baby-panic-book-skews-data-misses-actual-issue; Lynn Prince Cooke and Janeen Baxter, "Families in International Context," *Journal of Marriage and Family*, forthcoming; John Gottman, *Why Marriages Succeed or Fail* (New York: Simon & Schuster, 1994); Christine Whelan, *Why Smart Men Marry Smart Women* (New York: Simon & Schuster, 2006); Christie F. Boxer and Christine B. Whelan, "Changing Mate Preferences 1939–2008," unpublished working paper, University of Iowa, Iowa City, 2008; Robert Schoen, Stacy Rogers, and Paul Amato, "Wives' Employment and Spouses' Marital Happiness," *Journal of Family Issues* 27 (2006): 506–528; Paul Amato, Alan Booth, David Johnson, and Stacey Rogers, *Alone Together: How Marriage in America Is Changing* (Cambridge, MA: Harvard University Press, 2007); Lynn Prince Cooke, "'Doing Gender' in Context: Household Bargaining and the Risk of Divorce in Germany and the United States," *American Journal of Sociology* 112 (2006): 442–472; Lynn Prince Cooke, "'Traditional' Marriages Now Less Stable than Ones Where Couples Share Work and Household Chores," www.contemporaryfamilies.org/subtemplate.php?t=briefingPapers&ext=LynnCooke; Rosalind Barnett and Caryl Rivers, *She Works, He Works* (New York: HarperSanFrancisco, 1996); E. Wethington and R. Kessler, "Employment, Parental Responsibility, and

Psychological Distress," *Journal of Family Issues* 10 (1989): 527–546; Janet Hyde, John DeLamateur, and Erri Hewitt, "Sexuality and the Dual-Earner Couple: Multiple Roles and Sexual Functioning," *Journal of Family Psychology* 12 (1998): 354–368; Constance Gager and Scott Yabiku, "Who Has the Time? The Relationship Between Household Labor Time and Sexual Frequency," *Journal of Family Issues* 31 (2009): 135–163; Neil Chetnik, *Voicemale* (New York: Simon & Schuster, 2006); Sharon Meers and Joanna Strober, *Getting to 50/50* (New York: Bantam Books, 2009).

For changes in the household division of labor and time with children, see Oriel Sullivan and Scott Coltrane, "Men's Changing Contribution to Housework and Child Care," Discussion Paper on Changing Family Roles, briefing paper prepared for the 11th Annual Conference of the Council on Contemporary Families, April 25–26, 2008, www.contemporary families.org/subtemplate.php?t=briefingPapers&ext=menshousework, and Suzanne Bianchi, John Robinson, and Melissa Milkie, *Changing Rhythms of Family Life* (New York: Russell Sage, 2006).

On the complex determinants of gender equity at home and work, see Lynn Prince Cooke, *Gender-Class Equality in the Political Economy* (New York: Routledge, 2011). On the attitudes of young men and women toward gender equality and family arrangements, see Kathleen Gerson, *The Unfinished Revolution: How a New Generation Is Reshaping Family, Work, and Gender in America* (New York: Oxford University Press, 2010).

On the continuing mystiques of gender, sexuality, and consumerism, see: Barbara Risman and Elizabeth Seale, "Betwixt and Be Tween: Gender Contradictions Among Middle Schoolers," in *Families as They Really Are*, ed. Barbara Risman (New York: Norton, 2010); Susan Douglas, *Enlightened Sexism: The Seductive Message that Feminism's Work Is Done* (New York: Times Books, 2010); Sharon Lamb and Lyn Brown, *Packaging Girlhood: Rescuing Our Daughters from Marketers' Schemes* (New York: St. Martin's, 2006); Margaret Talbot, "Little Hotties," *New Yorker*, December 4, 2006; Peggy Orenstein, "Playing at Sexy," *New York Times*, June 7, 2010; Stephen Hinshaw with Rachel Kranz, *The Triple Bind: Saving Our Teenage Girls from Today's Pressures* (New York: Random House, 2009);

Deborah Tolman, *Dilemmas of Desire: Teenage Girls Talk About Sexuality* (Cambridge, MA: Harvard University Press, 2002); Ariel Levy, *Female Chauvinist Pigs: Women and the Rise of Raunch Culture* (New York: Free Press, 2005). On the motherhood mystique, see Judith Warner, *Perfect Madness: Motherhood in the Age of Anxiety* (New York: Riverhead Books, 2005) and Sharon Hays, *The Cultural Contradictions of Motherhood* (New Haven, CT: Yale University Press).

Good sources on the continuing discrimination against working women, especially mothers, include: Shelley Correll, Stephen Barnard, and In Paik, "Getting a Job: Is There a Motherhood Penalty?" *American Journal of Sociology* 112 (2007): 1297–1338; Catalyst, "Damned If You Do, Damned If You Don't," July 2007, www.catalyst.org/publication/83/the-double-bind-dilemma-for-women-in-leadership-damned-if-you-do-damned-if-you-don't; and Ann Crittendon, *The Price of Motherhood: Why the Most Important Job in the World Is Still the Least Valued* (New York: Metropolitan Books, 2001). Also see Linda Babcock and Sara Laschever, *Women Don't Ask: Negotiation and the Gender Divide* (Princeton, NJ: Princeton University Press, 2003).

For research on women's employment trends and the debate over "opting out," see: Claudia Goldin, "The Quiet Revolution that Transformed Women's Employment, Education, and Family," *American Economic Review* 96 (2006): 1–21; Heather Boushey, "Are Women Opting Out? Debunking the Myth," Center for Economic and Policy Research Briefing Paper, 2005; Linda Hirshman, *Get to Work: A Manifesto for Women of the World* (New York: Viking, 2006); Leslie Bennetts, *The Feminine Mistake* (New York: Hyperion, 2007); David Cotter, Paula England, and Joan Hermsen, "Moms and Jobs," in *American Families: A Multicultural Reader*, ed. Stephanie Coontz, Maya Parson, and Gabrielle Raley (New York: Routledge, 2008); Arielle Kuperberg and Pamela Stone, "The Media Depiction of Women Who Opt Out," *Gender & Society* 22 (August 2008): 497–517; Sylvia Ann Hewlett, *Off Ramps and On Ramps: Keeping Talented Women on the Road to Success* (Boston: Harvard Business School Press, 2007); Pamela Stone, *Opting Out? Why Women Really Quit Work and Head Home* (Berkeley: University of California Press, 2007); Joan Williams, Jessica Manvell, and Stephanie Bornstein, *"Opt Out" or Pushed Out? How the Press Covers Work/Family Conflict: The Untold Story of Why Women Leave the Workforce* (San Francisco: University of California, Hastings College of the Law, Center for WorkLife Law, 2006); Joan Williams, "The Opt-Out Revolution Revisited," *American Prospect*, March 2007; Claudia Goldin and Lawrence Katz, "Transitions: Career and Family Life Cycles of the Educational Elite," *American Economic Review: Papers & Proceedings* 98 (2008): 363–369.

For information on work-family issues, see: Phyllis Moen and Patricia Roehling, *The Career Mystique: Cracks in the American Dream* (Lanham, MD: Rowman & Littlefield, 2005); Heather Boushey and Joan Williams, "The Three Faces of Work-Family Conflict: The Poor, the Professionals, and the Missing Middle," Center for American Progress and the Center for WorkLife Law at the UC Hastings College of the Law, January 25, 2010; all the articles in Susanne Bianchi, Lynn Casper, and Rosalind King, eds., *Work, Family, Health, and Well-Being* (Mahwah, NJ: Lawrence Erlbaum Associates, 2005); Cathleen Benko and Anne Weisberg, *Mass Career Customization: Aligning the Workplace with Today's Nontraditional Workforce* (Boston: Harvard Business School Press, 2007); E. Wethington and R. Kessler, "Employment, Parental Responsibility, and Psychological Distress," *Journal of Family Issues* 10 (1989): 527–546; Rosalind Chait, "On Multiple Roles: Past, Present, and Future," and other chapters in Karen Korabik, Donna Leto, and Denise Whitehead, eds., *Handbook of Work-Family Integration* (Amsterdam: Elsevier, 2008); Deborah Carr, "The Psychological Consequences of Midlife Men's Social Comparisons with Their Young Adult Sons," *Journal of Marriage and Family* 67 (February 2005): 240–250; Jerry Jacobs and Kathleen Gerson, *The Time-Divide: Work, Family, and Gender Inequality* (Cambridge, MA: Harvard University Press, 2004); Ellen Galinsky, Kerstin Aurmann, and James T. Bond, National Study of the Changing Workforce, 2008, "Times Are Changing: Gender and Generation at Work and at Home" (New York: Families and Work Institute, 2009).

Index